Unbelievably
Gluten-Free!

Unbelievably Gluten-Free!

Dinner Dishes You Never Thought
You'd Be Able to Eat Again

Anne Byrn

Photographs by Lucy Schaeffer

WORKMAN PUBLISHING · NEW YORK

641.563
BYR

Library of Congress Cataloging-in-Publication Data is available.

ISBN 978-0-7611-7168-3

Designer: Ariana Abud
Photography: Lucy Schaeffer
Food stylist: Simon Andrews
Prop stylist: Deborah Williams

Workman books are available at special discounts when purchased in
bulk for premiums and sales promotions as well as for fund-raising or
educational use. Special editions or book excerpts can also be created to
specification. For details, contact the Special Sales Director at the
address below, or send an email to specialmarkets@workman.com.

Workman Publishing Company, Inc.
225 Varick Street
New York, NY 10014-4381

workman.com
WORKMAN is a registered trademark of Workman Publishing Co., Inc.
cakemixdoctor.com

Printed in the United States
First printing September 2012

10 9 8 7 6 5 4 3 2

Dedication

*For Martha Bowden, who accepts
every challenge with a smile.*

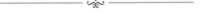

Acknowledgments

*Thanks again to all my readers who offered
suggestions for this book. Thanks to those cooks who provided
recipes, encouragement, and helpful gluten-free suggestions,
especially Sarah Ann Harwick, Hartley Steiner, Bev Lieven,
Cheryl Leslie, Suzanne Simpson, Jody Lehman,
Alison Fujito, and Allison Greiner.*

CONTENTS

Unbelievably Gluten-Free 101
page 2

Covering everything you need to know about cooking gluten-free, starting with the basics: What is gluten? Then, how to build a gluten-free pantry. Plus tips on saving money and which dinners to turn to when time is short.

Breakfast and Brunch All Day
page 13

Rise and shine to an array of breakfasts so delicious, you won't believe they don't contain gluten. Just to name a few: Allison's Gluten-Free Granola; Fresh Blueberry Pancakes; Cornmeal, Chile, and Cheese Waffles; and Classic but Simple Quiche Lorraine.

Little Snacks and Nibbles
page 33

Highly anticipated, these appetizers and little bites take the edge off hunger and entice the palate. Serve up Five-Minute Hummus; Greek Spinach and Feta Balls; Fresh Barbecue Chicken Spring Rolls; or Crab Fritters with Spicy Mayonnaise.

Soups and Stews
page 75

The comfort of soup in all its vegetal and meaty glory is represented here: Enjoy Chilled Cucumber and Tomato Soup; Cream of Tomato Soup with Basil; Mom's Chicken and Rice Soup; December Beef Stew.

Gluten-Free Bread
page 109

Breads and muffins for the gluten-free baker? Believe it! Starting with simple baking mixes and flour blends, you can create scrumptious gluten-free versions of classic recipes, such as Gluten-Free Banana Bread; Chocolate and Cherry Scones; Buttermilk Biscuits; and Zesty Parmesan Bread.

Chicken, Meats, and Other Mains
page 143

All the comforting, homey dishes you love get gluten-free makeovers, with stunning results. Real Deal GF Fried Chicken; Gluten-Free Chicken Potpie; Braised Pot Roast with Vidalia Onions; and The Best GF Meat Loaf—they're all here.

Pasta and Pizza Night
page 211

Serve up pasta dishes and pizza worthy of the Tuscan countryside, with nary a grain of wheat flour in sight. All these meals are possible, and more: Homestyle Spaghetti Carbonara; Unbelievable Spaghetti and Meatballs; Classic Gluten-Free Pizza; and Grilled Chicken and Pesto Pizza, to boot!

Salads and Sides
page 249

Here, all the great-tasting salads and sides get the wheat-free treatment, with some unexpected additions. Dish up the Best Caesar Salad with Gluten-Free Croutons; Easy Fried Rice; Gluten-Free Mac and Cheese; and Cheryl's Cornbread Dressing.

Sweets for Every Occasion
page 287

Go ahead—have your cake (and cookies, and pudding, and pie . . .) and eat it, too. Beloved dessert classics are perfect for any celebration: Gluten-Free Angel Food Cake; Gluten-Free Red Velvet Cake; even an easy crust that is the basis of an array of enviable pies. And irresistible Gluten-Free Saucepan Brownies.

Conversion Tables
page 360

Index
page 361

INTRODUCTION:

Welcome to the Gluten-Free Kitchen

T HIS BOOK IS ROOTED IN A BOOK TOUR. I WAS IN Austin, Texas, signing copies of *The Cake Mix Doctor Bakes Gluten-Free* when one of the attendees shared her secret for making gluten-free angel food cake and the room grew instantly quiet. I don't know how everyone else felt at that moment, but I felt like we had been handed a long hoped for secret.

And that was far from the end of it. In Denver readers asked me for recipes for gluten-free fried chicken, potpie, and pizza. And in Milwaukee, a group of gluten-free cooks gathered at their local bookstore to meet the Cake Mix Doctor and afterward swapped tips for using sweet rice flour in gumbo and how to make your own gluten-free bread crumbs. From city to city, it was the same routine. I came to speak about cake and ended up scribbling dinner notes at the podium. Gluten-free pie crust, lasagna, fried fish. It just made me hungry.

Once I was home I created a gluten-free angel food cake of sweet rice and sorghum flours. I attempted my first roux without the customary flour and butter, instead browning sweet rice flour until it was a deep tan color and adding this to simmering broth, tomatoes, and seasonings for seafood gumbo. I found spaghetti made from corn at my local Whole Foods and tossed it with chopped ripe tomatoes, basil, and garlic. I dredged chicken breasts in gluten-free *panko* crumbs and fried them until crispy. I made a gluten-free pie crust and turned it into a potpie crammed with chicken and veggies. I made pizza doughs, both thick and thin. I baked lasagna with brown rice noodles. And I made creamy rice pudding and a flourless chocolate cake so dark and delicious everyone begged for the recipe.

I am not someone who has to forego gluten for health reasons. I have been baking for forty years and cooking dinner for a family for more than twenty of those. I am curious and enjoy a challenge. And I love good food. Just because you can't eat gluten does not mean you have to do without those amazing comfort foods we all look forward to. And knowing that no busy mom should ever have to cook one dinner for the gluten-free family member and a second dinner for the rest of the family helped me develop a greater resolve to write this book. From appetizers to soups, to salads, to sides, to mains, to breads, and of course, desserts, these recipes are completely family friendly and unbelievably gluten-free. They are gluten-free either because of the ingredients they contain or the technique you employ to make them so. Come join me as we cook unbelievably good gluten-free dinners for everyone!

Anne Byrn
Nashville, Tennessee

Unbelievably Gluten-Free!

Unbelievably Gluten-Free 101

WHAT IS IT THAT GLUTEN—THE PROTEIN FOUND in wheat, barley, and rye—adds to dinner? It thickens sauces and soups, binds meatballs and meat loaf, adds structure to cakes, pie crust, and breads, and helps form a crust to seal in the juices of fried chicken and fish, to name just a few things. Take away gluten and can we still create those same homey soups and stews, sauces, fish fries, and desserts? That's what I wanted to know when working on this book.

Let's backtrack for a minute. It is estimated that 1 in every 133 people in the United States and Canada suffers from celiac disease whereby the body isn't able to metabolize gluten. Many more people are sensitive to gluten. On top of that, many who must eat gluten-free or are sensitive to gluten cannot tolerate dairy. I first wrote for a gluten-free audience in my cookbook *The Cake Mix Doctor Bakes Gluten-Free*. It was a book requested by readers who could no longer bake my cakes because either they or someone they loved had discovered they had to give up food containing gluten. I learned in researching that book that gluten-free cake mixes are a handy and inexpensive way to bake because you don't have to keep a lot of expensive ingredients on hand. But just like cake

{ *I hope you see how healthy and fresh gluten-free dinners can be.* }

flour mixes need doctoring up to improve their flavor, I found that acidic ingredients like sour cream, orange juice, and buttermilk improved the gritty texture of the rice flour used in gluten-free mixes, and an extra egg improved the finished cake's volume.

This dinner book came with its own set of challenges. How could I thicken without flour, bind stuffings, or coat chicken without my favorite bread crumbs, or make something as simple as French toast gluten-free? How could I make gumbo when the flour and butter roux was the very heart and soul of the soup? How could I enjoy pasta? And then came the requests from readers—could I share with them a recipe for an angel food cake, a red velvet cake, a potpie? Potpie? I got an uneasy feeling in my stomach trying to imagine how in the world I could make a perfect gluten-free pie crust.

Fortunately I have learned from my previous books that a cookbook is not written in a day. I reached out to other gluten-free cooks and had the creative assistance of Martha Bowden in the kitchen. As I write this intro-duction I think back on the nine months spent testing recipes, hoping

{ 10 FAST GLUTEN-FREE DINNERS YOU'LL LOVE }

1. Gluten-Free Chicken Potpie, page 162

2. Smashed Chicken Gluten-Free Style, page 149

3. Cornmeal-Crusted Fried Fish, page 198

4. Mexican Lasagna, page 185

5. Macho Nacho Taco Salad, page 261

6. Susan's Penne and Tomato Salad, page 254

7. Easy Fried Rice, page 273

8. The Best Skillet Lasagna, page 228 (you don't even have to cook the lasagna noodles ahead of time)

9. Meaty Macaroni, page 231

10. Spaghetti with Fresh Tomatoes, Basil, and Mozzarella, page 221

for just one success. And the successes came: The pie crust day was memorable and unlocked the door to potpies, cobblers, pecan pie, apple tarts, fried pies, you name it. The pizza crust day was a good one, too.

Along the way, I revisited easy cooking techniques I learned in my mother's kitchen, and also in cooking school in France, but had taken for granted—pureeing soups to thicken them, taking the lid off the soup pot to let the juices cook down and evaporate without adding a thickening ingredient, adding potato to a stew to let its natural starch thicken the juices. It didn't take long to realize that toasting gluten-free sandwich bread made it tastier. And it also made better bread crumbs. When I added a little Italian seasoning and Parmesan cheese to those bread crumbs I was in business.

How to Use This Book

Let my book be the beginning of great gluten-free home cooking for you. As you flip through it, I hope you will see how simple and delicious it is to prepare comforting, satisfying, and nostalgic recipes your family will enjoy, such as fried chicken, potpie, and meat loaf. And I hope you also see how healthy and fresh gluten-free dinners can be, too. For those meals, I lean toward the pastas, the chicken and vegetarian main dishes, and the salads and soups.

Eating gluten-free is not just an American phenomenon. Some of the most incredible choices come from a wide variety of other countries. So, I've incorporated flavors from around the world to enliven my recipes. Try chickpea (garbanzo bean) flour to thicken the onion batter when frying Indian *bhaji*. Wrap cold chicken and crisp veggies in softened Vietnamese rice paper rounds for a terrific addition to your next picnic. Dip shrimp in an Asian batter of sweet rice flour and fry them until crisp. Bake orange-scented Italian cornmeal cookies. Try Southern corn bread recipes and cornmeal coatings on fried green tomatoes.

Based on what my readers have told me, usually the gluten-free family can make do at breakfast and get by at lunch but it is dinner that presents the greatest dilemma. How to cook one meal for a family with both gluten-free and gluten-eating members is a challenge. Although these recipes were intended to solve the dinner conundrum, feel free to prepare them for lunch, brunch, or most any time of the day.

Who Knew It Was Gluten-Free?

That should be the mantra of this book. You see, when I tested each recipe on its own and then prepared a menu of recipes as a meal, I wanted no one to guess the food was gluten-free. I just wanted it to taste delicious and fresh. The recipes are grouped into appetizers and nibbles to serve before a meal or if you are having a party, then soups, salads, main dishes, side dishes, breads, and desserts. There are chapters devoted to pasta and pizza because they present particular challenges in the gluten-free kitchen, and they hold a special place in the heart of family cooking. There is a separate chapter for breakfast and brunch because kids love to eat breakfast for dinner. And there are a dozen breads because they're gluten-free and great and I think you'll enjoy making them.

{ HOW TO SAVE MONEY COOKING DINNER GLUTEN-FREE }

The secrets to saving money cooking any dinner, whether it is gluten-free or not, are to keep the ingredients simple and cook more of the meal at home. If you are eating gluten-free you are probably cooking at home more than most people you know. But to save further, bake your own cakes and pies, and freeze the pie crusts to have on hand, so you will be less tempted to purchase expensive store-bought gluten-free goodies. Also try to reduce the number of items that go into a recipe, and you will be buying less. Make more out of one meal. Freeze leftover soup in portions you can reheat. Freeze leftover cooked seasoned ground beef for the next time you make tacos. And keep the items you shop for simple. It's less expensive to buy beans and rice for dinner than it is halibut and shrimp.

My favorite gluten-free cheap eats in this book are the New Orleans Red Beans and Rice, Old-Fashioned Pigs in Blankets, Baked Potato Soup, Quick-Cook Rice Pudding, Gluten-Free Saucepan Brownies, and Easy Apple Tart.

Many of the recipes I've included suggest a specific gluten-free ingredient. Fortunately, gluten-free ingredients are a lot easier to locate than they used to be. Many supermarkets even have a dedicated gluten-free section. For a list of my favorite gluten-free ingredients, see The Gluten-Free Pantry on page 8. Some recipes you'll find here are just naturally gluten-free. Many are based on rice, such as the Quick-Cook Rice Pudding, or on cornmeal, such as the Indian Pudding with Pumpkin. Often recipes don't contain any flour at all, for example, the Texas Tortilla Soup thickened with corn tortilla chips or the Flourless Chocolate Cakes. This cake works because the chocolate and eggs hold the cake together. Plus it's so rich, dense, and delicious you don't realize that it doesn't contain flour.

Enjoy these recipes with family and friends, gluten-free or not. That is the goal, the highest compliment!

Suggestions from My Kitchen to Yours

If you have cooked from my cookbooks before, you know how I love to dole out advice at the end of a recipe. This advice comes from testing the recipe and learning something new, whether it is about an ingredient or a method, or a way to substitute and change up the recipe seasonally or increase or decrease servings for large or small crowds. Read through the recipe before you begin, and soak in all the information. It is especially important to read the method before you start making the pie crust or pizza crusts. Recipes call for a rising time or a cooling time, and I know how frustrating it is to be in the middle of a recipe and realize you don't have time to finish it. So read, shop, then cook. You don't want to miss anything!

Things to Remember

Some challenges remain for the gluten-free home cook.

1. Be vigilant when grocery shopping and especially when buying readymade food. Look for products labeled gluten-free (they are easier to find than ever). And when in doubt, ask.

2. Cooking and eating gluten-free does not mean the food will be calorie- or fat-free. You still need to maintain a balanced diet and get plenty of exercise. Many of the recipes readers requested for this book are not the healthiest recipes on the block—fried fish, casseroles, and puddings. But you can serve these dishes on special occasions.

3. According to Suzanne Simpson, dietitian at the Celiac Disease Center at Columbia University, you can increase iron in gluten-free recipes by adding green vegetables; meat, poultry, or fish; quinoa; legumes; and steel-cut gluten-free oats. To add fiber she suggests you include fruits and vegetables in the meal. And to add calcium, use dairy products (if you can tolerate them).

4. Find the time to cook at home, and try your hand at making some things you may normally buy premade, such as bread crumbs and pie crust. You'll save some money because you won't have to buy expensive ingredients.

The Gluten-Free Pantry

Here are suggestions for stocking your pantry, fridge, and freezer with gluten-free ingredients to make cooking dinner so much easier.

In the Pantry

Basic baking mixes: Bisquick, King Arthur, Bob's Red Mill, and Arrowhead Mills are all brands that make gluten-free all-purpose baking mixes. Each is slightly different, but most are mainly rice flour.

Multiuse flour: For coating fish and chicken and for last-minute thickening, this is a baking mix without the leavening.

Sweet rice flour: Add sweet rice flour to angel food cake, brown it on top of the stove to thicken and flavor gumbo, and turn it into batters to dip fish and vegetables in prior to frying.

Pie crust mix: I like the Gluten-Free Pantry Perfect Pie Crust mix. At 16 ounces, it makes three pie crusts. You can use one and freeze the other two.

{ I MAY NOT BE GLUTEN-FREE . . . }
{ BUT I SURE DO LIKE THESE RECIPES }

Now I am happy to say you can remove the gluten from dinner and never miss it. This cookbook may be a little different from other gluten-free books in that it is written from the perspective of a picky cook who is not gluten-intolerant. Because I don't have a gluten sensitivity, I was able to test my gluten-free recipes side by side with recipes made with wheat flour, and I wasn't satisfied until the gluten-free version tasted as good as the traditional one.

So what did I take away? What ingredients and recipes will I continue to make and enjoy in my kitchen? What did I learn that I didn't expect to learn? For one, I will continue to prepare gluten-free recipes. No doubt about it, they are lighter than their counterparts with gluten. I especially love the corn spaghetti from Italy. When tossed with olive oil, fresh tomatoes, basil, and mozzarella you would think you are sitting in a café in Rome in the heat of the summer. The bite of the pasta, the bright yellow color of it, is most appealing and a fun departure from regular pasta made from wheat.

The gluten-free baking mixes like Bisquick are an easy way to jump-start quick breads like scones. This book's photography team drooled over the moist, tender, and light Cranberry and Orange Scones. You know how some scones can get tough and dry? Not these scones, based on the baking mix with white rice flour. I love the tempura batter and the granola with oats, nuts, and fruit. I love dredging fish in cornmeal before panfrying. I love tortilla soup thickened with corn tortillas (and garnished with crunchy radishes like our food stylist Simon recommended). I adore angel food cake made with sticky rice and sorghum flours more than any angel food cake my mother made. And I am passionate about the Flourless Chocolate Cakes with cocoa and cornstarch because they are intensely chocolaty and gooey and so over-the-top everyone will think you have gone to a lot of trouble when you have not. Those kinds of recipes are my favorite recipes of all!

Pizza crust mix: I'm a fan of two mixes: the Gluten Free Pantry French bread and pizza mix, and the King Arthur pizza crust mix. Both include the yeast.

Brownie and cake mixes: These are useful to have on hand. Betty Crocker and Gluten Free Pantry cake mixes are both good, as is the King Arthur brownie mix.

Bread crumbs: If you don't make your own, try Gillian's bread crumbs, made from brown rice flour. They're perfect for adding to stuffed mushrooms and spinach balls.

***Panko*-style bread crumbs:** The Kinnikinnick *panko* crumbs are great pressed onto chicken tenders and fish before frying. These crumbs are very crunchy.

Gluten-free pasta: Keep a selection of pastas on hand for last-minute meals. I like the brown rice or corn spaghettis, the macaroni made of quinoa, and the rice lasagna for Italian meals. I also like the thin Asian rice vermicelli noodles you just soak in hot water before serving with a stir-fry.

Rice: Enjoy a variety of rice—long-grain basmati, jasmine, short-grain Asian sticky rices, and Italian Arborio.

Gluten-free cereals: Combine Chex rice or corn cereals and a gluten-free O-shaped oat cereal for the classic Chex mix. Or crush rice or corn cereals, toss them with melted butter, and use them to top casseroles before baking.

Oats: Make sure to buy gluten-free oats and use them when making granola and topping baked goods and to serve for breakfast.

Basic crackers: For topping a main dish or vegetable casserole. Crush the crackers, toss them with melted butter, and sprinkle them on the casserole before baking it. I like the Glutino crackers made with cornstarch and white rice flour.

Corn tortilla chips: As well as serving corn tortilla chips with gluten-free dips, use them for thickening soups and chilis.

Almond milk, rice milk, coconut milk: All of these make good dairy substitutes.

In the Fridge and Freezer

Orange juice: A flavorful addition to cakes and muffins.

Plain yogurt, sour cream, and buttermilk: Adding any of these makes batters with rice flour seem less gritty in texture.

Cornmeal: Both white and yellow cornmeal should be stored in the freezer. They are great for baking and coating.

Sandwich bread: Sample the breads in your stores and choose your favorite. Gluten-free sandwich breads improve with toasting. Choose crusty coarse bread for making French toast. For homemade bread crumbs, toast slices until browned, let them cool, then tear them into pieces and pulse in a food processor until they form crumbs. Gluten-free sandwich breads should be stored in the freezer.

Frozen pizza crust: Handy for last-minute meals, place the crust on a baking sheet and let it thaw briefly while you prepare the pizza toppings. I like Whole Foods Market Gluten Free Bakehouse pizza crust. It contains tapioca starch, white bean flour, sorghum flour, yeast, xanthan gum, lemon juice, olive oil, and salt.

Fresh corn tortillas: Use fresh corn tortillas when making enchiladas or to thicken soup.

Nuts of all types: Nuts also should be stored in the freezer so they don't turn rancid. They can be ground and used like flour in baking and coating.

{ ## WHERE TO GO FOR MORE INFORMATION ABOUT GLUTEN-FREE COOKING }

Find the local gluten-free support group in your community. Search for local gluten-free food bloggers who keep tabs on new products in your area. And check out the following good online sources:

www.celiacdiseasecenter.org—The Celiac Disease Center at Columbia University provides nutritional information and news of the latest research.

www.csaceliacs.info—The Celiac Sprue Association is a country-wide resource and referral organization with chapters throughout the United States.

www.celiac.com—A source for good basic information: Find out if there is a R.O.C.K. (Raising Our Celiac Kids) support group in your area.

Eight Unbelievably Gluten-Free Breakfasts and Brunches

Breakfast and Brunch All Day

I love this chapter of eclectic recipes, all gluten-free and all suitable any time of the day. Yes, they're mostly identified with breakfast or brunch, but when you find yourself in a dinner recipe rut, or when your kids don't seem to ever eat a good dinner, or when all else fails and you have few ingredients in the house, cook breakfast. Be they eggs, French toast, pancakes, or waffles, breakfast or brunch recipes work very well at dinner.

This is something the brunch crowd has known for a long time. Bake a quiche, add a fruit salad, and your brunch food can easily move to dinnertime. I found myself munching on Allison's Gluten-Free Granola all day long. It was great in the morning with sliced fruit and milk, perfect in the afternoon with a cup of my favorite yogurt, wonderful sprinkled on vanilla ice cream for a quick dessert, and tasty folded into my favorite chocolate chip cookie dough.

Be creative. Think outside the box. Even the unassuming Overnight Breakfast Casserole can be changed up with crumbled cooked Italian sausage or smoked chicken and chiles. And those Cornmeal, Chile, and Cheese Waffles? They are the bomb served alongside chili or underneath a freshly fried chicken breast.

Allison's Gluten-Free Granola

MAKES: A GENEROUS 6 CUPS
PREP: 10 TO 15 MINUTES
BAKE: 25 TO 30 MINUTES

MY FRIEND ALLISON GREINER SHARED THIS RECIPE WITH me. Her son Elliot calls the granola "squirrel food." But it is undoubtedly the most delicious food a squirrel will see, full of toasted oats and almonds and pumpkin seeds, flavored with maple syrup and a dash of cinnamon. Be sure to buy oats labeled gluten-free on the package. Oats do not contain gluten but because they are grown and transported in bulk with other grains, they may contain trace amounts of gluten from wheat, barley, or rye.

4 cups gluten-free old-fashioned oats (see Note)

1 cup sliced almonds

½ cup sweetened flaked coconut

¼ cup unsalted pepitas (hulled pumpkin seeds)

½ cup pure maple syrup

2 tablespoons vegetable oil

½ teaspoon kosher salt

Dash of ground cinnamon (optional)

1 cup dried fruit, such as cherries, cranberries, raisins, or currants

1 Place a rack in the center of the oven and preheat the oven to 350°F.

2 Place the oats, almonds, coconut, and *pepitas* in a large mixing bowl and stir to combine. Drizzle the maple syrup and oil over the oat mixture and add the salt and cinnamon, if using. Stir again to combine, then spread the oat mixture on a rimmed baking sheet in a single layer. Place the baking sheet in the oven.

An Unbelievably Gluten-Free Meal

WHERE EATEN: _____

_____

WHEN EATEN: _____

_____

WHO WAS THERE: _____

_____

_____

TIPS FOR MAKING AT HOME: _____

_____

_____

_____

_____

NEW INSPIRATIONS: _____

_____

_____

3 Bake the granola, tossing it once or twice with a spatula, until the oats and almonds are golden brown, 25 to 30 minutes.

4 Remove the baking sheet from the oven. Sprinkle the dried fruit over the granola and stir to combine. Let the granola cool for about 2 hours. The granola can be stored in a tightly covered container at room temperature for up to 3 weeks.

Note: Do not use quick-cooking oats in this recipe. Use regular, old-fashioned oats.

EXTRA! EXTRA!

This recipe is fun to make and adaptable to whatever ingredients you have in the pantry or freezer. Use chopped walnuts or pecans instead of almonds or omit the coconut if someone in your house doesn't like it. I have even used already toasted and salted *pepitas* because that is what I had on hand, and they worked fine.

Dairy-Free:
The granola is dairy-free.

New Orleans–Style French Toast

SERVES: 4
PREP: 18 TO 20 MINUTES
COOK: 8 TO 12 MINUTES

FRENCH TOAST HAS LONG BEEN A MAINSTAY OF NEW Orleans, where it was called *pain perdu* or lost bread. Discarded day-old crusty French bread makes the best French toast, but any sturdy gluten-free sandwich bread will do; revive it in egg and milk and fry it until golden. French toast is suitable to serve for breakfast, brunch, or an early dinner. For an added touch sauté bananas in a little butter and serve them atop the French toast.

8 slices gluten-free French bread or sandwich bread (see Note)

3 large eggs

¼ cup milk

1 teaspoon pure vanilla extract

¼ teaspoon ground cinnamon

½ to ¾ cup vegetable oil, for frying the French bread

2 tablespoons (¼ stick) butter, for frying the bananas

2 small bananas, peeled and sliced in half lengthwise

Cinnamon sugar and pure maple syrup, for serving

1 Trim the crusts from the slices of bread, if desired, and set the bread aside.

2 Place the eggs, milk, vanilla, and cinnamon in a medium-size bowl and whisk to combine. Set the egg mixture aside.

3 Fill a large frying pan with oil to a depth of 1 inch. Place the pan over medium heat.

4 Line a platter with paper towels. When the oil is hot, dip the bread slices into the egg mixture, coating them on all sides, and carefully slide them 2 or 3 at a time into the hot oil. Cook the slices until browned on one side, 1 to 1½ minutes, then turn them with a fork to brown on the second side, 2 to 3 minutes. Transfer the bread to the paper towel–lined platter to drain and cover the slices with a kitchen towel to keep warm. Repeat with the remaining slices of bread.

5 After frying all of the French toast, discard the cooking oil and wipe the pan clean. Add the butter and heat over medium heat. Add the sliced bananas to the sizzling butter and cook until lightly browned on both sides, 1 to 2 minutes total.

6 To serve, place 2 slices of French toast on each of 4 serving plates and top each serving with a banana half. Sprinkle the French toast with cinnamon sugar and serve with maple syrup.

Note: Use the most dense, coarse French bread or sandwich bread you can find for this French toast. Soft gluten-free sandwich bread will work but tastes greasy after frying. You want a sturdy bread with a substantial crust. Udi's White Sandwich Bread works well.

EXTRA! EXTRA!

Make this a Valentine's special by cutting the slices of bread into heart shapes before dunking them in the egg and milk mixture and frying them. Rather than serving the French toast with the bananas, serve a medley of lightly sweetened fresh raspberries and strawberries atop the French toast hearts.

Dairy-Free:
You can omit the milk and use unsweetened coconut milk or water instead when making the French toast. Cook the bananas in margarine.

Fresh Blueberry Pancakes

MAKES: 6 PANCAKES
PREP: 10 TO 15 MINUTES
COOK: 2 TO 3 MINUTES

CREATING GLUTEN-FREE DISHES IS LIKE CONDUCTING FUN science experiments. Here's an example. I made these pancakes first with buttermilk, then sour cream, and lastly with yogurt, knowing an acidic ingredient would improve the texture. The buttermilk made great pancakes, the yogurt puffier ones, and the sour cream more richly-flavored ones. Try this recipe with whichever of the three possibilities you have in your fridge!

½ cup fresh blueberries

Vegetable oil spray, for misting the skillet or griddle

½ cup gluten-free baking mix, such as Bisquick

1 tablespoon granulated sugar

½ cup buttermilk, or ¼ cup sour cream mixed with ¼ cup water, or ½ cup plain or vanilla yogurt

1 large egg

1 tablespoon vegetable oil

½ teaspoon pure vanilla extract

Butter and pure maple syrup or confectioners' sugar, for serving

1 Rinse and drain the blueberries and set them aside.

2 Mist a large nonstick skillet or griddle with vegetable oil spray and preheat it for 3 to 4 minutes over medium-low heat.

3 Place the baking mix, sugar, and buttermilk, sour cream and water, or yogurt, along with the egg, oil, and vanilla in a medium-size bowl. Stir until the batter is

smooth, 15 to 20 strokes. Fold in the blueberries.

4 Using a large spoon, scoop spoonfuls of batter, about ¼ cup each, onto the hot skillet. Cook the pancakes until bubbles start to form and the pancakes are lightly browned on the bottom, about 1½ minutes. Turn the pancakes over and cook until lightly browned on the second side, about 1 minute longer.

5 Serve the pancakes hot with butter and maple syrup or a sprinkling of confectioners' sugar.

EXTRA! EXTRA!

For a twist, instead of blueberries add ½ cup of thinly sliced bananas, ¼ teaspoon of cinnamon, and 1 tablespoon of finely chopped walnuts to the pancake batter.

Dairy-Free:
Use ½ cup of unsweetened coconut milk instead of the buttermilk, sour cream, or yogurt.

Sweet Cornmeal Waffles with Mashed Banana and Chocolate Chips

MAKES: 5 OR 6 WAFFLES
PREP: 10 MINUTES
COOK: 20 TO 24 MINUTES TOTAL

GLUTEN-FREE RECIPES MADE WITH RICE FLOUR HAVE A reputation of being unexpectedly gritty. But when you add cornmeal to the baking mix, as in this waffle recipe, you expect them to have texture, so the waffles have permission to be gritty. I added mashed ripe bananas and mini chocolate chips to the batter, making the waffles scrumptious and perfect for brunch or school-day breakfasts. If you have leftover cooked waffles, store them in a plastic bag and reheat them in the toaster.

⅔ cup gluten-free baking mix, such as Bisquick

⅔ cup yellow cornmeal

⅓ cup granulated sugar

3 tablespoons vegetable oil

2 large eggs

½ cup mashed ripe banana (from 1 large to 2 small bananas)

½ cup water

1 teaspoon pure vanilla extract

½ teaspoon ground cinnamon

½ cup miniature semisweet chocolate chips (optional)

Vegetable oil spray, for misting the waffle iron

Butter and pure maple syrup or confectioners' sugar, for serving

1 Preheat an electric or stovetop waffle iron.

2 Place the baking mix, cornmeal, and sugar in a large mixing bowl and whisk to combine. Add the oil, eggs, banana, water, vanilla, and cinnamon. Stir until the batter is combined, 15 to 20 strokes. Fold in the chocolate chips, if using.

3 Lightly mist the hot waffle iron with vegetable oil spray. Spoon about ½ cup of the batter into the center of the waffle iron and close the lid. Cook the waffle until golden brown, 3 to 4 minutes depending on the size of your waffle iron. Repeat with the remaining waffle batter. Serve the waffles with butter and maple syrup or with butter and a sprinkling of confectioners' sugar.

EXTRA! EXTRA!

Make orange-blueberry waffles: Substitute orange juice for the water. Fold in 1 cup of fresh blueberries instead of the banana and leave out the chocolate chips.

Dairy-Free:
If you don't serve them with butter, the waffles are dairy-free.

An Unbelievably Gluten-Free Meal

WHERE EATEN:

WHEN EATEN:

WHO WAS THERE:

TIPS FOR MAKING AT HOME:

NEW INSPIRATIONS:

Pumpkin and Spice Waffles

MAKES: 5 OR 6 WAFFLES
PREP: 10 MINUTES
COOK: 20 TO 24 MINUTES TOTAL

HANDY CANNED PUMPKIN IS A GREAT ADD-IN TO BREADS and waffles. It adds fiber and vitamin A, but you don't have to tell anyone. Pumpkin and cinnamon are universally loved, especially in the fall. For a twist, throw in a half cup of miniature chocolate chips. No one will complain!

⅔ cup gluten-free baking mix, such as Bisquick

⅔ cup yellow cornmeal

⅓ cup granulated sugar

3 tablespoons vegetable oil

2 large eggs

⅔ cup canned 100% pure pumpkin

½ cup water

1 teaspoon pure vanilla extract

½ teaspoon ground cinnamon

¼ teaspoon ground nutmeg

Vegetable oil spray, for misting the waffle iron

Butter and pure maple syrup or confectioners' sugar, for serving

1 Preheat an electric or stovetop waffle iron.

2 Place the baking mix, cornmeal, and sugar in a large mixing bowl and whisk to combine. Add the oil, eggs, pumpkin, water, vanilla, cinnamon, and nutmeg. Stir with a wooden spoon until the batter is combined, 15 to 20 strokes.

3 Lightly mist the hot waffle iron with vegetable oil spray. Spoon about ½ cup of the batter into the center of the waffle iron and close the

lid. Cook the waffle until golden brown, 3 to 4 minutes depending on the size of your waffle iron. Repeat with the remaining waffle batter. Serve the waffles with butter and maple syrup or with butter and a sprinkling of confectioners' sugar.

EXTRA! EXTRA!

Turn this batter into little pumpkin pancakes by spooning it onto a lightly oiled heated griddle or frying pan. Cook the pancakes until they are lightly browned on the bottom, 1 to 1½ minutes. Turn the pancakes over and cook until lightly browned on the second side, 1 to 1½ minutes longer. Serve the pancakes for brunch with maple syrup and toasted pecans. Or, serve them along with roast turkey and cranberry sauce.

Dairy-Free:

Pumpkin and spice waffles are dairy-free when served without butter.

An Unbelievably Gluten-Free Meal

WHERE EATEN: _____

_____

WHEN EATEN: _____

_____

WHO WAS THERE: _____

_____

_____

TIPS FOR MAKING AT HOME: _____

_____

_____

_____

NEW INSPIRATIONS: _____

_____

_____

Cornmeal, Chile, and Cheese Waffles

MAKES: 5 OR 6 WAFFLES

PREP: 10 MINUTES

COOK: 20 TO 24 MINUTES TOTAL

I LOVED THE SWEET WAFFLES MADE WITH BANANA AND chocolate chips so much, I wondered if the recipe could be taken in a savory direction. And it can! These waffles are wonderfully crisp and delicious on their own or served with chili or barbecue. They contain cheddar cheese and hot peppers, making them a great cool weather substitute for garlic bread.

⅔ cup gluten-free baking mix, such as Bisquick

⅔ cup yellow cornmeal

⅛ teaspoon ground cumin

3 tablespoons vegetable oil

2 large eggs

½ cup sour cream

½ cup water

½ cup shredded sharp cheddar cheese

2 teaspoons minced jalapeño pepper, or more to taste

Vegetable oil spray, for misting the waffle iron

1 Preheat an electric or stovetop waffle iron.

2 Place the baking mix, cornmeal, and cumin in a large mixing bowl and whisk to combine. Add the oil, eggs, sour cream, and water. Stir with a wooden spoon until the batter is combined, 15 to 20 strokes. Fold in the cheddar cheese and jalapeño pepper.

3 Lightly mist the hot waffle iron with vegetable oil spray. Spoon about ½ cup of the batter into the center of the waffle iron and close

{ *These waffles are great for dinner, too, alongside fried chicken* (see page 145) }

the lid. Cook the waffle until lightly browned, about 3 to 4 minutes depending on the size of your waffle iron. Repeat with the remaining waffle batter. Serve the waffles warm.

EXTRA! EXTRA!

Instead of heating up the waffle iron, make griddle cakes! Heat a cast-iron skillet or griddle and brush it with vegetable oil. Spoon 3 tablespoons of the batter onto the hot cooking surface and cook until lightly brown on both sides, 2 to 3 minutes total.

Dairy-Free:

Make the waffles dairy-free by using plain soy yogurt instead of the sour cream, and omit the cheese entirely.

5 FAST, FRESH { WAYS TO DOCTOR } THIS RECIPE

1. Substitute finely chopped scallions for the jalapeño pepper.

2. Add 1 tablespoon of minced fresh parsley or cilantro.

3. Instead of cheddar cheese, use Parmesan and add a grinding of black pepper; the jalapeño is optional.

4. Add ⅓ cup of grated fresh corn from the cob and a pinch of sugar in place of the cheddar cheese and jalapeño pepper.

5. Cook ½ cup of chopped sweet onion, such as Vidalia, in 1 teaspoon of butter until soft, 4 to 5 minutes. Fold the onion into the waffle batter instead of the cheddar cheese and jalapeño pepper.

Classic but Simple Quiche Lorraine

SERVES: 8

PREP: 25 MINUTES | BAKE: 43 TO 55 MINUTES

COOL: 30 MINUTES

QUICHE COMES IN ALL SHAPES AND SIZES, BUT MY FAVORITE recipe remains the classic quiche lorraine, which contains bacon and Swiss or Gruyère cheese. Add a little cayenne pepper to the custard mixture, a bit of dry mustard, and if you like, a dash of nutmeg on top before baking—this seems to bring out the sweetness of the onion. The gluten-free pie crust can be your homemade crust or a store-bought frozen one.

12 ounces bacon

1 unbaked gluten-free pie crust (9 to 10 inches), homemade (page 318) or store-bought, thawed if frozen

3 large eggs

1½ cups half-and-half

½ teaspoon dry mustard

Dash of cayenne pepper (optional)

Salt and freshly ground black pepper

1 medium-size sweet onion, such as Vidalia, chopped

2 cups (8 ounces) shredded Swiss cheese

½ cup (2 ounces) shredded cheddar cheese

Dash of ground nutmeg (optional)

1 Cook the bacon in a large skillet over medium heat until lightly browned, 3 to 4 minutes per side. Drain the bacon on paper towels, then break it into ½-inch pieces. Set the crumbled bacon aside. Discard all but 2 tablespoons of the bacon drippings and set the skillet aside.

2 Place a rack in the center of the oven and preheat the oven to 350°F. If the crust is homemade, fit it into a 10-inch tart pan or a 9-inch pie pan that is 2 inches deep.

the crumbled bacon over the bottom of the pie crust and top it with the onion. Scatter the Swiss and cheddar cheeses over the onion and pour the egg mixture on top. Sprinkle a dash of nutmeg over the egg mixture, if using. Place the pan in the oven.

5 Bake the quiche until the crust is golden brown and the egg mixture has just set, 43 to 47 minutes for a 10-inch tart pan, 50 to 55 minutes for a 9-inch pie pan.

6 Let the quiche cool for 30 minutes before slicing.

EXTRA! EXTRA!

If you don't have half-and-half in the house, look in the pantry for a 12-ounce can of evaporated milk. Feel free to change up the cheeses, using Monterey Jack or mozzarella instead of the Swiss.

Dairy-Free:

It is not possible to make this quiche dairy-free.

3 Place the eggs in a medium-size bowl and beat them with a whisk until the yolks are well blended. Whisk in the half-and-half, dry mustard, and cayenne pepper, if using. Season the egg mixture with salt and black pepper to taste. Set the egg mixture aside.

4 Place the onion in the skillet with the reserved bacon drippings and cook over low heat until soft, 4 to 5 minutes. Spread

Overnight Breakfast Casserole

SERVES: 6 TO 8
PREP: 20 MINUTES
COOK: 45 TO 55 MINUTES

MY FAMILY'S TRADITIONAL CHRISTMAS MORNING breakfast casserole can be assembled the night before and stashed in the fridge to bake up fresh and puffy, like a soufflé, the next morning. The secret is to make the casserole with soft white bread. But making it gluten-free? I was a little nervous as to whether the bread would fall apart or be able to hold the casserole together. Thankfully there are good gluten-free sandwich breads with enough structure to make this casserole work. Whole Foods bakery has a light white sandwich bread that works great. And Udi's White Sandwich Bread, while a little heavier than the one from Whole Foods, works well, too.

Vegetable oil spray, for misting the baking dish

3 cups cubed gluten-free white bread, crusts removed (about 8 slices)

3 ounces thinly sliced ham, cut into 1-inch pieces (about ¾ cup; optional)

2 cups (8 ounces) shredded cheddar cheese (see Note)

1 tablespoon minced onion

4 large eggs

2 cups milk

½ teaspoon Dijon mustard

⅔ cup crushed buttery gluten-free crackers (10 to 12 crackers)

3 tablespoons butter, melted

1 Lightly mist a 2-quart glass or ceramic baking dish with vegetable oil spray. Scatter half of the bread cubes in the baking dish. Top the bread with the ham, if using, and the

cheddar cheese and onion, followed by the remaining bread cubes. Set the baking dish aside.

2 Place the eggs, milk, and mustard in a medium-size bowl and whisk to combine. Pour the egg mixture over the bread cubes and press down on them so they are immersed in it. Cover the baking dish with plastic wrap and refrigerate it overnight.

3 When ready to bake, place a rack in the center of the oven and preheat the oven to 350°F. Remove the plastic wrap from the casserole.

4 Place the crackers and butter in a small bowl and toss to mix. Using your fingers, scatter the cracker mixture over the top of the soaked bread cubes. Bake the casserole until it puffs up like a soufflé and is golden brown, 45 to 55 minutes. Serve at once.

Easter Brunch

Overnight Breakfast Casserole
Fresh fruit platter
Steamed asparagus
Soft Yeast Rolls, page 137
Amazing Angel Food Cake, page 301, with fresh strawberries

Note: I often substitute shredded Gruyère or Comté or some other interesting hard and full-flavored cheese for half of the cheddar called for in the recipe.

EXTRA! EXTRA!

If you don't want to wait until the next day to bake this casserole, wrap it and place it in the fridge for at least 4 hours before baking. If you don't add the ham, the casserole will be vegetarian. For a Southwestern flavor add a pinch of cumin to the eggs and milk instead of the mustard along with 2 tablespoons of drained canned chopped green chiles or 1 tablespoon of minced hot pepper.

Dairy-Free:
It is not possible to make this casserole dairy-free.

Sixteen Unbelievably Gluten-Free Little Snacks and Nibbles

1. *Crispy Cheese Wafers*
2. *Good Old Nuts and Bolts*
3. *Greek Spinach and Feta Balls*
4. *Five-Minute Hummus*
5. *Warm Baked Onion Dip with Tortilla Chips*
6. *Toaster Oven Flatbread*
7. *Oven-Baked Sweet Potatoes with Green Goddess Dip*
8. *Big Stuffed Mushrooms*
9. *Fried Mushrooms à la 1970s*
10. *Onion Bhaji*
11. *Fried Green Tomatoes*
12. *Dee's Sausage Pinwheels*
13. *Mini Ham Biscuits*
14. *Fresh Barbecue Chicken Spring Rolls*
15. *Our Favorite Chicken Lettuce Wraps*
16. *Crab Fritters with Spicy Mayonnaise*

Little Snacks and Nibbles

Your mother might have told you not to fill up on snacks before dinner. But these little bites and nibbles are more than just snacks—to the starving schoolchild, coming into the afternoon kitchen, they are sustenance before dinner. To the hungry dinner guest, they are a pleasurable bite before the meal is served. They can be meals along with a green salad. They are the star of a buffet party. They are the gift you place on a plate and bring to a friend.

For gluten-free appetizers, seek inspiration in Asian, Italian, and Indian cuisines—these cultures offer many classic recipes that don't contain gluten. And you can adapt many of your own traditional recipes using such gluten-free products as premade pizza crust, baking mix, or panko-style rice crumbs.

Bake the Big Stuffed Mushrooms and Fresh Barbecue Chicken Spring Rolls for first courses at dinner parties. Serve Warm Baked Onion Dip with Tortilla Chips and Nuts and Bolts at football parties and tailgates. Bake Toaster Oven Flatbread and Oven-Baked Sweet Potatoes with Green Goddess Dip for the kids. And fry up Onion Bhaji and Crab Fritters with Spicy Mayonnaise when you are feeling decadent.

Crispy Cheese Wafers

MAKES: 6 TO 7 DOZEN WAFERS
PREP: 15 MINUTES | BAKE: 10 TO 12 MINUTES

CHEESE AND CRACKERS MAY NOT BE AN ACCEPTABLE gluten-free snack, but these cheese wafers you make from sharp cheddar surely are. Choose the best sharp cheese you can find—from Vermont or an English sharp Cheddar. Shred the cheese yourself and fold it into butter and a gluten-free baking mix. A hearty dash of cayenne pepper adds a little needed heat, and if you like, roll the dough in chopped pecans before slicing it. These wafers are a great make-ahead for busy times, and they freeze well.

8 tablespoons (1 stick) butter, chilled and cut into tablespoons

2 cups (8 ounces) shredded sharp cheddar cheese

1½ cups gluten-free baking mix, such as Bisquick

Big dash of cayenne pepper

⅓ cup finely chopped pecans (optional)

1 Place the butter, cheese, baking mix, and cayenne pepper in a food processor and pulse until the mixture comes together into a ball, about 20 seconds.

2 Cut off two 12-inch long pieces of waxed paper and place them on a work surface. Divide the dough in half, place one half on one of the pieces of waxed paper, and shape the dough into a log. Repeat with the second dough half and piece of waxed paper. Scatter the pecans, if using, over the top of the logs and roll the logs back and forth over the pecans so they stick. Draw the waxed paper up around a log and roll it gently on the work surface until the log has a uniform diameter of about an inch.

Repeat with the remaining log of dough. Chill the wrapped logs for at least 15 minutes or up to 1 day.

3 Place a rack in the center of the oven and preheat the oven to 375°F.

4 Unwrap the logs and cut them into ¼-inch slices. Arrange the slices 1 inch apart on baking sheets. Bake the wafers until they are lightly browned, 10 to 12 minutes. Using a metal spatula, transfer the wafers to a large wire rack to cool for about 15 minutes.

5 Store the wafers in tins or glass containers for up to 4 days.

EXTRA! EXTRA!

Place the baked wafers in resealable plastic bags and you can freeze them for up to 6 months. To thaw the wafers, place them on a serving tray and let them come to room temperature.

You can vary the seasoning in the wafers by adding black pepper instead of cayenne pepper or by adding a dash of Creole seasoning.

Dairy-Free:

Because a good sharp cheddar cheese is key to this recipe, you cannot make the wafers dairy-free.

{ *10 Must-Have Ingredients for a Gluten-Free Appetizer Kitchen* }

1. *Panko* crumbs made from rice flour

2. Frozen gluten-free pizza crusts

3. Rice paper rounds

4. Gluten-free Bisquick

5. Gluten-free cereals

6. Tortilla chips and corn tortillas—think corn

7. Potato starch for making batters for fried veggies

8. Sliced veggies (instead of crackers)

9. Popcorn

10. Good cheese, dried fruit, and toasted nuts

Good Old Nuts and Bolts

MAKES: 13 CUPS
PREP: 15 MINUTES
BAKE: 1½ HOURS | COOL: 2 HOURS

ONE OF MY FAVORITE HOMEMADE SNACKS IS NUTS AND Bolts. When it first became popular, the mix was nearly gluten-free. I say "nearly" because it contained Cheerios and pretzels, which are not gluten-free. Today's version is usually a combination of gluten-free cereals like Rice Chex and Corn Chex, plus gluten-free versions of cereals that mimic Cheerios. With so many choices, you can make a safe, fun Nuts and Bolts, using whatever cereal and nut combinations you have on hand. Bake the mix often and package it for the folks on your gift list who are following a gluten-free diet.

FOR THE NUTS AND BOLTS

2 cups mixed nuts, such as almonds, pecans, and peanuts, either whole or halves

3 cups Rice Chex cereal

3 cups Corn Chex cereal

3 cups gluten-free O-shaped oat cereal (see Notes)

2 cups gluten-free pretzel sticks (see Notes)

FOR THE SAUCE

8 tablespoons (1 stick) unsalted butter

¼ cup Worcestershire sauce

1½ teaspoons garlic powder

2 teaspoons seasoned salt of your choice (see Notes)

Dash of cayenne pepper or hot sauce (optional)

1 Place a rack in the center of the oven and preheat the oven to 200°F.

2 Prepare the Nuts and Bolts: Place the nuts, cereals, and pretzels in a large roasting pan and stir to combine. Set the pan aside.

3 Make the sauce: Place the butter in a small saucepan over low heat and stir until melted, 3 to 4 minutes. Remove the pan from the heat and stir in the Worcestershire sauce, garlic powder, seasoned salt, and cayenne or hot sauce, if using. Pour the butter mixture over the cereal mixture and toss gently to coat well. Place the pan, uncovered, in the oven.

4 Bake the mixture until it is lightly golden in color, about 1 ½ hours, stirring it every 20 minutes with a wooden spoon. Remove the pan from the oven and let the mixture cool completely, about 2 hours. To speed the cooling you can spread the hot Nuts and Bolts out on rimmed baking sheets to cool, about 45 minutes.

5 Store the Nuts and Bolts in tins or glass containers for up to 10 days.

Notes: Nature's Path Organic Whole O's cereal is a gluten-free version of the popular Cheerios. You can find gluten-free pretzel sticks at stores carrying gluten-free products. The Glutino brand is a good one.

I like Lawry's seasoned salt and Creole seasoning, but read the label to make sure the seasoned salt is gluten-free.

EXTRA! EXTRA!

Feel free to toss in such dried fruit as raisins or cherries after the mixture has cooled. And think of pretty ways to package Nuts and Bolts for gifts—cellophane bags with ribbons, recycled tins, stainless steel canisters, and decorative glass jars.

Dairy-Free:

Substitute margarine for butter in the sauce and the Nuts and Bolts will be dairy-free.

Greek Spinach and Feta Balls

MAKES: 32 BALLS
PREP: 15 MINUTES
CHILL: 15 MINUTES | BAKE: 10 TO 12 MINUTES

ONE OF THE EASIEST APPETIZERS TO MAKE FOR A HUNGRY holiday crowd, spinach balls have been a favorite of mine for years. But the original recipe is based on stuffing mix, which is not exactly gluten-free. So I did some experimenting, using gluten-free bread crumbs instead of the stuffing mix, and adding feta, which gave these spinach balls a spanikopita-like flavor and now we like to call these Greek spinach balls!

1 package (10 ounces) frozen chopped spinach

3 large eggs

5 tablespoons butter, melted

½ cup gluten-free bread crumbs (see Note)

½ cup (2 ounces) grated Parmesan cheese

¼ cup (1 ounce) crumbled feta cheese

½ teaspoon salt

Dash of cayenne pepper

1 Thaw the frozen spinach quickly by removing it from the package and placing it in a microwave-safe bowl. Microwave the spinach on high power for 1 minute. Remove the bowl from the microwave and stir the spinach. Return the bowl to the microwave and microwave the spinach on high power until completely thawed, 45 seconds to 1 minute longer. Stir the spinach, then press it through a fine mesh sieve to get rid of the liquid. Set the spinach aside.

2 Place the eggs in a large bowl and lightly beat them with a fork until they are lemon colored. Add the drained spinach, butter, bread crumbs, Parmesan cheese, feta cheese, salt, and cayenne pepper. Stir until the ingredients come together. Cover the bowl with plastic wrap and refrigerate the spinach mixture for 15 minutes.

3 Preheat the oven to 350°F. Using your hands, roll the spinach mixture into balls about 1 inch across; you will get 32 balls.

4 Place the spinach balls on ungreased baking sheets, arranging them 1 inch apart. Bake the spinach balls until they are browned around the edges, 10 to 12 minutes. Transfer them to a serving platter and serve warm.

Note: I used Gillian's bread crumbs in this recipe. They are made from brown rice flour, and they have a lot of texture to them, and a toasted quality, which makes them very absorbent in this recipe but not gummy. You could also use gluten-free *panko*-style bread crumbs, but they're more expensive and not necessary in this case.

EXTRA! EXTRA!

You can easily double this recipe for big groups. And you can freeze the unbaked balls for up to 1 month. Arrange unbaked balls on a baking sheet and place them in the freezer until firm, about 1 hour. Transfer the frozen spinach balls to resealable plastic freezer bags and return them to the freezer. The frozen spinach balls can be baked without thawing and will be done in 13 to 15 minutes baked in a 350°F oven.

Dairy-Free:
Because of the Parmesan and feta cheese needed in this recipe, it is not possible to make the spinach balls dairy-free.

Five-Minute Hummus

SERVES: 6 TO 8
MAKES: ABOUT 2 CUPS
PREP: 5 MINUTES

I'LL ADMIT I BUY STORE-BOUGHT HUMMUS WHEN I'M IN A hurry. But as easy as it is to pick up and put it in my shopping cart, so is hummus simple and fast to make in a food processor at home. You just need a can of chickpeas, a little garlic, some seasonings, and olive oil. Oh sure, you can add a dash of lemon juice or tahini, but the most basic hummus is just chickpeas blended with oil until smooth and seasoned as you like. And it only takes five minutes!

2 cloves garlic, peeled

1 can (about 15 ounces) chickpeas
   (garbanzo beans)

Pinch each of ground cumin, salt,
   freshly ground black pepper, and
   cayenne pepper, or more to taste

3 tablespoons olive oil

Kalamata olives, chopped tomatoes,
   and/or chopped fresh parsley,
   for garnish

Gluten-free corn tortilla chips,
   for serving

1 Using a food processor or a blender, while the motor is running, drop the garlic through the feed tube and process until minced, about 5 seconds. Stop the machine.

2 Drain the chickpeas, setting aside the liquid. Add the chickpeas, cumin, salt, black pepper, and cayenne to the minced garlic. Process in short pulses until the chickpeas are minced, about 5 seconds. Stop the

machine and scrape down the side of the bowl with a rubber spatula.

3 Add the olive oil and up to 2 tablespoons of the reserved chickpea liquid to the processor bowl. Process until the hummus is smooth, adding more chickpea liquid as needed. The hummus should be smooth and thick like a milkshake. Taste for seasoning, adding more cumin, salt, pepper, and/or cayenne pepper as necessary. Garnish the hummus with kalamata olives, chopped tomatoes, chopped fresh parsley, whatever is quick and on hand. Serve the hummus with tortilla chips for dipping.

EXTRA! EXTRA!

Make a festive red pepper hummus by pulsing 1 cup of roasted red peppers along with the garlic and then adding the chickpeas, seasonings, and oil.

PLAN AHEAD: The hummus can be stored in a tightly sealed glass container in the refrigerator for up to 4 days. You do not need to stir it before serving.

Dairy-Free:
Hummus is naturally dairy-free—enjoy!

{ **HOW TO MAKE A GLUTEN-FREE HUMMUS FLOWER** }

In my cookbook *What Can I Bring?* I shared how to make a hummus flower by arranging pita crisps on top of hummus like the petals on a flower. You can do a gluten-free version by using steamed artichoke leaves. First of all, steam a whole artichoke about 45 minutes in water to cover the artichoke halfway. When it is done, you can gently pull off the artichoke leaves and set them aside. Now, make the hummus and spread it on a large round serving plate. Beginning at the center, place an artichoke leaf in the hummus with the pointed end up. Arrange the remaining artichoke leaves in the same way so they form a spiral of leaves resembling a flower. You can get fancy by placing basil leaves around the hummus to look like the leaves on the plant, and you can place a spoonful of olive tapenade or chopped tomatoes in the middle for the center of the flower.

Warm Baked Onion Dip with Tortilla Chips

SERVES: 8 TO 10

MAKES: ABOUT 4 CUPS OF DIP

PREP: 10 MINUTES | BAKE: 20 TO 25 MINUTES

WHAT DOES EVERY FOOTBALL PARTY, HOLIDAY GET-together, and potluck supper need? A big, hot, cheesy dip! Thankfully you don't have to go without a recipe like this when you are following a gluten-free diet. Shred your own cheese, use sweet onions, add a bit of cayenne to this warm onion dip, and serve gluten-free chips on the side.

2 medium-size sweet onions, such as Vidalia or Walla Walla

2 cups shredded Swiss or Manchego cheese

2 cups mayonnaise (preferably Hellmann's, see Note)

¼ teaspoon cayenne pepper, or more to taste

Pinch of paprika (optional), for sprinkling

Gluten-free corn tortilla chips, for serving

1 Place a rack in the center of the oven and preheat the oven to 375°F.

2 Chop the onions finely to make 2 cups. Place the chopped onions, cheese, mayonnaise, and cayenne pepper in a large mixing bowl and stir to combine. Taste for seasoning, adding more cayenne as necessary. Transfer the mixture to a 2-quart glass or ceramic baking dish. Sprinkle the

{ *Serve this dip at a Super Bowl party or at a winter DVD film fest.* }

top with paprika, if desired. Place the baking dish in the oven.

3 Bake the dip until it is golden brown and bubbling, 20 to 25 minutes. Serve the warm dip with tortilla chips.

Note: I use Hellmann's mayonnaise. It is gluten-free.

Dairy-Free:
You cannot make this dip dairy-free.

PLAN AHEAD: The dip can be assembled up to 8 hours in advance—cover it with plastic wrap and refrigerate it until you're ready to bake.

EXTRA! EXTRA!

Make this a more colorful appetizer and add some vitamins, too, by serving steamed asparagus spears, long cucumber wedges, carrot sticks, celery sticks, and strips of bell pepper along with the tortilla chips.

Toaster Oven Flatbread

SERVES: 2 OR 3

MAKES: 3 PIECES

PREP: 10 MINUTES | BAKE: 4 TO 5 MINUTES

IMAGINE YOUR KIDS COMING HOME FROM SCHOOL HUNGRY for a filling yet healthy snack. Not too hard to imagine, is it? But imagine now that you have at the ready the fixings for a homemade flatbread pizza, made from a thin gluten-free pizza crust onto which your kids pile their favorite toppings and then pop their creations in the toaster oven. Now, Mom, you're a hero.

1 frozen 9-inch gluten-free pizza crust
 (4 ounces)

1 cup pizza sauce

2 tablespoons sliced gluten-free pepperoni
 (optional)

2 cups (8 ounces) shredded mozzarella
 cheese

1 Remove the pizza crust from the freezer and place it on the kitchen counter to thaw just enough to slice it into strips.

2 Preheat the toaster oven or a conventional oven to 375°F.

3 Cut the pizza crust into three 3-inch strips. Place each strip on a cutting board and spoon about ⅓ cup of pizza sauce on top of each. Spread the sauce smoothly to the edges of the crust. Top the sauce with pepperoni, if desired, followed by the cheese.

4 Carefully transfer the pizza strips, one at a time, to the

An Unbelievably Gluten-Free Meal

WHERE EATEN: _____

_____

WHEN EATEN: _____

_____

WHO WAS THERE: _____

_____

_____

TIPS FOR MAKING AT HOME: ____

_____

_____

_____

NEW INSPIRATIONS: _____

_____

_____

_____

toaster oven to bake. Bake until the topping is bubbly, 4 to 5 minutes.

EXTRA! EXTRA!

It's convenient to keep some gluten-free pizza crusts in the freezer for making not only pizzas, but also oven flatbreads. Try one of these topping combinations if you're feeling creative:

- Turkey strips with dollops of pesto (pictured)

- Diced grilled chicken, eggplant, and roasted red peppers

- Diced ham and pineapple

Dairy-Free:

Omit the cheese and top the pizza sauce with pepperoni and dollops of a cream cheese substitute.

Oven-Baked Sweet Potatoes with Green Goddess Dip

SERVES: 6
PREP: 20 MINUTES
BAKE: 20 TO 25 MINUTES

BOY, DO I LOVE SWEET POTATOES. AND NOT IN THE Thanksgiving sort of way, mashed and sweetened and topped with marshmallows. I love them plain, roasted with a little salt and pepper, and then eaten along with a good grilled burger or steak, or simply enjoyed on their own. This easy appetizer highlights the natural sweetness of sweet potatoes, which really comes out in roasting. Served with a shockingly delicious dip of parsley and garlic and anchovies, it is perfect for grown-ups with a glass of wine or for adventurous children who love a good roasted veggie.

FOR THE SWEET POTATOES

4 sweet potatoes (about 2 pounds), peeled and cut into 1-inch-thick wedges

¼ cup olive oil

Salt and freshly ground black pepper

FOR THE GREEN GODDESS DIP
(Makes about 2 cups)

2 cloves garlic, peeled

2 cups fresh parsley leaves

2 scallions, light green parts only, chopped

3 anchovy fillets

1 teaspoon fresh lemon juice, or more to taste

½ teaspoon freshly ground black pepper

½ cup mayonnaise (preferably Hellmann's)

¼ cup reduced-fat sour cream

1 Bake the sweet potatoes: Place a rack in the center of the oven and preheat the oven to 400°F.

2 Place the sweet potato wedges in a large mixing bowl, add the olive oil, and toss to coat. Season the sweet potatoes with salt and pepper to taste and toss to coat. Arrange the sweet potatoes in a single layer on a large baking sheet. Place the baking sheet in the oven.

3 Bake the sweet potatoes until they are lightly browned and tender, 20 to 25 minutes. Remove the baking sheet from the oven and let the sweet potatoes cool.

4 Meanwhile, make the Green Goddess Dip: Using a food processor with the motor running, drop the garlic through the feed tube and process until minced, about 5 seconds. Stop the machine. Add the parsley, scallions, anchovies, lemon juice, and pepper. Pulse until minced, about 10 seconds. Add the mayonnaise and sour cream and pulse until smooth, about 15 seconds. Taste for seasoning, adding more lemon juice if necessary.

5 Spoon the dip into a serving dish. Place the dish in the center of a platter and surround it with the cooled sweet potato wedges. Serve at once.

EXTRA! EXTRA!

Instead of sweet potatoes, roast Brussels sprouts. I trim the stem ends just a smidgen, cut the sprouts in half, toss them with olive oil, salt, and pepper and then roast them in a 400°F oven until they are tender and crisp, 10 minutes. Serve the Brussels sprouts with toothpicks.

Dairy-Free:
Omit the sour cream and use ¾ cup mayonnaise in the Green Goddess Dip.

PLAN AHEAD: The dip can be prepared a day in advance—cover it with plastic wrap and refrigerate it until you're ready to serve.

Big Stuffed Mushrooms

SERVES: 12 TO 15 AS AN APPETIZER, 4 AS A MAIN DISH
PREP: 25 MINUTES
BAKE: 30 TO 35 MINUTES

W HEN YOU SEE *STUFFED* ON A RESTAURANT MENU YOU think breading, and for gluten-free diners it's normally a red alert. But you can make restaurant-style stuffed mushrooms, and you can make them gluten-free. The key ingredient is *panko*-style bread crumbs made from rice flour. Begin with extra-large white mushroom caps, and you can serve these big mushrooms for appetizers (cut them into quarters and serve them with toothpicks) or as a main dish served alongside rice pasta and a green salad.

15 extra-large white mushrooms

3 tablespoons olive oil

8 ounces sweet or hot Italian sausage meat

⅓ cup finely minced onion

2 cloves garlic, minced

⅓ cup gluten-free *panko*-style rice bread crumbs

4 ounces (8 tablespoons) reduced-fat cream cheese

⅓ cup grated Parmesan cheese

3 tablespoons minced fresh parsley

1 large egg, lightly beaten

Salt and freshly ground black pepper

1 Place a rack in the center of the oven and preheat the oven to 325°F.

2 Wipe the mushrooms with paper towels to remove dirt and grit. Remove the stems and set them aside. Place the caps in a large shallow baking dish that will hold the caps in one layer. Brush them on all sides with the olive oil. Set the baking dish aside.

3 Crumble the Italian sausage into a nonstick frying pan and cook

over medium-low heat, stirring, until browned, 6 to 7 minutes. Turn off the heat and add the onion and garlic. Finely chop the mushroom stems. Add these to the frying pan and cook, stirring, over low heat until the onion and mushroom stems soften, about 3 minutes. Stir in the *panko* crumbs, then the cream cheese, and cook until the cream cheese softens, about 2 minutes. Turn off the heat and stir in the cheese, parsley, and egg. Season with salt and pepper to taste. Cool slightly, about 5 minutes.

4 Spoon the stuffing generously into each mushroom cap, pressing it down to fill the caps. Bake until the mushrooms are cooked through, 30 to 35 minutes.

5 If you're serving the mushrooms as an appetizer, cut them in quarters and arrange on a large platter before serving.

Dairy-Free:

Substitute dairy-free cream cheese, for the cream cheese and omit the Parmesan cheese.

EXTRA! EXTRA!

For a change of taste, parboil 8 small zucchini. Cut them in half top to stem end and scoop out the centers to form boats. Fill with *panko* stuffing (minus the mushroom stems) and bake at 325°F until cooked through, 30 to 35 minutes. Serve warm with marinara sauce.

Fried Mushrooms à la 1970s

SERVES: 4
PREP: 10 MINUTES
COOK: 12 TO 15 MINUTES

I REMEMBER WHEN FRIED MUSHROOMS WERE THE HOTTEST appetizer around. Served with a horseradish-seasoned mayonnaise, they were crisp on the outside and warm and oozy inside. You can create your own fried mushrooms at home, beginning with simple white button mushrooms. The batter is a blend of potato starch, beaten eggs, and Lawry's seasoned salt. If desired, serve the mushrooms with mayonnaise seasoned with prepared horseradish. Use 1 teaspoon horseradish per ½ cup mayonnaise. Yum!

1 pound white button mushrooms

½ cup potato starch

2 large eggs, beaten

½ teaspoon seasoned salt, such as Lawry's

2 cups vegetable oil, for frying

1 Wipe the mushrooms with paper towels to remove dirt and grit. Thinly slice the tough end off each mushroom stem. Set the mushrooms aside.

2 Place the potato starch and beaten eggs in a large mixing bowl. Stir in the seasoned salt. Set the egg mixture aside.

An Unbelievably Gluten-Free Meal

. . . .

WHERE EATEN:

_____

_____

WHEN EATEN:

_____

_____

WHO WAS THERE:

_____

_____

_____

TIPS FOR MAKING AT HOME:

_____

_____

_____

_____

NEW INSPIRATIONS:

_____

_____

_____

_____

3 Place the oil in a heavy deep frying pan or electric skillet and heat until the oil registers 365°F on a candy thermometer. When ready to cook, place the mushrooms in the egg mixture and stir with a fork to coat. Place 3 or 4 mushrooms in the hot oil and cook until they are lightly browned all over, about 3 minutes. Using a slotted spoon, transfer the cooked mushrooms to paper towels to drain. Repeat with the remaining mushrooms. Serve the mushrooms warm.

EXTRA! EXTRA!

Instead of mushrooms, you can fry onion rings (¼ inch thick) sliced from 1 large onion. Or, fry zucchini sticks: Cut 1 large or 2 medium zucchini into sticks 2 inches long by ¼ inch thick. Serve with lemon wedges for squeezing and grated Parmesan cheese, if desired.

Dairy-Free:
These fried mushrooms are dairy-free.

Onion Bhaji

SERVES: 6
MAKES: 12 TO 15 *BHAJI*
COOK: 4 TO 6 MINUTES

WHEN YOU NEED INSPIRATION FOR COOKING GLUTEN-free, look to the cuisines of other countries. One such country is India, where its brightly flavored wheat-free foods can energize tired menus. This recipe for onion *bhaji,* a classic Indian fried onion fritter that uses chickpea flour as a binder, is adapted from Madhur Jaffrey's cookbook, *Quick & Easy Indian Cooking,* which I love. Fry these to serve alongside grilled lamb or chicken curry. Or just have them with drinks during the holidays.

1 cup chickpea flour, also known as gram flour (see Notes)

1 teaspoon ground cumin

1 teaspoon garam masala (see Notes)

½ teaspoon salt

¼ teaspoon cayenne pepper

2 tablespoons chopped fresh cilantro

½ cup water

1 tablespoon fresh lemon juice

1 large egg, lightly beaten

1½ cups chopped onion

3 cups vegetable oil, for frying

Fresh Green Chutney (recipe follows) or chutney of your choice

1 Place the chickpea flour, cumin, garam masala, salt, cayenne pepper, and cilantro in a large bowl and stir to combine. Make a well in the center of the flour mixture and add the water, lemon juice, and egg. Using a fork, beat the egg and water mixture to blend them together. Use a fork to

An Unbelievably Gluten-Free Meal

WHERE EATEN:

_____

_____

WHEN EATEN:

_____

WHO WAS THERE:

_____

_____

TIPS FOR MAKING AT HOME:

_____

_____

_____

_____

NEW INSPIRATIONS:

_____

_____

_____

_____

combine the egg mixture with the dry ingredients until it looks like pancake batter. Spoon the onion on top of the chickpea batter without stirring it, then set the batter aside.

2 Place the oil in a heavy, deep frying pan or electric skillet and heat until the oil registers 365°F on a candy thermometer. When ready to cook, stir the onion into the batter. Carefully drop tablespoons of the chickpea batter into the hot oil, cooking 5 or 6 *bhaji* at a time, being careful not to overcrowd the pan. Cook the *bhaji* on one side until browned, about 1 minute, then using a slotted spoon, turn the *bhaji* over and cook them until browned on the second side, about 1 minute longer. Transfer the *bhaji* to paper towels to drain.

3 Repeat with the remaining chickpea batter until all of the *bhaji* have been fried. Serve the *bhaji* warm with the Fresh Green Chutney or chutney of your choice.

Notes: You can find chickpea flour in health food stores, Indian groceries, and wherever gluten-free ingredients are sold.

Garam marsala is an Indian spice mixture, more delicious than your average curry powder. It is often made from scratch but you can buy pretty good blends at the supermarket. In a pinch you can use regular curry powder.

EXTRA! EXTRA!

The *bhaji* batter is not only delicious made with onions but also with other veggies such as zucchini sticks and eggplant slices. Use 1 to 1½ cups very thinly sliced (⅛ inch thick) eggplant or zucchini sliced ¼ inch thick in place of the onion. Then stack the slices and cut them into 3 or 4 matchsticks. Toss the eggplant or zucchini sticks in the chickpea batter immediately prior to cooking. As with the onions, the zucchini and eggplant sticks will cook for about 1 minute on each side.

Dairy-Free:

The *bhaji* are dairy-free. Serve them with a dairy-free sauce such as mango chutney.

Fresh Green Chutney

This refreshing yogurt dip is a perfect accompaniment to fried finger foods like the Onion Bhaji and other vegetable fritters.

MAKES: ABOUT ½ CUP

6 tablespoons plain yogurt

2 tablespoons chopped fresh mint leaves

2 tablespoons chopped fresh cilantro leaves

1 tablespoon fresh lemon juice

Dash of salt

Place 2 tablespoons of the yogurt and the mint, cilantro, lemon juice, and salt in a blender or food processor and pulse until a paste forms. Fold in the remaining 4 tablespoons of yogurt and stir to mix. The chutney can be refrigerated, covered, for 3 to 4 days.

Fried Green Tomatoes

SERVES: 4
PREP: 10 MINUTES
COOK: 10 MINUTES

I NEVER TIRE OF WATCHING THE MOVIE *FRIED GREEN TOMATOES,* and I never tire of eating those tomatoes, either. And considering that I grew up in the South and have lived in the South most of my adult life, I have eaten a good number of fried green tomatoes. My favorite way to prepare them is the most simple of all—just a dredging of white cornmeal seasoned with salt and pepper. The cornmeal sticks right to the sliced tomatoes, and it sticks even better if you dunk the tomato slices in beaten egg and dredge them a second time in the cornmeal. Then fry the tomatoes in hot vegetable oil in, what else, a cast-iron skillet!

I cup white or yellow cornmeal

2 large eggs

Salt and freshly ground black pepper

3 large green tomatoes

3 cups vegetable oil, for frying

1 Place the cornmeal in a shallow bowl. Place the eggs in a small bowl and beat them with salt and pepper to taste.

2 Rinse, core, and, using a serrated knife, cut the tomatoes into ¼-inch slices. Dredge the tomato slices on both sides in the cornmeal. Using a fork, dunk the tomato slices in the egg mixture, then dredge them again in the cornmeal on both sides. Set the tomato slices aside on a cutting board or platter.

3 Preheat the oven to 200°F. Line a baking sheet with paper towels.

4 Place the oil in a 12-inch cast-iron frying pan over medium-high heat and heat until the oil registers 365°F on a candy thermometer. Slide 3 or 4 tomato slices into the hot oil and cook them for 2 to 3 minutes, then turn them and cook until golden brown, about 2 minutes longer. Transfer the fried tomato slices to the paper towel–lined baking sheet and place the baking sheet in the oven to keep the tomatoes warm. Repeat with the remaining tomato slices. Serve warm in a towel–lined basket.

EXTRA! EXTRA!

For the ultimate treat, create fried tomato stacks. Place one fried tomato slice on a serving plate and top it with a dab or smear of goat cheese and a grinding of black pepper. Top that fried tomato with a second tomato slice and a little goat cheese and chopped fresh chives or basil. Then top everything with a third tomato slice, a drizzling of good olive oil, and chopped ripe tomato.

Dairy-Free:

Fried green tomatoes are naturally dairy-free!

An Unbelievably Gluten-Free Meal

WHERE EATEN: _____

_____

WHEN EATEN: _____

_____

WHO WAS THERE: _____

_____

_____

TIPS FOR MAKING AT HOME: _____

_____

_____

_____

NEW INSPIRATIONS: _____

_____

_____

_____

Dee's Sausage Pinwheels

MAKES: 3 DOZEN
PREP: 30 MINUTES
CHILL: 2 HOURS | BAKE: 10 TO 15 MINUTES

MY GRANDMOTHER, WHOM WE AFFECTIONATELY CALLED Dee, baked these spicy snacks during the Christmas holidays. And our family continues to bake them today. They are as suitable for brunch as they are a cup of cheer at a festive party. I was curious how Dee's recipe would take to a gluten-free baking mix and, with some adaptations, I was happy with the outcome. Since these baking mixes, such as Bisquick, are based on rice flour, they are not as easy to roll out with a rolling pin. So I wrapped the dough in waxed paper and pressed it out before chilling. Then after spreading the dough with spicy sausage, I rolled the dough up into a log and froze it for easy slicing. The colder the dough, the easier it is to slice!

2 cups gluten-free baking mix,
    such as Bisquick

2 tablespoons white or yellow cornmeal

⅓ cup solid vegetable shortening

½ cup milk or buttermilk

8 ounces spicy pork breakfast sausage meat

1 Place the baking mix and cornmeal in a food processor. Pulse a few times to combine. Scatter tablespoons of the shortening around the bowl of the processor. Pulse until the dough resembles large peas, 12 to 15 times. With the motor running, pour in the milk or buttermilk and process until combined.

2 Turn the dough out onto a 12-inch piece of waxed paper.

Fold the edges up and over the dough as if you were wrapping a present. Wrap another 12-inch piece of waxed paper around the dough to secure it. Using your hands gently knead the dough so that it comes together into a ball. Flatten the dough ball into a disk about 1 inch thick. Place it in the refrigerator for 1 hour.

3 Remove the dough from the refrigerator and unwrap the waxed paper. Leave the dough on top of the waxed paper and, using a rolling pin, carefully but quickly roll it out to a ¼-inch thickness. Scatter the sausage over the top of the dough and carefully spread it with a knife to cover it. Using the waxed paper, roll the dough into a log, taking care not to roll the waxed paper into the log. Wrap the log back up in one piece of the waxed paper and place the log in the freezer to chill for 2 hours.

4 When you are ready to bake the pinwheels, place a rack in the center of the oven and preheat the oven to 375°F.

5 Remove the dough from the freezer and unwrap it. Using a sharp knife, slice the log into ½-inch-thick slices and place them on ungreased baking sheets, 1 inch apart.

6 Bake the pinwheels until they are golden brown around the edges and the sausage is cooked through, 10 to 15 minutes. Transfer the pinwheels to a rack to cool before serving.

EXTRA! EXTRA!

The pinwheels can be baked in advance and frozen for up to 1 month. They are easy to reheat and serve warm. If you need just a dozen, place the frozen pinwheels on baking sheets and reheat them in a 350°F oven for 4 to 5 minutes. If you are reheating them for a party, wrap the pinwheels in aluminum foil and reheat them at 350°F for 5 minutes, then turn off the oven and keep warm.

Dairy-Free:
Substitute rice milk, soy milk, or water for the milk or buttermilk in the dough.

Mini Ham Biscuits

MAKES: 18 MINI BISCUITS
PREP: 35 MINUTES
BAKE: 7 TO 8 MINUTES

ONE OF MY FAVORITE APPETIZERS AND BRUNCH OFFERINGS is little ham biscuits. Once I mastered the art of making gluten-free buttermilk biscuits, I was ready to make ham biscuits. You don't need to roll out the dough, just drop the dough onto baking sheets and bake it. If making eighteen minis seems too tedious, you can bake larger biscuits, then split them in half and fill them with the ham filling. Cut the biscuits in half and serve.

1 cup gluten-free baking mix, such as Bisquick

1 tablespoon minced fresh chives

2½ tablespoons solid vegetable shortening

1 large egg

½ cup buttermilk or plain yogurt

6 ounces cooked ham

2 to 3 tablespoons mayonnaise (preferably Hellmann's)

2 teaspoons pickle relish

1 Place a rack in the center of the oven and preheat the oven to 400°F. Set aside an ungreased baking sheet.

2 Place the baking mix and chives in a medium-size mixing bowl. Add the shortening and, using a pastry blender or 2 small sharp knives, cut the shortening into the mix until it resembles small peas.

3 Place the egg and buttermilk or yogurt in a small bowl and whisk to mix. Add the egg mixture to the baking mix and stir with a fork until a soft dough forms.

4 Scoop the dough by heaping teaspoons onto the baking sheet, spacing the chive biscuits 1 to 2 inches apart. You will have enough dough for about 18 biscuits. Place the baking sheet in the oven.

5 Bake the biscuits until they are very lightly browned, 7 to 8 minutes. Remove the baking sheet from the oven and let the biscuits cool on the baking sheet for 1 to 2 minutes before filling them.

6 Cut the ham into 2-inch pieces and place in a food processor. Process until the ham is ground and crumbly, about 10 pulses. Transfer the ham to a mixing bowl and fold in the mayonnaise and pickle relish.

7 Split the biscuits in half and spoon a small teaspoonful of ham filling on one half, then replace the second half. Place the filled biscuits on a serving tray and serve at once.

EXTRA! EXTRA!

Don't have time to bake biscuits? Make the ham filling and spread it open-face on gluten-free sandwich bread. Cut the bread into small squares and serve these garnished with chopped parsley.

Dairy-Free:
Substitute rice or soy milk for the buttermilk in the biscuits.

PLAN AHEAD: The ham filling can be made 1 day ahead. Transfer it to an airtight container and refrigerate. Remove the filling from the fridge 1 hour before assembling the biscuits.

Fresh Barbecue Chicken Spring Rolls

SERVES: 8
PREP: 30 MINUTES

IT'S NO WONDER SPRING ROLLS ARE SO POPULAR—THEY'RE versatile, delicious, light, and fun to eat. The important ingredient here is edible rice paper rounds known to the Vietnamese as *bánh tráng.* These crisp rounds need only to be softened in warm water for less than a minute and they become pliable so you can wrap them around your favorite ingredients—boiled shrimp, julienne sliced pork tenderloin, and in this recipe chicken enlivened with barbecue sauce. Begin by tossing cooked chicken with a half cup (or more) of your favorite barbecue sauce, whatever is in the fridge. (Just make sure it's gluten-free!) Then gather your other filling ingredients—a shredded carrot, cilantro leaves, sliced cucumber—and start rolling! What makes this appetizer even more lovable is that it can be made ahead and stashed in the fridge.

8 ounces shredded cooked chicken (about 2 cups)

½ cup gluten-free barbecue sauce of your choice

1 large carrot

2 small cucumbers

8 rounds edible rice paper

8 small lettuce leaves

24 cilantro leaves

Favorite Spring Roll Sauce (optional); recipe follows

Finely chopped roasted peanuts (optional)

1 Place the chicken in a small bowl, add the barbecue sauce, and toss to coat. Set the chicken mixture aside. Peel and shred the carrot and set it aside. Peel the cucumbers and slice

them very thinly crosswise. Set the cucumbers aside.

2 Moisten one rice paper round at a time in a small bowl of warm water. It will take less than a minute. Remove the round and stretch it out on a work surface. Place a lettuce leaf on the bottom third of the round. Top with 2 tablespoons of the chicken mixture, 1 tablespoon of shredded carrot, and 6 to 8 slices of cucumber. Roll the rice paper halfway up into a cylinder. Fold the sides in and scatter some of the cilantro leaves at the crease. Continue to roll the round into a cylinder. Place the spring roll on a plate and cover it with a damp paper towel. Continue making the rest of the spring rolls.

3 Serve the spring rolls with my Favorite Spring Roll Sauce and/ or chopped peanuts, if desired.

Dairy-Free:

These spring rolls are naturally dairy-free. Love it!

{ *Start this easy dish with a store-bought rotisseried chicken and it becomes even easier.* }

EXTRA! EXTRA!

These easy appetizers can also be made with sliced turkey or smoked salmon. Omit the barbecue sauce and add thinly sliced radishes, watercress, mint, or arugula for crunch and freshness. Add a drizzle of gluten-free peanut sauce for the turkey or sour cream for the salmon. Really, the sky is the limit.

PLAN AHEAD: The spring rolls can be assembled up to 2 hours in advance— cover them with plastic and refrigerate them until you're ready to serve.

Favorite Spring Roll Sauce

Here is a delicious dipping sauce for these spring rolls and all Asian appetizers or grilled fish and chicken. If desired, add a dash of Asian (dark) sesame oil. For a more Vietnamese flavor, omit the soy sauce and use fish sauce.

MAKES: ABOUT ½ CUP
PREP: 5 MINUTES

¼ cup rice vinegar

¼ cup low-sodium soy sauce

1 clove garlic, minced

1 teaspoon granulated sugar

Pinch of red pepper flakes

1 teaspoon grated fresh ginger (optional)

1 scallion, white and green parts trimmed and chopped (optional)

Dash of Asian (dark) sesame oil (optional)

Whisk together the vinegar and soy sauce. Stir in the garlic, sugar, and red pepper flakes. Add the fresh ginger, scallion, or Asian (dark) sesame oil, if desired.

{ LET'S PARTY! }

Arrange the spring rolls in a spoke pattern on your favorite serving plate. Make the easy dipping sauce, pour it into a small bowl, and place it in the center of the plate for dunking. If you want smaller bites, cut the spring rolls in halves or thirds, and spear them with toothpicks for easy handling.

Our Favorite Chicken Lettuce Wraps

SERVES: 4 TO 6

MAKES: 12 WRAPS

PREP: 20 MINUTES | COOK: 8 TO 10 MINUTES

THIS IS EASILY MY KIDS' FAVORITE MEAL—WARM SAUTEED ground chicken and seasoning piled into crisp lettuce. We like it in the summertime when light meals seem right. And it's great party food, too, because it is a do-ahead dish—make the chicken in advance and keep it warm till party time. Place the lettuce on a serving platter, then fill and serve. To eat, just pick up a lettuce leaf and wrap it around the filling. Iceberg lettuce works, but if you're feeling fancy opt for butterhead or buttercrunch or other varieties of crispy leafy lettuces.

1 large head iceberg lettuce, or 2 small
    heads butterhead lettuce

1 tablespoon vegetable oil

1 pound ground chicken

3 cloves garlic, minced

1 cup chopped scallions, green parts only
    (1 bunch)

1 tablespoon minced peeled fresh ginger

¾ cup gluten-free hoisin sauce

4 teaspoons gluten-free soy sauce

1 teaspoon Asian (dark) sesame oil

¾ cup finely chopped water chestnuts

1 Using a small paring knife, cut the core out of the head of lettuce and discard it. Rinse the lettuce under cool running water and drain it well on paper towels. Set the lettuce aside.

2 Place the oil in a large frying pan over medium heat. Add the chicken, breaking it up with a wooden spoon into as small pieces as possible. Add the garlic, and cook, stirring, until the chicken is cooked through,

4 to 5 minutes. Turn off the heat. Stir in the scallions, ginger, hoisin sauce, soy sauce, sesame oil, and water chestnuts. Turn the heat back on to medium-low and cook, stirring, until the filling bubbles and is heated through, 4 to 5 minutes. Keep the filling warm if not serving immediately.

3 When ready to serve, carefully pull apart the head of lettuce to separate the leaves. Pat the leaves dry with paper towels and arrange them like bowls on a serving platter. Fill the lettuce leaves with a couple tablespoons of chicken filling. You should have enough for 12 wraps. Serve at once.

EXTRA! EXTRA!

Using the basic recipe, substitute ground turkey or pork for the chicken. And to make the wraps very festive, top the lettuce leaves with a few mandarin orange slices and some dried cranberries.

Dairy-Free:
Yes, the chicken lettuce wraps are dairy-free.

An Unbelievably Gluten-Free Meal

WHERE EATEN:

WHEN EATEN:

WHO WAS THERE:

TIPS FOR MAKING AT HOME:

NEW INSPIRATIONS:

Crab Fritters with Spicy Mayonnaise

MAKES: 24 TO 28 TEASPOON-SIZE FRITTERS,
OR 8 TO 10 TABLESPOON-SIZE FRITTERS
PREP: 30 MINUTES | COOK: 8 TO 10 MINUTES PER BATCH

N O ONE WILL SUSPECT THAT THESE CRISP POCKETS OF crab are gluten-free. Even Mr. Picky himself, my fourteen-year-old son John, loves these. Based on a gluten-free baking mix, into which you fold lump crabmeat and seasoning, these fritters are perfect for holidays or birthdays, any time you want that out-of-the-ordinary appetizer.

FOR THE SPICY MAYONNAISE

¼ cup mayonnaise (preferably Hellmann's)

¼ cup Creole or other spicy mustard

Dash of hot pepper sauce

FOR THE FRITTERS

½ cup gluten-free baking mix, such as Bisquick

3 tablespoons buttermilk

1 large egg, lightly beaten

¼ cup chopped scallions, both white and green parts

2 tablespoons chopped fresh parsley, plus parsley for garnishing the fritters (optional)

Dash of hot pepper sauce

Pinch of finely ground black pepper

8 ounces lump crabmeat, drained and picked over for cartilage

2 cups vegetable oil, for frying

1 Make the spicy mayonnaise: Place the mayonnaise, mustard, and dash of hot pepper sauce in a small bowl and stir to combine. Place the spicy mayonnaise in an airtight container in the refrigerator until ready to serve. It can be prepared up to 4 days in advance.

{ *Make plenty—these hot crispy fritters go quickly.* }

2 Make the crab fritters: Place the baking mix, buttermilk, egg, scallions, parsley, dash of hot pepper sauce, and the black pepper in a medium-size mixing bowl. Stir to combine well. Fold in the crabmeat. Place the bowl in the refrigerator to firm up the batter while the oil heats, about 10 minutes.

3 Place the oil in a heavy deep frying pan or electric skillet and heat over medium-high until the oil registers 365°F on a candy thermometer. While the oil is heating, remove the bowl of fritter batter from the refrigerator.

4 Carefully drop the fritter batter by the teaspoon or tablespoon into the hot oil, being careful not to overcrowd the pan. You should cook 6 to 7 small fritters and 3 to 4 large fritters per batch. Cook the small fritters 1 minute per side and the large fritters 1½ to 2 minutes per side. As they fry, turn them, pushing them down gently into the oil with a slotted spoon. When the fritters are deeply brown, transfer them to paper towels to drain. Repeat with the remaining batter.

5 To serve, spoon the spicy mayonnaise into a small serving bowl set in the center of a large plate. Surround it with the drained hot crab fritters. Sprinkle more parsley over the fritters, if desired.

EXTRA! EXTRA!

Turn this super appetizer into a main dish by doubling the size of the fritters and frying them until browned and cooked through, 3 to 4 minutes. Serve atop a bed of salad greens with sliced tomatoes in the summertime or sliced fresh oranges and avocado in the wintertime.

Dairy-Free:

Use rice milk instead of the buttermilk in the fritters.

An Unbelievably Gluten-Free Meal

WHERE EATEN: _____

_____

WHEN EATEN: _____

_____

WHO WAS THERE: _____

_____

_____

TIPS FOR MAKING AT HOME: _____

_____

_____

_____

NEW INSPIRATIONS: _____

_____

_____

Thirteen Unbelievably Gluten-Free Soups and Stews

1. *Chilled Cucumber and Tomato Soup*

2. *Cold Pimento Soup*

3. *Cream of Tomato Soup with Basil*

4. *Easy Black Bean Soup*

5. *Quick Tuscan White Bean Soup*

6. *Hearty Vegetarian Chili*

7. *Oven-Broiled French Onion Soup*

8. *Cream of Cauliflower Soup*

9. *Baked Potato Soup*

10. *Mom's Chicken and Rice Soup*

11. *Texas Tortilla Soup*

12. *December Beef Stew*

13. *Simple Seafood Gumbo*

Soups and Stews

They say the best way to spot a great restaurant is to taste its soup. Making soup is simple and yet it takes finesse. Anyone can open a can, but not everyone can make delicious soup from scratch. Practice makes perfect. These fast, flavorful, and gluten-free recipes will have you on the road to delicious soup in no time.

I seldom relied on flour to thicken my soups and stews before this book, and so when testing recipes for this chapter I already had tricks up my sleeve for thickening—evaporation, purees, potatoes, cream. I would rather taste a soup that has been thickened by cooking down in an open pot, its juices reducing and its flavor becoming more concentrated than look to flour for the task. I would rather eat a vegetable soup that is fresh and clean and pureed, without a speck of flour. I love adding potatoes to soup to add that silent thickener. And cream, well, who doesn't like a bit of cream added to a potato, tomato, or cauliflower soup?

Sometimes only a cold soup will do and on those days look to the pimento and the chilled cucumber and tomato. Other days call for warm soups like the Cream of Tomato Soup with Basil, the Cream of Cauliflower Soup, and the Baked Potato Soup. And nothing is more comforting than Mom's Chicken and Rice Soup. Nothing says cold weather fare better than December Beef Stew or Oven-Broiled French Onion Soup. Whichever you choose, you won't be disappointed.

Chilled Cucumber and Tomato Soup

SERVES: 6
PREP: 15 MINUTES
CHILL: 3 HOURS

YOU KNOW IT'S SUMMERTIME WHEN RIPE TOMATOES AND crisp local cucumbers fill market bins. Those warm sunny days call for a simple, refreshing cold soup. Because both cukes and tomatoes are watery you have to add a little thickener, which in this recipe is cornstarch. It helps pull the soup together and yet doesn't take away from the fresh flavor.

1 cup chopped onions

2 tablespoons (¼ stick) butter

2 tablespoons cornstarch

4 cups (1 quart) low-sodium chicken or vegetable broth, at room temperature

4 cups (about 2 pounds) chopped, peeled, and seeded cucumbers

4 cups (about 2 pounds) chopped, peeled, and seeded tomatoes

½ cup heavy (whipping) cream or crème fraîche

Salt and freshly ground black pepper

2 tablespoons chopped fresh basil or parsley, for garnish

1 Place the onions and butter in a large saucepan over medium-low heat and cook, stirring, until the onions are soft, 4 to 5 minutes. Remove the pan from the heat and whisk in the cornstarch and then the broth until well combined.

2 Working in batches, place the broth mixture and the cucumbers and tomatoes in a blender or food processor and puree until smooth. Pour the vegetable mixture into a large mixing bowl and stir in the cream. Season with salt and pepper to taste.

An Unbelievably Gluten-Free Meal

WHERE EATEN:

_____

WHEN EATEN:

_____

WHO WAS THERE:

_____

_____

TIPS FOR MAKING AT HOME:

_____

_____

_____

NEW INSPIRATIONS:

_____

_____

_____

Cover and refrigerate the soup until cold, about 3 hours. The soup can be refrigerated for 3 or 4 days.

3 Ladle the soup into serving bowls and garnish it with the fresh basil or parsley.

EXTRA! EXTRA!

For a fresh gazpacho-like version of this soup, substitute sweet red bell peppers for half of the cucumbers. Serve this soup with the Crispy Cheese Wafers (page 35) on the side.

Dairy-Free:

To make the soup dairy-free, replace the butter with olive oil; instead of the cream use unsweetened coconut milk.

Cold Pimento Soup

SERVES: 4 TO 6
PREP: 25 MINUTES
CHILL: 3 HOURS (OPTIONAL)

I'VE MADE THIS SOUP FOR YEARS, EVER SINCE I FIRST TASTED it in an Atlanta take-out gourmet grocery called Proof of the Pudding. Through the years I have adapted it to use what I have on hand, such as Greek yogurt instead of the original sour cream, scallions instead of white onion, and roasted red peppers from the garden instead of pimentos from a jar. This version is a blend of my experimentation, and the version I like best. It uses store-bought roasted red peppers, a little cornstarch to help thicken the soup, and that thick and wonderful Greek yogurt to pull it together. Make this when it is really hot outside and you want to stay cool.

FOR THE SOUP

2 tablespoons olive oil

2 tablespoons minced white onion or
  scallions

1 tablespoon cornstarch

3 cups low-sodium chicken broth,
  at room temperature

1 cup store-bought roasted red peppers or
  pimentos

1 cup plain Greek yogurt or sour cream

Salt and freshly ground black pepper
  (see Note)

FOR GARNISH

Plain Greek yogurt or sour cream (optional)

Chopped chives

1 Place the olive oil and onion in a large saucepan over medium-low heat and cook, stirring, until the onion is soft, about 4 minutes. Whisk in the cornstarch and then the chicken broth, whisking until the

mixture comes together and thickens slightly, 5 to 6 minutes. Turn off the heat and let the broth mixture cool.

2 Working in batches, place the broth mixture and the peppers in a blender or food processor and puree until smooth. Return the mixture to the saucepan and stir in the yogurt or sour cream. Season the soup with salt and black pepper to taste. Serve the soup at once at room temperature or transfer it to a large bowl and refrigerate it until cold, about 3 hours. The soup can be refrigerated for 2 or 3 days.

3 Ladle the soup into bowls and serve it with a drizzle of yogurt or sour cream, if desired, and a sprinkling of chives.

Note: When food is served cold it tends to taste less seasoned than if it were served warm or hot. So you need to add a bit more salt and pepper than you are used to adding to season this cold soup appropriately.

EXTRA! EXTRA!

To garnish the soup beautifully, place the yogurt or sour cream in a clean plastic squirt bottle and decoratively drizzle it over the soup, then scatter the chives on top.

Dairy-Free:

You can make this soup without adding the sour cream or yogurt. Puree the roasted peppers with the broth mixture, then season the soup with salt and black pepper. Serve the soup garnished with chopped chives.

Cream of Tomato Soup with Basil

SERVES: 4
PREP: 15 MINUTES
COOK: 35 TO 40 MINUTES

THERE IS NO NEED TO THICKEN THIS SOUP WITH FLOUR OR even cornstarch because the tomatoes cook down and you puree the soup and stir in cream at the end to thicken things up beautifully. I prefer the flavor of soups made this way, with no thickener added. Because it is based on canned tomatoes, you can serve the soup when tomatoes are not in season.

1 cup chopped onions

2 cloves garlic, minced

1 tablespoon butter

1 tablespoon olive oil

1 can (28 ounces) good Italian tomatoes with their juice

2 cups low-sodium chicken broth

1 bay leaf

½ cup heavy (whipping) cream

Salt and freshly ground black pepper

1 cup fresh basil, sliced into thin strips

1 Place the onions and garlic in a large heavy pot and add the butter and olive oil. Cook, stirring, over medium-low heat until the onion softens, 4 to 5 minutes. Add the tomatoes and juice, chicken broth, and bay leaf. Cover the pot and increase the heat enough to bring the mixture to a boil. Reduce the heat to low and let simmer, covered, until the flavors come together, 30 to 35 minutes.

2 Remove and discard the bay leaf. Stir in the cream and season

{ *When it comes
to favorite comfort
foods, does anything
rank higher than
creamy tomato
soup?* }

the soup with salt and pepper to taste. Working in batches puree the soup in a food processor until it is smooth but the tomatoes are still a little chunky. Return the soup to the pot, stir in the basil, and serve. The soup can be refrigerated for 2 or 3 days. Reheat it over low heat to just a simmer.

EXTRA! EXTRA!

Make this a meal by adding sautéed shrimp to the soup and serving a green salad alongside. Add a pinch of red pepper flakes to the soup pot if you like your soup spicy.

Dairy-Free:

In lieu of the heavy cream, to thicken the soup use ½ cup of canned unsweetened coconut milk or ¼ cup of dairy-free cream cheese, such as Better Than Cream Cheese, stirring to let it melt.

Easy Black Bean Soup

SERVES: 4 TO 6
PREP: 10 MINUTES
COOK: 25 TO 30 MINUTES

THIS SOUP IS SUCH A BREEZE TO MAKE THAT I AM A LITTLE embarrassed to share the recipe! It begins with canned black beans and a can of beef broth. Let them cook together with a bay leaf and some oregano and cumin. Then puree the soup to your preferred degree of smoothness—no need to thicken it—and serve it with your favorite garnishes.

FOR THE SOUP

1 cup chopped onions

1 clove garlic, minced

2 tablespoons olive oil

2 cans (about 15 ounces each) black beans, undrained

1 can (14½ ounces) low-sodium beef broth (see Note)

1 teaspoon ground cumin

1 teaspoon dried oregano

1 bay leaf

FOR GARNISH

¼ cup sour cream

1 tablespoon fresh oregano leaves

Avocado cubes

1 Place the onions and garlic in a large saucepan and add the olive oil. Cook, stirring, over medium heat until the onions soften, 4 to 5 minutes. Add the black beans, beef broth, cumin, oregano, and bay leaf.

2 Increase the heat to medium-high and let the soup come to a boil,

An Unbelievably Gluten-Free Meal

....

WHERE EATEN:

WHEN EATEN:

WHO WAS THERE:

TIPS FOR MAKING AT HOME:

NEW INSPIRATIONS:

then reduce the heat to low and cover the pan. Let the soup simmer until thickened, 20 to 25 minutes. Remove and discard the bay leaf. Working in batches, puree the soup in a food processor until it is smooth. If desired, reheat the soup after pureeing. The soup may be refrigerated for 2 or 3 days. Serve it with a small dollop of sour cream, topping it with oregano leaves and avocado cubes.

Note: Make sure you use beef broth and not consommé, which contains wheat gluten. And use chicken broth instead of beef if that is what is on the pantry shelf.

EXTRA! EXTRA!

This soup is a blank canvas when it comes to garnishes. Add gluten-free croutons, crumbled bacon, diced ham, or crabmeat.

Dairy-Free:
Omit the sour cream garnish for a dairy-free soup.

Quick Tuscan White Bean Soup

SERVES: 6 TO 8
PREP: 15 TO 20 MINUTES
COOK: 20 MINUTES

NATURALLY GLUTEN-FREE, THIS SOUP IS A GREAT EXAMPLE of the wonderful food you can create and never miss the gluten. Beans are a natural thickener, and you can make the soup seem creamier just by pureeing them. I usually base my soups on dried beans but this is a quick version that relies on canned white beans. Use cannellini or great northern beans and serve a loaf of gluten-free French bread on the side.

3 tablespoons olive oil

¼ cup finely chopped cooked ham

¾ cup finely chopped onion

1 rib celery, finely chopped

1 medium-size carrot, peeled and finely chopped

3 cloves garlic, minced

6 cups (1½ quarts) low-sodium chicken broth

3 cans (about 15 ounces each) cannellini or great northern beans, rinsed and drained

1 tablespoon fresh thyme leaves

Salt and freshly ground black pepper

½ cup (2 ounces) grated Parmesan cheese, for garnish

Gluten-free French bread slices (see *Extra! Extra!*), toasted, for serving

1 Place the olive oil in a large heavy soup pot over medium-low heat. Add the ham, onion, celery, carrot, and garlic and cook, stirring, until the onion is soft, 4 to 5 minutes. Add the broth, beans, and thyme and season with salt and pepper to taste. Let simmer, covered, over low heat until slightly thickens, 15 minutes.

An Unbelievably Gluten-Free Meal

WHERE EATEN: _____

_____

WHEN EATEN: _____

_____

WHO WAS THERE: _____

_____

_____

TIPS FOR MAKING AT HOME: _____

_____

_____

_____

NEW INSPIRATIONS: _____

_____

_____

_____

2 Remove the pot from the heat and, working in batches, puree the soup in a food processor or blender until nearly smooth. Return the soup to the pot, taste for seasoning, adding more salt and/or pepper as necessary, and reheat the soup before serving. The soup may be refrigerated for 3 to 4 days.

3 To serve, spoon the soup into serving bowls and top it with the Parmesan cheese. Serve toasted French bread on the side.

EXTRA! EXTRA!

My favorite gluten-free French-style bread is the crusty baguette from Everybody Eats, a Brooklyn, New York, bakery. The bread is crusty on the outside, soft and fluffy inside. Check its website—www.everybodyeatsinc.com—for a store near you that carries its breads. Everybody Eats also ships its products directly to you. You can order several loaves and freeze them.

Dairy-Free:
Omit the Parmesan cheese garnish and this soup is dairy-free.

Hearty Vegetarian Chili

SERVES: 8
PREP: 25 MINUTES
COOK: 40 TO 45 MINUTES

SOMETIMES, BELIEVE IT OR NOT, I DON'T WANT MEAT IN MY chili. So I make a vegetarian version. This is a kid-friendly dish with Southwestern flavors. And it cooks down quickly thanks to the canned beans. Garnish the chili with shredded cheese, and serve gluten-free tortilla chips on the side or, even better, Southern Skillet Corn Bread (see page 134). If you would like to add meat, first brown a half pound of lean ground beef or turkey in two tablespoons of olive oil, then proceed with the recipe.

2 tablespoons olive oil

1 cup chopped onions

1 cup chopped carrots

1 cup chopped red bell pepper

1 cup chopped green bell pepper

½ jalapeño pepper, seeds and veins removed, pepper finely chopped

2 cloves garlic, minced

2 cans (about 15 ounces each) pinto or kidney beans, rinsed and drained

1 cup corn, fresh or frozen

2 teaspoons chili powder, or more to taste

2 teaspoons ground cumin, or more to taste

½ teaspoon salt, or more to taste

1 can (28 ounces) diced tomatoes with their juices

2 cups low-sodium vegetable broth

1 small zucchini, cut into ½-inch dice

Freshly ground black pepper

1 to 2 cups shredded cheddar cheese, for serving

{ *Easy, filling, and a kid favorite, add more or less spice depending on your family's tolerance.* }

1 Place the olive oil in a large heavy soup pot. Add the onions, carrots, red and green bell peppers, jalapeño pepper, and garlic and cook over medium heat, stirring, until the vegetables soften, 6 to 7 minutes.

2 Add the beans, corn, chili powder, cumin, salt, tomatoes, and vegetable broth. Let come to a boil over medium heat, then reduce the heat to low and let simmer, covered, until cooked down, about 30 minutes.

3 Add the zucchini to the pot, and taste for seasoning, adding more chili powder, cumin, and/or salt as necessary and black pepper to taste. Cook the chili, covered,

until the zucchini is tender, about 5 minutes. The chili can be refrigerated for 3 or 4 days (made with meat it can be refrigerated for 2 or 3 days).

4 To serve, ladle the chili into bowls and serve sprinkled with the cheese.

EXTRA! EXTRA!

This is a great side dish for grilled steaks or sausages when you are serving a crowd. It beats the usual baked beans, and it is jam-packed with veggies. The chili is even better made in the summertime when the veggies are at the peak of freshness and many of them can come from your garden.

Dairy-Free:
Omit the cheese garnish and the chili will be dairy-free.

Oven-Broiled French Onion Soup

SERVES: 6

PREP: 15 TO 20 MINUTES

COOK: 1 HOUR TO 1 HOUR, 10 MINUTES

CLASSIC AND TIMELESS, ONION SOUP HAS BEEN A FAVORITE for decades. And now you can enjoy it gluten-free. The secret to great French onion soup is a perfect balance between caramelized onions, cheese, and bread. The onions cook slowly—it's a little labor intensive—but they become sweet and nut brown in color. The cheese should be flavorful but melt easily—like Gruyère, fontina, or Havarti. And the bread has to have some structure to it, which is difficult to find in gluten-free breads. The best choices are French-style baguette or a high-protein, multigrain bread. You will need six 6-ounce broiler-safe ramekins for this recipe.

2 tablespoons olive oil

2 pounds onions, peeled and sliced ¼ inch thick

Salt and freshly ground black pepper

⅓ cup dry sherry

8 cups (2 quarts) low-sodium beef broth

2 sprigs fresh thyme

6 slices (½ inch thick) gluten-free French bread (see Note)

1 clove garlic, cut in half

6 slices (about 6 ounces total) Gruyère, fontina, or Havarti cheese

1 Place the olive oil in a large heavy soup pot and add the onions. Place the pot over medium heat. Cook the onions, stirring constantly, until they soften and then darken and caramelize, about 35 minutes.

2 Season the onions with salt and pepper to taste. Add the sherry and let come to a boil. Add the beef broth and thyme, reduce the heat, and let the soup simmer, covered, until the flavors come together, 25 to 30 minutes.

3 While the soup cooks, preheat the broiler.

4 Place the bread on a baking sheet and broil it on one side until light brown, 30 to 45 seconds. Rub the toasted bread with the cut side of the garlic. Set the bread toasts aside. Leave the broiler on.

5 When the soup is done, divide it evenly among six 6-ounce ramekins. Top each portion with a toasted slice of bread. Place the cheese on top of the bread and place the ramekins on the baking sheet. Broil until the cheese bubbles and is lightly browned, 1 to 2 minutes. Remove the ramekins from the baking sheet and serve the soup at once.

Note: Use the best quality gluten-free French bread you can find. Whole Foods and some supermarkets carry sturdy gluten-free sourdough bread. The bread needs to be firm or else it will get mushy in the soup.

EXTRA! EXTRA!

This soup is a meal in itself. It needs only a green salad to be complete. For vegetarians, you can prepare this with vegetable broth instead of beef broth.

Dairy-Free:

Omitting the cheese will make the onion soup dairy-free. Serve the soup with the toasts; you can cut the toasts in half.

Cream of Cauliflower Soup

SERVES: 4 TO 6
PREP: 18 TO 22 MINUTES
COOK: 20 TO 25 MINUTES

I WAS RAISED ON STEAMED CAULIFLOWER SERVED WITH A creamy cheese sauce my mother would make and pour over the hot vegetable at the table. Those were the days! It's no wonder I am partial to the flavors of cream with cauliflower, and think they blend well in this pureed soup. The cumin and cayenne add that needed bit of heat my mother's cheese sauce never had. No cheese in this soup, however, and the thickener here is potato. A little cream added at the end makes the soup, well, creamy and delicious!

1 cup chopped onions

2 cloves garlic, minced

2 tablespoons vegetable or olive oil

1 teaspoon ground cumin

¼ teaspoon cayenne pepper

2 cups cauliflower florets

2 cups chopped peeled potatoes

5 cups low-sodium chicken broth

Salt and freshly ground black pepper

⅔ cup heavy (whipping) cream

2 tablepoons chopped fresh parsley, for garnish

1 Place the onions and garlic in a large heavy soup pot and add the oil. Cook, stirring, over medium-low heat until the onions soften, 4 to 5 minutes. Add the cumin and cayenne pepper and stir to coat the onion mixture. Add the cauliflower, potatoes, and chicken broth. Season with salt and black pepper to taste. Let come to a boil over medium-high heat, then reduce the heat to low and let simmer until the potatoes are tender, 15 to 20 minutes.

2 Working in batches, ladle the soup into a blender or food processor and puree until smooth. Return the soup to the pot, add the cream, and reheat before serving. The soup can be refrigerated for 2 or 3 days.

3 To serve, ladle the soup into bowls and garnish it with the parsley.

EXTRA! EXTRA!

For a change of pace and a beautiful color, use sweet potatoes or butternut squash instead of white potatoes. Garnish the soup with salted, toasted pumpkin seeds (*pepitas*).

Dairy-Free:
For a dairy-free soup omit the cream.

An Unbelievably Gluten-Free Meal

WHERE EATEN: _____

_____

WHEN EATEN: _____

_____

WHO WAS THERE: _____

_____

_____

TIPS FOR MAKING AT HOME: _____

_____

_____

_____

NEW INSPIRATIONS: _____

_____

_____

_____

Baked Potato Soup

SERVES: 6 TO 8 | PREP: 20 MINUTES (IF MICROWAVING POTATOES)
OR 1 HOUR, 10 MINUTES (IF OVEN ROASTING)
COOK: 15 TO 20 MINUTES

P UREED VEGETABLE SOUPS SUCH AS THIS ONE ARE SELF thickening. I love to make potato soup at the spur of the moment, when the weather is cold and my kids are having friends over to the house. If you've got the time, the flavor of oven-roasted potatoes is really delicious—the potatoes taste sweeter. But in a pinch, microwaving them is fine. I have included both methods.

FOR THE SOUP

4 large baking potatoes

2 tablespoons (¼ stick) butter, or 2
  tablespoons olive oil

½ cup chopped onion

8 cups (2 quarts) low-sodium chicken
  broth

Salt and freshly ground black pepper

½ cup heavy (whipping) cream

2 cups (8 ounces) shredded Colby or mild
  cheddar cheese

FOR GARNISH

1 cup crumbled cooked bacon

¼ cup chopped fresh chives or parsley

1 If you are baking the potatoes,
  preheat the oven to 425°F.

2 Rinse the potatoes under warm
  running water and pat them dry
with paper towels. Prick each of the
potatoes several times with a fork or
sharp knife to let steam escape. Place
the potatoes in the oven and bake

them until cooked through, about 1 hour. When done the potatoes will be easily pierced with a knife.

If you are microwaving the potatoes: Place the potatoes in a microwave oven and cook them on high power for 5 minutes. Then, turn the potatoes over and cook them for another 5 minutes. Remove the potatoes from the microwave and let them rest for about 1 minute. Check for doneness by cutting into one potato with a sharp knife. If the potatoes are not done, return them to the microwave to cook for about another 1 minute, then repeat the test for doneness.

3 Set the potatoes aside. Place the butter or olive oil in a large heavy soup pot. Add the onion and cook over medium-low heat until the onion softens, 4 to 5 minutes. Turn off the heat. Cut the baked potatoes in half lengthwise and scoop out the cooked potato flesh into the pot with the onions. Add the chicken broth and season with salt and pepper to taste. Let come to a boil over medium heat, stirring, and then reduce the heat to low,

{ *Freshly crumbled bacon adds flavor and a great crunch to a pureed potato soup.* }

cover the pot, and let simmer until the potatoes are very tender and the soup is well combined, about 15 minutes. Stir in the cream.

4 Working in batches, ladle the warm soup into a blender or food processor and puree until smooth. Return the soup to the pot and add 1 cup of the cheese. Cook, stirring, over low heat until the cheese has melted, 1 to 2 minutes. The soup can be refrigerated for 2 or 3 days.

5 To serve, ladle the soup into bowls and garnish it with the remaining 1 cup of cheese and crumbled bacon and chives or parsley.

An Unbelievably Gluten-Free Meal

....

WHERE EATEN: _____

_____

WHEN EATEN: _____

_____

WHO WAS THERE: _____

_____

_____

TIPS FOR MAKING AT HOME: _____

_____

_____

_____

NEW INSPIRATIONS: _____

_____

_____

_____

When you have leftover mashed potatoes, you can easily turn them into mashed potato soup the next day. Place the mashed potatoes in a saucepan and add chicken broth to cover. Add a pinch of salt and pepper. Let come to a simmer over low heat and cook, whisking, until smooth, adding more chicken broth or a little milk, whatever is needed to arrive at the right soup consistency. Serve the soup warm, garnished with shredded cheese, crumbled bacon, and chopped chives.

Dairy-Free:

For a dairy-free potato soup omit the cream and whisk in ¼ cup of a dairy-free cream cheese, such as Better Than Cream Cheese instead. Omit the shredded cheese and garnish the soup with just the bacon and chives.

Mom's Chicken and Rice Soup

SERVES: 10 TO 12
PREP: 15 TO 20 MINUTES
COOK: 2 TO 3 HOURS

PART OF THE JOB OF BEING MOM IS TAKING CARE OF everyone in the family when they don't feel well. And one of the best ways I nurture my household is to make chicken soup. It may be sniffles or a sore throat, little aches, pains, even a broken heart. No matter the malady, everyone feels better after a bowl of homemade chicken soup. The secret is cooking a whole organic chicken because the skin, fat, and bones all add to the flavor of the broth. And when it comes down to it, the broth is what makes the soup. Here is my basic blueprint. Add the veggies you like. And if you make this soup a day ahead, you can refrigerate it and skim off the fat before reheating.

1 whole organic chicken (3 to 4 pounds), giblets removed (see Notes)

1 small onion, peeled and quartered

3 carrots, 1 peeled and coarsely chopped, 2 peeled and finely chopped

1 sprig fresh parsley

1 bay leaf

Salt and freshly ground black pepper

3 gluten-free chicken bouillon cubes (optional; see Notes)

1 cup frozen or fresh peas

1 cup frozen or fresh green beans

1 large zucchini, diced

½ cup uncooked rice

3 packed cups fresh spinach leaves

Parmesan cheese (optional), for serving

1 Rinse the chicken inside and out under cold running water and pat it dry with paper towels. Place the chicken in a large soup pot and add

water to cover it completely. Add the onion, coarsely chopped carrot, parsley, and bay leaf and season with salt and pepper to taste. Add the chicken bouillon cubes, if desired. Cover the pot and let come to a boil over medium-high heat. Reduce the heat to low and let simmer, covered, for 1 to 1½ hours, depending on how much time you have to watch the pot. (You need at least 1 hour to cook the chicken through but the longer you cook it the more flavorful the broth becomes.)

2 Turn off the heat and carefully transfer the chicken to a 13 by 9-inch glass baking dish to cool. Strain the broth, discarding the onion, carrot, parsley, and bay leaf, then return the broth to the pot.

3 When the chicken is cool enough to handle, remove the meat from the bones. Discard the bones and skin. You can shred the meat or you can coarsely chop it with a chef's knife. If desired, set aside some of the breast meat for a sandwich the next day. There will be 4 to 5 cups of chicken.

4 Add the finely chopped carrots, peas, green beans, zucchini, and shredded or chopped chicken to the soup pot. Let come to a boil over medium-high heat, then reduce the heat to medium-low and let the soup simmer, partially covered, until the vegetables are cooked, about 30 minutes. Add the rice. Cover the pot and let simmer until the rice has cooked through, about 20 minutes. Then add the spinach, turn off the heat, and let the spinach wilt into the soup. The soup can be refrigerated for 2 or 3 days.

5 Taste the soup for seasoning, adding more salt and pepper as necessary. Serve the soup in bowls with grated Parmesan cheese, if desired.

Notes: Organic chickens have a lot of flavor, and they make this soup unbelievably good.

When I am in a hurry I add bouillon cubes to the soup to deepen the flavor. They are not as pure as just adding salt and pepper, so if you don't like to use them, that is okay. If you do, make

sure the label reads gluten-free and watch the amount of salt you add so you don't oversalt the soup. If you are not in a hurry, let the chicken simmer for the full 1½ hours.

EXTRA! EXTRA!

Clean out your refrigerator or freezer when you make this soup, adding the veggies you have on hand or the veggies your family enjoys. I look at this as a great time to give my family all five servings of their daily vegetables in one meal! To make the soup more Italian, add a can of white beans in addition to the grated Parmesan, and top it with fresh basil and a drizzle of good olive oil.

Dairy-Free:

If you don't add the Parmesan, this soup is absolutely dairy-free!

An Unbelievably Gluten-Free Meal

WHERE EATEN: _____

_____

WHEN EATEN: _____

_____

WHO WAS THERE: _____

_____

_____

TIPS FOR MAKING AT HOME: _____

_____

_____

_____

NEW INSPIRATIONS: _____

_____

_____

_____

Texas Tortilla Soup

SERVES: 4 TO 6
PREP: 20 MINUTES
COOK: 19 TO 25 MINUTES

I LOVE TRAVELING TO TEXAS—IT'S WHERE I GET MY FILL OF tortilla soup. The soup is on just about every restaurant menu, in all sorts of wonderful variations. I started making my own tortilla soup a few years back and found that the corn tortillas provide flavor and thickening. So when planning this book I realized this soup was a natural. Buy gluten-free tortillas or tortilla chips. The toppings are up to you—chopped tomatoes, cilantro, sour cream, shredded cheese, avocado cubes—whatever you and your family like.

FOR THE SOUP

3 tablespoons olive oil

1 red bell pepper, stemmed, seeded, and sliced into thin strips

½ cup chopped onion

2 cloves garlic, minced

1 can (about 15 ounces) tomatoes with green chiles with their juice

4 cups (1 quart) low-sodium chicken broth

2 cups shredded cooked chicken

2 fresh gluten-free corn tortillas, cut into strips, or ½ cup gluten-free tortilla chips, crushed

½ cup frozen corn (see *Extra! Extra!*)

FOR THE TOPPINGS

1 jalapeño pepper, seeds and veins removed, pepper thinly sliced

1 avocado, cubed

½ cup fresh cilantro sprigs

1 cup (4 ounces) shredded Mexican cheese blend or crumbled Cotija cheese

1 cup gluten-free corn tortilla chips

1 Place the olive oil in a large soup pot over medium heat. Add the bell pepper strips, onion, and garlic. Reduce the heat to medium-low and cook until the vegetables are soft, 4 to 5 minutes.

2 Add the tomatoes and juice, chicken broth, chicken, tortilla strips or crushed tortilla chips, and corn. Cover the pot and let simmer over low heat until the tortillas are cooked through, 15 to 20 minutes. The soup can be refrigerated for 3 to 4 days.

3 Serve the soup in shallow bowls, topped with jalapeño pepper, avocado, cilantro, cheese, and tortilla chips.

EXTRA! EXTRA!

Any frozen corn will do, but my favorite corn is the roasted corn you can buy frozen at Trader Joe's.

Dairy-Free:

The soup is dairy-free, but omit the cheese as a topping.

December Beef Stew

SERVES: 6 TO 8
PREP: 20 TO 25 MINUTES
COOK: 1 HOUR, 15 MINUTES

I GUESS YOU COULD SAY THIS STEW IS NATURALLY GLUTEN-free, but I think it is more intentionally gluten-free. Instead of dredging the beef cubes in seasoned flour, I just sear the beef in oil. What encourages the thickening process are white beans and potatoes, starchy elements that help to bring the stew together.

2 tablespoons olive oil

4 cups lean stew beef cubes

2 medium-size onions, chopped

4 cloves garlic, minced

4 cups (1 quart) low-sodium beef broth

1 cup canned white beans, rinsed and drained

2 cups diced, peeled potatoes, cut ½ inch thick

3 carrots, peeled and cut into 1-inch pieces

1 tablespoon fresh rosemary, crushed (optional)

1 bay leaf

Salt and freshly ground black pepper

1 Place the olive oil in a large heavy soup pot over medium-high heat. Working in batches, add the beef cubes and brown well on all sides, 4 to 5 minutes. Do this in batches so you don't crowd the beef and it browns on all sides. Set the browned beef aside.

2 Reduce the heat to medium. Add the onions and garlic to the pot and cook, stirring, until they just begin to brown, about 3 minutes. Add the beef broth and let it come to a simmer, scraping the bottom of the pan to loosen the cooked bits of beef.

Add the reserved beef, white beans, potatoes, carrots, rosemary, and bay leaf. Cover the pot and reduce the heat to low. Let the stew simmer until the beef is cooked through and tender, about 1 hour. The stew can be refrigerated for 3 or 4 days.

3 Before serving, taste for seasoning adding salt and pepper to taste and remove and discard the bay leaf.

EXTRA! EXTRA!

This stew is a great recipe for entertaining. You can make it a day in advance, refrigerate it, then reheat it when the guests arrive. Add a green salad and a festive dessert, such as the Pear and Cranberry Crostata, Flourless Chocolate Cakes, or Easy Apple Tart. If you prefer, you can make the stew with lamb instead of beef.

Dairy-Free:
This stew is dairy-free!

An Unbelievably Gluten-Free Meal

WHERE EATEN: _____

_____

WHEN EATEN: _____

_____

WHO WAS THERE: _____

_____

_____

TIPS FOR MAKING AT HOME: ____

_____

_____

_____

_____

NEW INSPIRATIONS: _____

_____

_____

_____

Simple Seafood Gumbo

SERVES: 8
PREP: 30 MINUTES
COOK: 48 TO 50 MINUTES

ONE OF THE AUTHENTIC COMPONENTS OF GUMBO—something that gives it flavor, color, and texture—is the roux. A blend of flour and oil, a roux is cooked until it turns dark red in color and then is added to the remaining gumbo ingredients. For this reason gumbo has often been off the list of acceptable recipes for the gluten-free. But traveling to Milwaukee on tour and listening to the suggestions of long-time gluten-free cook Bev Lieven and others, I learned you can make gumbo using sweet rice flour. No oil is needed for the roux since you just slowly cook the sweet rice flour until it browns and smells like toasting nuts. Then remove it from the heat and proceed with the recipe. Enjoy!

2 tablespoons sweet rice flour (see Notes)

4 tablespoons (½ stick) butter, or
4 tablespoons vegetable oil

2 cups chopped onions

5 cloves garlic, minced

4 ounces cooked ham or
cooked spicy sausage

1 cup sliced fresh okra

4 sprigs fresh thyme

2 bay leaves

2 tablespoons chopped fresh parsley

1 can (28 ounces) diced tomatoes with
their juices (do not discard the can)

Salt and freshly ground black pepper

1 pound shrimp, shelled and deveined
(see Notes)

1 pound lump crabmeat, drained and
picked over for cartilage

Steamed rice, for serving

An Unbelievably Gluten-Free Meal

WHERE EATEN:

WHEN EATEN:

WHO WAS THERE:

TIPS FOR MAKING AT HOME:

NEW INSPIRATIONS:

{ *Make plenty of rice to sop up all the delicious gumbo liquid.* }

1 Place the sweet rice flour in a heavy frying pan over low heat. Cook, stirring constantly, until the rice flour turns from light brown to reddish tan, about 10 minutes. Remove the pan from the heat and set it aside.

2 Place the butter or oil in a large heavy soup pot. Add the onions, garlic, and ham and cook over medium heat, stirring, until the onions are soft, about 3 minutes. Add the okra, thyme, bay leaves, parsley, and tomatoes and juices. Fill the tomato can 1½ times with water, adding the water to the soup pot. Season the tomato mixture with salt and pepper to taste. Let come to a boil over medium-high heat, then reduce the heat to low and let simmer, covered, until the flavors come together, about 15 minutes. Remove the pot from the heat and stir in the browned rice flour. Place the pot back over low heat and let the mixture simmer, covered, until the gumbo thickens and the rice flour dissolves, about 30 minutes.

3 Add the shrimp and crabmeat and let simmer until the shrimp is just cooked through, 2 to 3 minutes. Remove and discard the bay leaves. Serve the gumbo with steamed rice. The gumbo can be refrigerated for 1 day.

Notes: Sweet rice flour can be found in many markets carrying Asian or gluten-free ingredients. Or, order it online at Gluten-Free Trading Company (www.food 4celiacs.com).

For an even more flavorful gumbo, you can buy shrimp in the shell and peel and devein them yourself. Place the shrimp shells in a small saucepan and cover them with 2 cups of water. Place the pan over medium heat and let the water come to a boil, then
reduce the heat and let simmer until the shells are pink, about 15 minutes. Strain the liquid and add 1 can's worth of this liquid to the gumbo in place of 1 can of the water.

EXTRA! EXTRA!

For a true Louisiana gumbo, add 1 pint of fresh oysters with their liquid and use cooked spicy andouille sausage instead of ham.

Dairy-Free:
If you use vegetable oil for sautéing the onions, this gumbo is dairy-free.

A Dozen Unbelievably
Gluten-Free Bread Recipes

1. *Pumpkin Spice Bread*

2. *Full of Flavor Banana Bread*

3. *Easy Irish Soda Bread*

4. *Big Blueberry Muffins*

5. *Cinnamon Streusel Muffins*

6. *Chocolate and Cherry Scones*

7. *Cranberry and Orange Scones*

8. *Buttermilk Biscuits*

9. *Cornmeal Drop Biscuits*

10. *Southern Skillet Corn Bread*

11. *Soft Yeast Rolls*

12. *Zesty Parmesan Bread*

Gluten-Free Bread

The words bread and gluten-free don't usually go together well. But with some creativity and the help of a few baking mixes and flour blends, you can make great quick breads and yeast breads at home. The quick breads are pretty simple—begin with a baking mix or flour blend, add flavoring, eggs, oil, and a few other ingredients, and you can easily make pumpkin bread, banana bread, soda bread, muffins, scones, biscuits, and corn bread. The yeast breads, however, are a little trickier.

Gluten-free yeast bread is dense, sticky, and wet. You have to mix it with an electric mixer fitted with a dough hook or a food processor fitted with a steel blade. Oil your fingers before pressing the dough into the baking pan. And after baking, eat the bread fresh and warm. Toast leftover bread for a freshly baked texture.

That being said I think you'll enjoy the selection I've included here. Especially the biscuits—I really like them and I am picky about biscuits what with being a Southern cook. The drop biscuits with cornmeal are surprisingly light and simple to make, and the classic Buttermilk Biscuits are the best gluten-free biscuits I have tasted. As with all my recipes that begin with a mix, be sure to follow my recipe and not the instructions on the box for the best results.

Pumpkin Spice Bread

MAKES: 1 LOAF

SERVES: 8

PREP: 15 MINUTES | BAKE: 48 TO 53 MINUTES

I DON'T BELIEVE ANY BREAD SIGNALS THE BEGINNING OF fall, the Halloween party season, or the festivities of the winter holidays bet-ter than pumpkin bread. To make a great gluten-free pumpkin bread, begin with a baking mix, then add canned pumpkin, spices, eggs—the usual goodies. What results is a spicy, fragrant, and moist loaf. This recipe makes one big loaf, but if you wish, you can make three mini loaves (I use 6 by 3¼ by 2¼-inch pans); bake them for twenty-five to thirty minutes.

Vegetable oil spray, for misting the loaf pan

Rice flour, for dusting the loaf pan

1½ cups canned 100% pure pumpkin (see Notes)

¾ cup granulated sugar (see Notes)

½ cup vegetable oil

2 large eggs

2 teaspoons pure vanilla extract

1¾ cups gluten-free baking mix, such as Bisquick

2 teaspoons ground cinnamon

¼ teaspoon ground ginger

½ teaspoon salt

1 Place a rack in the center of the oven and preheat the oven to 350°F. Mist a 9 by 5-inch loaf pan with vegetable oil spray and dust it with rice flour. Set the loaf pan aside.

2 Place the pumpkin, sugar, oil, eggs, and vanilla in a large mixing bowl and beat with an electric mixer on medium speed until smooth, about 1 minute. Set the pumpkin mixture aside.

3 Place the baking mix, cinnamon, ginger, and salt in a small mixing bowl and stir to combine. Add the dry ingredients to the pumpkin mixture and beat with the electric mixer on low speed until the dry ingredients are just combined, 45 seconds to 1 minute. The batter will be thick. Spoon the batter into the prepared loaf pan and place the loaf pan in the oven.

4 Bake the pumpkin bread until the top springs back when lightly pressed with a finger, 48 to 53 minutes. Transfer the loaf pan to a wire rack and let the pumpkin bread cool for about 5 minutes.

5 Run a knife around the edges of the pan and give the pan a good shake to loosen the bread. Invert the pumpkin bread onto a wire rack, then invert it again onto another rack to cool right side up for about one hour before slicing.

Notes: I used not quite the whole 15-ounce can of pumpkin because using the entire can made the loaf too heavy.

Sugar contributes flavor as well as tenderness in this recipe and keeps the loaf from becoming gummy in texture.

EXTRA! EXTRA!

Vary the seasonings by adding ground nutmeg instead of ginger or by folding in a teaspoon or two of grated orange zest. If you add the orange zest, make a quick orange glaze by blending ½ cup of confectioners' sugar and 1 tablespoon of orange juice. Drizzle the glaze over the loaf after it cools.

Dairy-Free:
Pumpkin Spice Bread is dairy-free.

PLAN AHEAD: Pumpkin Spice Bread will keep covered in plastic wrap up to 4 days at room temperature.

Full of Flavor Banana Bread

MAKES: 1 LOAF

SERVES: 8

PREP: 15 MINUTES | BAKE: 40 TO 45 MINUTES

N O BREAD CHAPTER IS COMPLETE WITHOUT BANANA bread, so I was determined to create one that is gluten-free. Thankfully, a gluten-free baking mix is a great way to start the process and, as it has the leavening built in, I just needed very ripe bananas and a few other ingredients. It took several tries to get the proportions just right, but I am happy to say this is a dandy of a bread. It is moist and packed with fresh banana flavor.

Vegetable oil spray, for misting the loaf pan

Rice flour, for dusting the loaf pan

⅓ cup vegetable oil

⅓ cup packed light brown sugar

2 large eggs

2 tablespoons buttermilk

2 teaspoons pure vanilla extract

1½ cups gluten-free baking mix, such as Bisquick

¼ teaspoon ground cinnamon

1 cup mashed ripe bananas (from about 2 medium-size or 3 small bananas)

⅓ cup finely chopped pecans (optional)

1 Place a rack in the center of the oven and preheat the oven to 350°F. Mist a 9 by 5-inch loaf pan with vegetable oil spray and dust it with rice flour. Set the loaf pan aside.

2 Place the oil, brown sugar, eggs, buttermilk, and vanilla in a medium-size bowl and beat with an electric mixer on medium speed until combined, about 45 seconds. Scrape down the side of the bowl with a rubber spatula and set it aside.

3 Place the baking mix and cinnamon in a small mixing bowl and stir to combine. Place a third of the dry ingredients in the bowl with the egg mixture and beat with the electric mixer on low speed until just combined. Add ½ cup of the mashed bananas and beat until combined. Add another third of the dry ingredients and beat, then add the remaining ½ cup of bananas, followed by the remaining dry ingredients and beat to combine. Fold in the pecans, if using. Spoon the batter into the prepared loaf pan.

4 Bake the banana bread until it is lightly golden brown, 40 to 45 minutes. Transfer the loaf pan to a wire rack and let the banana bread cool for about 5 minutes.

5 Run a knife around the edges of the pan and give the pan a good shake to loosen the bread. Invert the banana bread onto a wire rack, then invert it again onto another rack to cool right side up for about 1 hour before slicing. The banana bread will keep covered in plastic wrap for up to 4 days at room temperature.

EXTRA! EXTRA!

To bake banana muffins, line muffin cups with paper liners and spoon the batter into them, filling each two-thirds full. Bake the muffins at 350°F until golden brown, 20 to 25 minutes. Makes 12 to 16 muffins.

Dairy-Free:

For a dairy-free banana bread use almond milk or coconut milk instead of buttermilk.

Easy Irish Soda Bread

MAKES: 1 LOAF
SERVES: 6 TO 8
PREP: 10 MINUTES | BAKE: 30 TO 35 MINUTES

FOR ST. PATRICK'S DAY BREAKFASTS AND DINNERS OR JUST because you miss the taste of soda bread, here is a quick and hearty recipe that begins with a gluten-free baking mix. It is best served warm, and it is delicious toasted. I like it for breakfast, but you might serve it with dinner using one tablespoon of caraway or dill seeds instead of the raisins.

1 teaspoon vegetable oil

2 cups gluten-free baking mix (see Note)

¼ cup granulated sugar

½ teaspoon xanthan gum (see *Extra! Extra!*)

1 cup buttermilk

1 large egg, lightly beaten

½ cup raisins (optional)

1 tablespoon unsalted butter, melted

1 Place a rack in the center of the oven and preheat the oven to 350°F. Brush the bottom of a 9-inch round cake pan with the oil and set it aside.

2 Place the baking mix, sugar, and xanthan gum in a medium-size mixing bowl and stir to combine. Set the dry ingredients mixture aside.

3 Place the buttermilk and egg in a small bowl and whisk to combine. Pour the buttermilk mixture into the dry ingredients and stir with a wooden spoon until just well blended, 20 to 25 strokes. Fold in the raisins, if using. The batter will be like biscuit dough. Transfer the dough to the prepared cake pan, spreading it to the edge. Place the pan in the oven.

An Unbelievably Gluten-Free Meal

WHERE EATEN:

_____

_____

WHEN EATEN:

_____

_____

WHO WAS THERE:

_____

_____

_____

TIPS FOR MAKING AT HOME:

_____

_____

_____

_____

NEW INSPIRATIONS:

_____

_____

_____

4 Bake the bread until it is very lightly browned on top, 30 to 35 minutes. Brush the top of the bread with the melted butter before slicing it and serving it warm.

Note: Arrowhead Mills all-purpose baking mix works well in this recipe.

EXTRA! EXTRA!

Xanthan gum is a corn product used in gluten-free cooking because it acts as a binder, thickener, and emulsifier. You can find it at Whole Foods or online. Xanthan gum brings ingredients together, but be careful not to use too much as it can make baked goods heavy and gummy.

Set aside some of the soda bread, if possible. Toast the leftover slices and serve them with butter.

Dairy-Free:

For a dairy-free soda bread, use almond milk instead of the buttermilk and serve the bread without the butter.

Big Blueberry Muffins

MAKES: 16 MUFFINS
PREP: 15 TO 20 MINUTES
BAKE: 16 TO 19 MINUTES

U NHAPPY WITH THE FLAVOR AND TEXTURE OF SOME OF the commercial gluten-free blueberry muffins, I set out to bake my own. These begin with a muffin mix, but I don't follow the package directions; instead I add sour cream and fresh blueberries and top the muffins with a glaze. They are far superior to any gluten-free muffins you can buy!

FOR THE MUFFINS

16 paper liners for muffin pans (2½-inch size)

1½ to 2 cups fresh blueberries, rinsed and drained well

1 package (15 to 16 ounces) gluten-free muffin mix (see Note)

6 tablespoons (¾ stick) cold unsalted butter, cut into 18 pieces

2 large eggs

1 cup sour cream

1 tablespoon pure vanilla extract

2 tablespoons warm water

FOR THE GLAZE (OPTIONAL)

1 cup confectioners' sugar

2 to 3 tablespoons milk

1 Make the muffins: Place a rack in the center of the oven and preheat the oven to 375°F. Line 16 muffin cups with paper liners and set the muffin pans aside.

2 Place the blueberries in a small bowl. Pour the muffin mix into a large mixing bowl and measure out 1 teaspoon of the mix. Toss the

blueberries with the 1 teaspoon of muffin mix. Set the bowl aside.

3 Distribute the butter on top of the muffin mix. Using 2 sharp knives or a pastry blender, cut the butter into the mix until the mixture looks like small peas. Set aside.

4 Place the eggs in a small bowl and whisk them slightly. Add the sour cream, vanilla, and warm water and whisk until well combined. Pour the egg mixture into the muffin mixture. Stir just until incorporated, about 20 strokes. The batter will be thick. Fold in the blueberries.

5 Spoon a scant ¼ cup of batter into the paper liners, filling each two thirds full. Place the muffin pans in the oven side by side.

6 Bake the muffins until they are very lightly browned, 16 to 19 minutes. Remove from the oven and let the muffins cool in the pans for 2 to 3 minutes to serve warm without the glaze, or transfer the pans to a wire rack and let the muffins cool for 15 to 20 minutes before glazing.

7 Make the glaze, if using. Place the confectioners' sugar in a small bowl, add 2 tablespoons of milk, and whisk until smooth, adding up to 1 more tablespoon of milk if the glaze is too thick. Spoon the glaze over the muffins and serve. The blueberry muffins will keep covered in plastic wrap for up to 3 days at room temperature.

Note: I used Gluten Free Pantry muffin and scone mix.

EXTRA! EXTRA!

Turn these into orange-blueberry muffins by adding orange juice instead of water to the batter and by using orange juice instead of milk in the glaze.

Dairy-Free:

For dairy-free blueberry muffins use margarine instead of butter, coconut milk instead of sour cream, and water or orange juice instead of milk in the glaze.

Cinnamon Streusel Muffins

MAKES: 16 MUFFINS
PREP: 20 MINUTES
BAKE: 16 TO 19 MINUTES

HERE IS ANOTHER DELICIOUS WAY TO JUMPSTART MUFFINS by beginning with a gluten-free mix. Sour cream adds richness and tenderness to the batter and seems to take away the gritty texture of the rice flour. Making an easy brown sugar, cinnamon, and pecan topping takes these muffins completely over the top; they're wonderful.

16 paper liners for muffin pans
    (2½-inch size)

½ cup firmly packed light brown sugar

⅓ cup finely chopped pecans

1 teaspoon ground cinnamon

1 package (15 ounces) gluten-free muffin
    mix (see Note)

6 tablespoons (¾ stick) cold unsalted
    butter, cut into 18 pieces

2 large eggs

1 cup sour cream

1 tablespoon pure vanilla extract

¼ cup warm water

1 Place a rack in the center of the oven and preheat the oven to 375°F. Line 16 muffin cups with paper liners and set the muffin pans aside.

2 Place the brown sugar, pecans, and cinnamon in a small bowl and stir to mix. Set the streusel aside.

3 Pour the muffin mix into a large mixing bowl. Distribute the butter on top of the mix. Using 2 sharp knives or a pastry blender, cut the butter into the mix until the mixture looks like small peas. Set aside.

An Unbelievably Gluten-Free Meal

WHERE EATEN:

_____

_____

WHEN EATEN:

_____

_____

WHO WAS THERE:

_____

_____

_____

TIPS FOR MAKING AT HOME:

_____

_____

_____

_____

NEW INSPIRATIONS:

_____

_____

_____

_____

4 Place the eggs in a small bowl and whisk them slightly. Add the sour cream, vanilla, and warm water and whisk until well combined. Pour the egg mixture into the muffin mixture. Stir with a large spoon just until the ingredients are incorporated, about 20 strokes. The batter will be thick.

5 Measure out ¼ cup of batter. Spoon half of this (2 tablespoons) into a paper liner.

Sprinkle 1 teaspoon of the streusel on top. Add the remaining two tablespoons of batter. Top this with about 1 teaspoon of streusel. Repeat with the remaining batter and streusel. Place the muffin pans in the oven side by side.

6 Bake the muffins until they are very lightly browned, 16 to 19 minutes. Remove from the oven and let the muffins cool in the pans for 2 to 3 minutes to serve warm or transfer the pans to a wire rack and let the muffins cool completely, 15 to 20 minutes.

Note: I used Gluten Free Pantry muffin and scone mix in this recipe.

Vary the streusel topping as you like, adding half shredded coconut instead of all pecans. Or, add ¼ teaspoon of nutmeg in addition to the cinnamon. These muffins and streusel are extremely versatile. You can turn this batter and the streusel into a coffee cake by layering them in an 8-inch square baking pan. Simply layer half the batter followed by half the streusel. Layer the remaining batter on top of that, followed by the remaining streusel. Bake it at 350°F until lightly browned, 35 to 40 minutes.

Dairy-Free:
Substitute margarine for the butter and unsweetened coconut milk for the sour cream to make dairy-free muffins.

PLAN AHEAD: Cinnamon Streusel Muffins will keep covered in plastic wrap for up to 3 days at room temperature.

Chocolate and Cherry Scones

MAKES: 15 TO 16 SCONES
PREP: 20 MINUTES
BAKE: 12 TO 15 MINUTES

SORT OF A BREAD, SORT OF A DESSERT, THESE SCONES ARE undeniably yummy and totally gluten-free. Cherries are just the right partner for chocolate. And the scones need no glaze because you sprinkle them with sugar before baking. If you must, drizzle a simple chocolate glaze over them.

Vegetable oil spray (optional)

2 cups gluten-free baking mix, such as Bisquick

¼ cup granulated sugar, plus 2 tablespoons sugar, for sprinkling on top of the scones (see Note)

6 tablespoons (¾ stick) cold unsalted butter, cut into 12 pieces, plus butter for serving

2 large eggs, lightly beaten

1 cup buttermilk

⅔ cup (about 3 ounces) chopped dried cherries

¼ cup miniature semisweet chocolate chips

1 Place a rack in the center of the oven and preheat the oven to 375°F. Line a baking sheet with parchment paper or mist it with vegetable oil spray.

2 Place the baking mix and the ¼ cup of sugar in a large mixing bowl and stir to combine. Distribute the butter on top of the baking mixture. Using 2 small sharp knives or a pastry cutter, cut the butter into the mix until the mixture looks like small peas. Add the eggs, buttermilk, cherries, and chocolate chips. Stir

with a large spoon until the dough just comes together, about 25 strokes.

3 Place large spoonfuls of dough, about ¼ cup each, on the prepared baking sheet, spacing them about 2 inches apart. You will have enough room for about 8 scones, or half of the dough. Do not flatten or spread the dough out. Sprinkle 1 tablespoon sugar on top of the spoonfuls of dough, distributing it evenly among them. Place the baking sheet in the oven.

4 Bake the scones until they are golden brown on the bottom and firm to the touch, 12 to 15 minutes. They will not brown on top. Transfer the baked scones to a wire rack to cool for about 10 minutes. Repeat with the remaining dough and 1 tablespoon of sugar.

5 Serve the scones warm with butter.

Note: If you'd rather sprinkle the scones with cinnamon sugar, combine a generous ¼ teaspoon cinnamon with the 2 tablespoons of sugar.

EXTRA! EXTRA!

No chocolate chips? Use a bar of semisweet or bittersweet chocolate. With a sharp, heavy knife, cut the chocolate into chip-size pieces. Measure ¼ cup for this recipe.

Dairy-Free:

To make the scones dairy-free, use margarine instead of the butter and use almond milk instead of the buttermilk. Use dairy-free chocolate chips.

PLAN AHEAD: The scones will keep covered in plastic wrap for up to 2 days at room temperature.

Gotta Have Glaze

For a milk chocolate glaze place 1 cup of confectioners' sugar in a small bowl and stir in 1 heaping tablespoon of unsweetened cocoa powder. Whisk in 2 tablespoons of milk until smooth, adding up to 2 more tablespoons of milk if the glaze is too thick.

Cranberry and Orange Scones

MAKES: 15 TO 16 SCONES
PREP: 20 MINUTES
BAKE: 12 TO 15 MINUTES PER BATCH

THE FLAVOR COMBO OF CRANBERRY AND ORANGE IS perfect for the holidays. These scones go well with turkey and ham so serve them at a festive brunch, tea, or along with dinner. They also make a nice gift for a gluten-intolerant friend. Place the scones in a cellophane bag and tie it with a bright red bow.

FOR THE SCONES

Vegetable oil spray (optional)

2 cups gluten-free baking mix, such as Bisquick

¼ cup granulated sugar, plus 2 tablespoons sugar, for sprinkling on top of the scones

6 tablespoons (¾ stick) cold unsalted butter, cut into 12 pieces

2 large eggs, lightly beaten

1 cup buttermilk

⅔ cup chopped dried cranberries

1 packed tablespoon orange zest (from 1 orange)

½ cup chopped walnuts (optional)

FOR THE ORANGE GLAZE

1 cup confectioners' sugar

2 to 3 tablespoons orange juice

1 Make the scones: Place a rack in the center of the oven and preheat the oven to 375°F. Line a baking sheet with parchment paper or mist it with vegetable oil spray.

2 Place the baking mix and the ¼ cup of granulated sugar in a large mixing bowl and stir to combine. Distribute the butter on top of the

baking mixture. Using 2 small sharp knives or a pastry cutter, cut the butter into the mix until the mixture looks like small peas. Add the eggs, buttermilk, cranberries, orange zest, and walnuts, if using. Stir with a large spoon until the dough just comes together, about 25 strokes.

3 Place large spoonfuls of dough, about ¼ cup each, on the prepared baking sheet, spacing them about 2 inches apart. You will have room for about 8 scones, or half of the dough. Do not flatten or spread the dough out. Sprinkle 1 tablespoon of the granulated sugar on top of the spoonfuls of dough, distributing it evenly among them. Place the baking sheet in the oven.

4 Bake the scones until they are golden brown on the bottom and firm to the touch, 12 to 15 minutes. They will not brown on top. Transfer the baked scones to a wire rack to cool for about 10 minutes. Repeat the process with the remaining dough and 1 tablespoon of granulated sugar.

5 While the scones cool, make the glaze. Place the confectioners' sugar in a small bowl and whisk in 2 tablespoons of orange juice, adding up to 1 more tablespoon of juice if the glaze is too thick. Drizzle the glaze on top of the cooled scones and serve.

EXTRA! EXTRA!

If you want to cut back on sugar and time, omit the glaze and serve the scones warm with a little butter.

Dairy-Free:
Use margarine instead of butter and coconut milk instead of the buttermilk for dairy-free scones.

PLAN AHEAD: The scones will keep covered in plastic wrap for up to 2 days at room temperature.

Buttermilk Biscuits

MAKES: 6 BISCUITS
PREP: 10 MINUTES
BAKE: 13 TO 16 MINUTES

IN RECIPE DEVELOPMENT THE SIMPLEST RECIPES OFTEN prove to be the most complicated to perfect. In coming up with this biscuit recipe, I began by following the directions on the package of gluten-free Bisquick. But the results were too "eggy," more like Southern spoonbread than biscuits. So I replaced the milk with buttermilk the next go-around. And I reduced the eggs to just one. These biscuits were better. Wondering if acidity was the key, I tried using plain yogurt instead of buttermilk and it also worked. My takeaway lesson? The best gluten-free biscuits have an acidic ingredient such as buttermilk or yogurt.

1 cup gluten-free baking mix (see Note)

2½ tablespoons solid vegetable shortening

1 large egg

½ cup buttermilk or plain yogurt

Butter and honey, for serving

1 Place a rack in the center of the oven and preheat the oven to 400°F.

2 Place the baking mix in a medium-size mixing bowl. Add the shortening and, using 2 small sharp knives or a pastry blender, cut the shortening into the baking mix until the mixture looks like small peas. Place the egg and buttermilk or yogurt in a small bowl and whisk to mix. Add the egg mixture to the baking mixture and stir with a fork until a soft dough forms.

{ BISCUIT VARIATIONS }

With a basic biscuit recipe under your belt, add a few twists and you have even more interesting biscuits.

Ham and cheese biscuits:
Add ¼ cup of diced ham and ½ cup of shredded sharp cheddar cheese to the biscuit dough after the dry ingredients have been incorporated.

Cheddar and chive biscuits:
Add ½ cup of shredded sharp cheddar cheese and 1 tablespoon of minced fresh chives to the dough after the dry ingredients have been incorporated.

Strawberry biscuits:
Add ¼ cup of drained, chopped fresh strawberries to the biscuit dough after the dry ingredients have been incorporated. Dust the tops of the biscuits with granulated sugar before baking.

3 Using a large spoon, scoop 6 spoonfuls of dough onto an ungreased baking sheet, spacing them 2 inches apart. Place the baking sheet in the oven.

4 Bake the biscuits until they are very lightly browned, 13 to 16 minutes. Remove the baking sheet from the oven and let the biscuits cool on the baking sheet for 1 to 2 minutes before serving them warm with butter and honey.

An Unbelievably Gluten-Free Meal

WHERE EATEN:

_____

_____

WHEN EATEN:

_____

_____

WHO WAS THERE:

_____

_____

TIPS FOR MAKING AT HOME:

_____

_____

_____

_____

NEW INSPIRATIONS:

_____

_____

_____

Note: Gluten-free Bisquick works well in this recipe. It is a good basic ingredient to keep on hand. The 16-ounce box contains 3 cups. You need 1 cup to make 6 biscuits.

EXTRA! EXTRA!

If you don't have buttermilk or buttermilk powder, stir 2 teaspoons of lemon juice into ½ cup milk and let rest at room temperature for 30 minutes.

Dairy-Free:
Use plain soy yogurt instead of buttermilk or yogurt.

Cornmeal Drop Biscuits

MAKES: 3 DOZEN
PREP: 5 TO 6 MINUTES
BAKE: 12 TO 14 MINUTES PER BATCH

THE PERFECT ACCOMPANIMENT TO CHILI, BEEF STEW, AND homemade vegetable soup, these little biscuits are supereasy to make. Mix them in one bowl, drop them from a spoon onto baking sheets, and bake them until golden. I love these freshly baked, but leftovers are easy to freeze and taste good when reheated. The key ingredient is a gluten-free baking mix, plus white cornmeal.

1½ cups gluten-free baking mix, such as Bisquick

¼ cup white cornmeal

8 tablespoons (1 stick) unsalted butter, melted

1 cup reduced-fat sour cream

1 large egg, lightly beaten

1 Place a rack in the center of the oven and preheat the oven to 400°F.

2 Place the baking mix and cornmeal in a large mixing bowl and stir to combine. Add the butter, sour cream, and egg. Stir until the batter is smooth, about 1 minute. Drop the batter by generous teaspoons onto an ungreased baking sheet, spacing them 1 to 2 inches apart. Place the baking sheet in the oven.

3 Bake the biscuits until they are lightly browned on the bottom and firm on top, 12 to 14 minutes. Remove the baking sheet from the oven and let the biscuits cool on the baking sheet for 1 to 2 minutes before

repeating with the remaining batter. Serve the biscuits warm.

Note: Cooled cornmeal drop biscuits can be frozen, wrapped in heavy aluminum foil, for up to 1 month. To serve, warm the defrosted biscuits inside the foil in a 350°F oven for 10 minutes.

EXTRA! EXTRA!

For a fun change of pace, turn these drop biscuits into cornmeal johnnycakes. Heat about 3 tablespoons of vegetable oil in a cast-iron skillet over medium-high heat. When the oil is hot, drop the cornmeal biscuit batter into the skillet by generous tablespoons and flatten them out slightly with a spatula. Cook the johnnycakes until they are lightly browned on one side, about 1 minute, then turn them and brown the second side, about 1 minute longer. You can jazz up the johnnycakes by adding a couple tablespoons of minced scallion or jalapeño pepper to the batter.

Dairy-Free:

It is not possible to make the biscuits dairy-free.

An Unbelievably Gluten-Free Meal

WHERE EATEN:

_____

_____

WHEN EATEN:

_____

WHO WAS THERE:

_____

_____

TIPS FOR MAKING AT HOME:

_____

_____

_____

_____

NEW INSPIRATIONS:

_____

_____

_____

Southern Skillet Corn Bread

MAKES: 1 LOAF | SERVES: 8
PREP: 10 TO 15 MINUTES
BAKE: 20 TO 25 MINUTES

O N NEW YEAR'S DAY IN THE SOUTH WE COOK A POT OF black-eyed peas and a pot of turnip greens, barbecue ribs on the smoker outside, and bake a pan of corn bread. It's just routine, and no year starts without this. The corn bread recipe I have used for years is adapted from the Martha White cornmeal package, and as I started researching this book I was delighted to know my cornbread is naturally gluten-free. Look for white cornmeal if you can find it and not cornmeal mix as that contains flour. If you must use yellow cornmeal, it's okay, but real Southern corn bread begins with white meal.

¼ cup plus 1 tablespoon vegetable oil

1 large egg

1¾ cups buttermilk, or more as needed

2 cups white cornmeal

1 tablespoon baking powder

½ teaspoon salt

Butter, for serving

1 Place a rack in the center of the oven and preheat the oven to 450°F.

2 Place 1 tablespoon of the oil in a 9-inch cast-iron skillet or a 8- to 9-inch square baking pan. Place the skillet or baking pan in the oven until it is hot. (Heating the skillet before adding the batter gives the corn bread a crispy crust.)

3 Meanwhile, place the egg in a large mixing bowl and stir in the buttermilk and remaining ¼ cup of oil until the yolk has blended in. Place the cornmeal, baking powder, and salt in a small bowl and stir to mix. Add the cornmeal mixture to the egg mixture and stir until just combined. You should be able to pour the batter into the skillet, so add another tablespoon of buttermilk if needed to make it pourable. Carefully remove the hot skillet or pan from the oven and pour the batter into it.

4 Return the skillet or pan to the oven and bake the corn bread until it is golden brown, 20 to 25 minutes. Remove the skillet or pan from the oven and turn it upside down onto a cutting board to remove the corn bread. Slice the corn bread into serving pieces and serve it warm with butter. Leftovers can be reheated under the broiler for 2 to 3 minutes.

{ *Corn bread is gluten-free to begin with, and this is just a good old-fashioned version.* }

EXTRA! EXTRA!

To turn this recipe into corn muffins, spray a muffin pan with vegetable oil spray. Place the muffin pan in the oven until it is hot. Scoop the batter into the hot tin, filling the muffin cups two-thirds full. Bake the muffins at 450°F until golden brown, 15 to 20 minutes. Makes about 12 muffins.

Dairy-Free:
Use 1⅓ cups of almond milk instead of the buttermilk for a dairy-free corn bread. Serve warm with margarine.

Soft Yeast Rolls

MAKES: 20 TO 24 ROLLS
(A HALF RECIPE MAKES 10 TO 12 ROLLS)
PREP: 40 MINUTES | BAKE: 12 TO 14 MINUTES

THESE ROLLS ARE AS CLOSE AS IT GETS TO CLASSIC DINNER rolls made with wheat flour—light, soft, and yeasty. Yum! They begin with a gluten-free flour blend. I have even turned the rolls into cinnamon rolls (see page 139) and found these are more delicious toasted the next morning for breakfast.

1 tablespoon plus 2 teaspoons butter, melted (see Notes)

1 package (16 ounces; 3¼ cups) all-purpose gluten-free flour (see Notes)

2 teaspoons (1 package), instant dry yeast, also known as RapidRise yeast

½ teaspoon salt

6 tablespoons vegetable oil

1 teaspoon cider vinegar

2 large eggs, at room temperature

2 tablespoons honey

1 cup warm milk (see Notes)

1 Brush the bottom of each of two 9-inch round baking pans with 1 teaspoon of butter. Set the baking pans aside.

2 Place the flour, yeast, and salt in a large mixing bowl and stir to combine. Set the flour mixture aside.

3 Place 5 tablespoons of the oil and the vinegar, eggs, and honey in a medium-size mixing bowl and whisk to combine. Add the warm milk and whisk until smooth. Pour the liquid mixture into the flour mixture and,

using an electric mixer fitted with a dough hook, beat at medium-high speed for about 3 minutes. You can also process the dough in a food processor fitted with a steel blade. The dough will be very thick but smooth.

4 Place a rack in the center of the oven and preheat the oven to 400°F.

5 Dip your fingers in the remaining 1 tablespoon of oil. Pinch off a 2-tablespoon size piece of dough. Using your fingers, stretch the piece of dough into a 3-inch round, then fold it in half and place it in one of the prepared baking pans. Continue to form rolls until all of the dough has been used, arranging the rolls side by side in the pans. You will have between 20 to 24 rolls.

6 Cover the pans with plastic wrap and put them in a warm place for the rolls to rise for about 15 minutes. The rolls will not quite double in volume.

7 When the rolls have risen, remove the plastic wrap and place the pans in the oven side by side. Bake the rolls until they are very lightly browned on top, 12 to 14 minutes. Remove the pans from the oven and brush the tops of the rolls with the remaining 1 tablespoon of melted butter. Serve the rolls warm; they will be soft when they come out of the oven and firm up as they cool.

Notes: If you prefer, you can use vegetable oil instead of the 2 teaspoons of melted butter for brushing the baking pans.

I used Gluten Free Pantry all-purpose flour when making these rolls.

The milk should be as warm as warm tap water. Heat cold milk in a microwave oven on high power for 40 seconds.

Toast leftover rolls for breakfast the next day. Slice them in half crosswise, dot them with butter, and toast them under the broiler until the butter melts and the rolls are crispy, about 2 minutes. Serve the rolls with your favorite honey or jam.

Dairy-Free:

Use margarine instead of butter and almond milk instead of the cow's milk for dairy-free rolls.

How to Make Cinnamon Rolls

As you shape the rolls into 3-inch rounds, sprinkle the center of each round liberally with a cinnamon-sugar mixture before folding the rounds in half. For the cinnamon sugar, mix 1 teaspoon of cinnamon with 5 tablespoons of granulated sugar. Place the cinnamon rolls in the prepared baking pans, then continue with the recipe beginning with Step 6.

An Unbelievably Gluten-Free Meal

WHERE EATEN:

WHEN EATEN:

WHO WAS THERE:

TIPS FOR MAKING AT HOME:

NEW INSPIRATIONS:

Zesty Parmesan Bread

MAKES: 2 LOAVES

SERVES: 12 TO 16

PREP: 1 HOUR, 40 MINUTES | BAKE: 23 TO 27 MINUTES

T HIS RECIPE IS BASED ON A FAVORITE BREAD RECIPE OF mine. In order to make it gluten-free, I used a little xanthan gum with the gluten-free flour to bring the dough together. The Parmesan cheese, parsley, onion, and sun-dried tomatoes are all part of the original recipe.

2 teaspoons olive oil or vegetable oil, plus oil for coating the bowl and your fingers

3 cups all-purpose gluten-free flour

1 tablespoon granulated sugar

2 teaspoons (1 package) instant dry yeast, also known as Rapid Rise yeast

½ teaspoon salt

1¼ teaspoons xanthan gum (see *Extra! Extra!*, page 116)

1 cup very warm milk

4 tablespoons (½ stick) unsalted butter, at room temperature

3 large eggs, at room temperature

1 cup grated Parmesan cheese

2 tablespoons chopped fresh parsley

1 tablespoon minced onion

2 tablespoons chopped oil-packed sun-dried tomatoes

1 Brush each of two 8-inch round baking pans with 1 teaspoon of oil. Set the baking pans aside.

2 Place the flour, sugar, yeast, salt, and xanthan gum in a large mixing bowl and stir. Set aside.

3 Using an electric mixer fitted with a dough hook, drizzle very warm milk over the flour mixture, while beating on low speed. Continue beating until all of the milk has been

added and the mixture is crumbly. Stop the mixer, add the butter, and beat on low speed until combined. Add the eggs, one at a time, beating well before adding the next egg. Turn off the machine and, using a rubber spatula, scrape down the side of the bowl. Beat on medium-high speed until the dough is thick and smooth, about 3 minutes. Turn off the mixer, and fold in the remaining ingredients.

4 Brush or mist another large mixing bowl with oil and place the dough in the bowl. Cover the bowl with plastic wrap and place it in a warm place for the dough to rise until doubled, about 1 hour.

5 Scrape down the side of the bowl with the rubber spatula, pushing down with the spatula to deflate the dough. Divide the dough in half. Place each half in a prepared pan. Oil your fingers, then shape each piece of dough into a round 6 or 7 inches in diameter. Put the pans in a warm place to let the dough rise until slightly increased in volume, about 30 minutes.

6 Place a rack in the center of the oven and preheat the oven to 350°F.

7 Place the baking pans in the oven side by side and bake the bread until pale golden and a toothpick inserted in the center comes out clean, 23 to 27 minutes.

8 Remove the breads from the oven and run a knife around the edge of the pans. Invert the breads onto a cutting board, slice them into wedges, and serve warm.

EXTRA! EXTRA!

Cut the ingredients for the recipe in half and you can bake just one loaf. For one half egg, beat an egg slightly in a measuring cup and use half of the beaten egg, discarding the rest.

Dairy-Free:
Use almond milk and omit the Parmesan cheese. This will not be a Parmesan-flavored bread, but it will still be delicious.

Twenty-Five Unbelievably Gluten-Free Chicken, Meats, and Other Mains

1. *Real Deal Gluten-Free Fried Chicken*

2. *Love Me Chicken Tender*

3. *Smashed Chicken Gluten-Free Style*

4. *Indian Chicken Kebabs*

5. *Parmesan Chicken Rolls*

6. *Country Captain Chicken*

7. *Martha's Baked Chicken*

8. *Gluten-Free Chicken Potpie*

9. *Chicken and Biscuit Pie*

10. *Martha's Chicken and Dumplings*

11. *Artichoke Chicken Casserole*

12. *Clay's Chicken Enchiladas*

13. *Country-Fried Steak with Gravy*

14. *Braised Pot Roast with Vidalia Onions*

15. *The Best GF Meat Loaf*

16. *Mexican Lasagna*

17. *Hartley's Mexican Rice Supper*

18. *French Baked Pork Chops with Mustard Sauce*

19. *Golden-Brown Ham and Cheese Impossible Pie*

20. *New Orleans Red Beans and Rice*

21. *Old-Fashioned Pigs in Blankets*

22. *Cornmeal-Crusted Fried Fish*

23. *Fried Shrimp and Tempura Veggies*

24. *Baked Eggplant and Zucchini Parmesan*

25. *Cheese Grits Soufflé*

Chicken, Meats, and Other Mains

A s I compiled this main dish chapter and looked at its list of recipes—from savory pies to a biscuit pie to casseroles, kebabs, braised pot roast, and a soufflé made with cheese grits—I was reminded of the days I spent in the kitchen partnering new ingredients and old techniques: the new gluten-free ingredients I found on store shelves combined with cooking methods I have used over the years.

Please note that this eclectic chapter is like a playlist at a wedding with tunes requested from the bride and groom that might not necessarily go together. These are the gluten-free recipes readers have requested. They are the must-have recipes. They are fried and battered and comforting and cozy. Add a green salad or some steamed broccoli, serve them with fresh sliced tomatoes in the summertime or a plateful of fresh orange sections in the winter and you have a complete meal.

Most of all, enjoy them. Be sure not to miss Martha's Chicken and Dumplings, my gluten-free version of smashed chicken, and Clay's Chicken Enchiladas. And don't pass up the French baked pork chops, the braised pot roast, and the Best GF Meat Loaf. I savor the meat loaf leftovers on sandwiches the next day.

Real Deal Gluten-Free Fried Chicken

SERVES: 6
PREP: 10 MINUTES
COOK: 30 TO 35 MINUTES

I WAS RAISED ON FRIED CHICKEN SOAKED IN SALT WATER OR buttermilk then dredged in flour seasoned with salt, pepper, and some Lawry's seasoned salt. My mother fried chicken in an electric skillet, browning the chicken on both sides, then reducing the heat, covering the skillet, and continuing to cook the chicken pieces until they were cooked through. With gluten-free flour blends more readily available, frying chicken is quite simple. King Arthur or Gluten Free Pantry use rice flour as a base and both are easy to buy online or if you can't find a local source. If you like a more crispy coating on the chicken, follow the directions for cooking chicken tenders on page 147. Fry up this very authentic chicken. You won't miss the wheat flour.

1 chicken (3 to 4 pounds),
   cut into 8 pieces

2 cups buttermilk or salted ice water

1 cup gluten-free flour (see Note)

Salt, freshly ground black pepper,
   and seasoned salt, such as Lawry's

6 cups (48 ounces) vegetable oil,
   for frying

1 Rinse the chicken pieces under cold running water and pat them dry with paper towels. Place the chicken in a glass or stainless steel bowl and pour the buttermilk or salted ice water over the chicken to cover it. Cover the bowl with plastic wrap and place it in the refrigerator to chill for at least 1 hour, preferably longer.

2 Remove the chicken piece by piece from the buttermilk or ice water and pat it dry. Place the flour in a large bowl or brown paper bag and season it generously with salt, pepper, and seasoned salt. Stir to combine the flour and seasoning. Add a few pieces of chicken to the flour and toss or shake to coat well. Repeat with the remaining chicken.

3 Heat the oil to a depth of 2 inches in a large frying pan or electric skillet over medium-high heat until the oil registers 360° to 370°F on a candy thermometer. The skillet needs to be at least 14 inches across so that you do not crowd the chicken in the pan. If your skillets are smaller, fry the chicken in 2 pans, filling each with oil to a depth of 2 inches. Place the chicken pieces in the oil (skin side down for breasts and thighs) and brown on one side, about 5 minutes. Using tongs, turn the chicken over and brown the second side, about 5 minutes. Reduce the heat, cover the pan, and cook the chicken until it is cooked through and has an internal temperature of 170°F

measured on an instant-read meat thermometer, 20 to 25 minutes. (Remove the cover from the skillet during the last few minutes of frying for a crispy crust.)

4 Transfer the chicken to brown paper bags or paper towels to drain, then serve it warm.

Note: I used Gluten Free Pantry, King Arthur, and Bob's Red Mill all-purpose flour blends when testing this recipe. These are not gluten-free baking mixes, which contain leavening.

EXTRA! EXTRA!

To drain fried chicken and also keep it its crispiest, place it on brown paper bags instead of paper towels.

Dairy-Free:
Use water instead of buttermilk or milk when soaking the chicken.

Love Me Chicken Tender

SERVES: 4
PREP: 30 MINUTES
COOK: 6 TO 7 MINUTES

KIDS LOVE CHICKEN TENDERS, BUT FOR THOSE WHO ARE gluten-intolerant, they're not even a once-in-a-while treat. Now they can be. Most likely kids will like them plain, but the grown-ups will enjoy the dipping sauce. For extra-crispy fried chicken tenders dredge them in seasoned flour, dip them in the egg and milk mixture, then dredge them in *panko*-style bread crumbs, pressing the bread crumbs into the chicken so they stick.

FOR THE BLUE CHEESE DIPPING SAUCE

1 cup mayonnaise (preferably Hellmann's)

½ cup sour cream

2 cloves garlic, crushed in a garlic press

2 tablespoons lemon juice

½ cup (2 ounces) crumbled blue cheese

FOR THE CHICKEN TENDERS

1 pound chicken tenders (about 12)

½ cup gluten-free flour (see Note on page 146)

2 teaspoons seasoned salt, such as Lawry's

1 large egg

1 tablespoon milk or water

4 cups (32 ounces) vegetable oil, for frying

1 Make the blue cheese dipping sauce: Place the mayonnaise, sour cream, garlic, and lemon juice in a small bowl and stir to mix. Fold in the blue cheese, cover the bowl with plastic wrap, and refrigerate until ready to use.

2 Prepare the chicken tenders: Rinse the chicken tenders under

An Unbelievably Gluten-Free Meal

....

WHERE EATEN:

_____

_____

WHEN EATEN:

_____

_____

WHO WAS THERE:

_____

_____

TIPS FOR MAKING AT HOME:

_____

_____

_____

_____

NEW INSPIRATIONS:

_____

_____

_____

_____

cold running water and pat them dry with paper towels. Combine the flour and seasoned salt in a shallow bowl. Place the egg and milk or water in a small bowl and beat with a fork to blend.

3 Dredge the chicken tenders in the seasoned flour first, dip them in the egg mixture, then dip them again in the flour, coating each piece. Place the chicken tenders on a baking sheet and refrigerate them for about 15 minutes to help the coating stick better.

4 When ready to cook, heat oil to a depth of 1 inch in a large deep heavy skillet over medium-high heat until the oil registers 360° to 370°F on a candy thermometer. Fry a few tenders at a time, being careful not to crowd the skillet. Turn the chicken tenders a few times while they fry. The tenders are done when they are browned on all sides and their juices run clear when pricked with the tip of a sharp knife, 6 to 7 minutes. Drain the fried tenders on brown paper bags or paper towels.

Smashed Chicken Gluten-Free Style

SERVES: 4
PREP: 20 MINUTES
COOK: 8 TO 10 MINUTES TOTAL

AFTER ORDERING CHICKEN MILANESE IN A FAVORITE restaurant, I was determined to come up with my own version of the recipe at home. Now I have mastered the art of smashing chicken breasts with a heavy rolling pin. Dredged in seasoned bread crumbs and then sautéed, my kids love them. Because gluten-free bread crumbs are so easy to make yourself—or to buy—I wanted to include a gluten-free version of this easy recipe. I have never met a child, teenager, or adult who doesn't like smashed chicken.

4 skinless boneless chicken breast halves (1¼ pounds total), frozen slightly

2 cups coarse, dry gluten-free bread crumbs (see Note)

½ cup (2 ounces) grated Parmesan cheese

2 cloves garlic, minced

¼ teaspoon dried oregano (optional)

¼ teaspoon dried basil (optional)

¼ teaspoon salt

¼ teaspoon freshly ground black pepper

½ cup olive oil, or more as needed, for frying

Arugula leaves and chopped fresh tomatoes, or your favorite pasta sauce, warmed, for serving

1 Place each chicken breast in a separate gallon-size resealable plastic bag. It is easier to smash the chicken if the chicken is cold, preferably a little frozen. Place the bags on a sturdy kitchen counter and smash the chicken breasts with a mallet, heavy rolling pin, or cast-iron skillet until they are ¼ inch thick.

This will take about 2 minutes per chicken breast. Set the chicken aside or, if you like to plan for future meals, place the smashed chicken in the plastic bags in the freezer until you need to cook them.

2 Place the bread crumbs, Parmesan cheese, garlic, oregano and basil, if using, and the salt and pepper in a large mixing bowl and stir to mix. Set the crumb mixture aside.

3 Pour the olive oil in a large frying pan and place the pan over medium-high heat. Carefully remove the chicken breasts from the plastic bags as they are delicate and can tear. Place 1 breast at a time in the bread crumb mixture and dredge it on both sides.

4 Line a platter with paper towels. When the oil is hot, slide the breaded chicken breasts into the pan, 1 or 2 at a time, depending on how many will fit in the pan. Cook the chicken breasts on one side until golden, 2 to 3 minutes, then turn them with tongs

and cook them on the second side until the chicken is cooked through and the bread crumbs are golden, 1 to 2 minutes. Transfer the chicken breasts to the paper towel–lined platter to drain. Repeat with the remaining chicken breasts, adding more olive oil to the pan, if necessary.

5 Remove the paper towels and serve the chicken on the platter, garnished with arugula and chopped tomatoes or with pasta sauce on the side.

Note: Buy *panko*-style gluten-free crumbs, or make your own. I use whatever gluten-free white bread I have on hand, toast it, then pulse it in the food processor until it forms coarse crumbs. You can put the garlic into the processor first, pulse to finely mince it, then add the toasted bread and pulse the processor to make crumbs. Stir in the Parmesan cheese and seasonings and you are ready to go!

EXTRA! EXTRA!

Leftover smashed chicken is superb sliced atop a salad or placed in a shallow baking dish, covered with your favorite pasta sauce, and topped with shredded mozzarella and Parmesan cheese. Bake it in a hot oven until the cheese bubbles and you have chicken Parmesan.

Dairy-Free:

Omit the Parmesan cheese when making the bread crumb mixture and the chicken will be dairy-free.

An Unbelievably Gluten-Free Meal

WHERE EATEN:

_____

_____

WHEN EATEN:

_____

_____

WHO WAS THERE:

_____

_____

_____

TIPS FOR MAKING AT HOME:

_____

_____

_____

_____

NEW INSPIRATIONS:

_____

_____

_____

Indian Chicken Kebabs

SERVES: 4 | PREP: 10 TO 12 MINUTES

MARINATE: AT LEAST 15 MINUTES, AS LONG AS OVERNIGHT

COOK: 8 TO 9 MINUTES

I ADAPTED THIS KEBAB RECIPE FROM MADHUR JAFFREY'S book *Quick & Easy Indian Cooking.* I love the way you can quickly marinate chicken with salt and lemon juice, adding flavor with a tenderizing combination of yogurt, curry spices, and a little chickpea (or gram) flour. The spices and yogurt cling to the chicken and create a nice coating while the chicken broils. Serve the kebabs over rice or with a green salad.

4 skinless boneless chicken breast halves
    (1¼ pounds total)

¾ teaspoon sea salt

2 tablespoons fresh lemon juice
    (from 1 lemon)

3 tablespoons plain yogurt

1 tablespoon chickpea flour,
    also known as gram flour

2 cloves garlic, crushed in a garlic press

1 teaspoon grated fresh ginger

½ teaspoon ground cumin

½ teaspoon garam masala

¼ teaspoon cayenne pepper

¼ teaspoon ground turmeric

3 to 4 tablespoons olive oil (see Note),
    for basting

1 Cut the chicken breasts into 1-inch pieces. Place the chicken pieces in a medium-size glass bowl and sprinkle ½ teaspoon of the salt and the lemon juice over them. Using clean hands, rub the salt and lemon juice into the chicken to combine well. Set the chicken aside.

2 Place the yogurt and chickpea flour in a small bowl and stir

to combine. Stir in the garlic, ginger, cumin, garam masala, cayenne pepper, turmeric, and the remaining ¼ teaspoon of salt. Pour the yogurt mixture over the chicken and stir to combine. Set the chicken aside for about 15 minutes, or let it marinate as long as overnight, covered with plastic wrap, in the refrigerator.

3 When you are ready to cook the chicken, preheat the broiler.

4 Remove the chicken pieces from the marinade, discarding the marinade. Thread the pieces onto 4 to 6 long skewers or 8 short skewers and set the skewers over a baking dish so that the ends of the skewers are balanced on the edges of the baking dish. Brush the chicken kebabs with olive oil. Broil the kebabs about 4 inches from the heat for about 5 minutes on one side. Turn the kebabs over, baste them again with olive oil, and broil them until the chicken is just cooked through, 3 to 4 minutes. Serve the chicken kebabs warm.

Note: In place of the olive oil you could use any vegetable oil for basting the kebabs or you could use butter. I always have olive oil on hand so I use it.

EXTRA! EXTRA!

Use this same recipe for cooking lamb, marinating a little more than a pound of lean lamb cubes that are no more than 1 inch in size. To cook the lamb through will take a total of 8 to 10 minutes. Serve the lamb kebabs over rice pilaf with fresh mint, cucumbers, and tomatoes.

Dairy-Free:
Use soy yogurt or unsweetened coconut milk instead of the yogurt when marinating the chicken.

Fall Football Tailgate Supper

Cream of Cauliflower Soup, page 92
Indian Chicken Kebabs
Green salad
Easy Apple Tart, page 325

Parmesan Chicken Rolls

SERVES: 6
PREP: 20 MINUTES
BAKE: 1 HOUR, 5 MINUTES TO 1 HOUR, 15 MINUTES

MY MOTHER WAS KNOWN FOR HER GOOD COOKING AND these Parmesan Chicken Rolls were one of her specialties. Sometimes we were fortunate enough to have them for dinner, but that was usually if they were left over from a ladies' luncheon, where they were the main course. To make them gluten-free, use gluten-free *panko*-style bread crumbs either purchased or made from your own sandwich bread. Toast the bread first until it is very dry, or dry it out in a 300°F oven for about twenty minutes. Then pulse the bread in a food processor until you have coarse crumbs.

6 skinless boneless chicken breast halves
(2 to 2½ pounds total)

4 tablespoons (½ stick) unsalted butter

1 cup coarse, dry gluten-free bread crumbs

¾ cup (3 ounces) grated Parmesan cheese

1 clove garlic, crushed in a garlic press

½ teaspoon salt

¼ teaspoon freshly ground black pepper

6 toothpicks

1 Place a rack in the center of the oven and preheat the oven to 325°F.

2 Rinse the chicken under cold running water, pat it dry with paper towels, and set it aside.

3 Melt the butter in a saucepan over low heat. Combine the bread crumbs, Parmesan cheese, garlic, salt, and pepper in a bowl.

{ *An easy company dish to serve with the Tomato Panzanella Salad on page 258.* }

...on page 258.

EXTRA! EXTRA!

Serve the chicken rolls at room temperature or sliced cold at a picnic with your favorite salad.

Add ½ teaspoon of Italian seasoning or a pinch each dried basil and oregano to the bread crumb mixture for an Italian flavor.

Dairy-Free:
Use margarine instead of butter and omit the Parmesan cheese and these chicken rolls can be dairy-free.

4 Dip the chicken, one breast at a time, in the melted butter, then dredge it in the crumb mixture. Beginning at the narrow end of a chicken breast, roll it up into a fat cigar shape. Insert a toothpick in the chicken breast to keep it from unrolling. Place the chicken roll seam side down in a 2-quart baking dish. Repeat with the remaining chicken breasts. Drizzle any leftover butter over the top.

5 Place the baking dish in the oven. Bake the chicken until it is tender and cooked through (you should be able to insert a fork with ease) and the top is golden brown, 1 hour, 5 minutes to 1 hour, 15 minutes. Carefully remove the toothpicks before serving.

Country Captain Chicken

SERVES: 6
PREP: 20 MINUTES
COOK: 46 TO 57 MINUTES

I SPENT TWENTY YEARS IN GEORGIA AND AM FOND OF THE state. While I was there a good cook in Savannah passed along this recipe for Country Captain Chicken, a favorite with people who like to entertain because it can be made a day in advance, then reheated and served over rice. Country Captain is legendary on the Georgia coast, and I love how the chicken thighs simmer down with tomatoes, onion, bell pepper, and exotic spices until they are very tender. Use any gluten-free flour blend you have on the pantry shelf to dredge the chicken before searing. If the sauce needs more thickening, just remove the lid of the pan to let the liquid evaporate. If the sauce is just the right consistency, leave the lid on the pan.

2 tablespoons gluten-free flour blend

1 tablespoon plus ½ teaspoon curry powder

Salt and freshly ground black pepper

6 skinless boneless chicken thighs
 (1½ pounds total)

3 tablespoons vegetable oil

1 cup chopped onions

1 cup chopped green bell pepper

3 cloves garlic, minced

2 cans (14½ ounces each) diced tomatoes
 with their juices

⅓ cup raisins

Steamed rice, for serving

Shredded coconut, chopped peanuts,
 mango chutney, chopped scallions, and
 cooked crumbled bacon, for garnish

1 Place the flour blend and ½ teaspoon of curry powder in a medium-size bowl. Season with salt and black pepper to taste and stir to combine. Add the chicken thighs and toss to coat them on all sides. Set the chicken aside.

2 Place the oil in a large frying pan over medium-high heat. When the oil is hot, add the chicken and brown on one side, about 2 minutes, then turn and brown on the other side, 1 to 2 minutes. Remove the pan from the heat and transfer the browned chicken to a plate to stay warm.

3 Place the pan back over medium heat and add the onions, bell pepper, and garlic. Cook, stirring, until the vegetables soften, about 3 minutes. Add the tomatoes and remaining 1 tablespoon of curry powder and season with salt and black pepper to taste. Let the mixture simmer, uncovered, until the liquid has reduced a bit, about 10 minutes. Return the chicken to the pan, spooning the tomato mixture over it. Cover the pan

and reduce the heat to low. Let the chicken simmer until it is tender and cooked through, 30 to 35 minutes. Add the raisins to the pan and stir to combine. If the sauce is too thin, uncover the pan and simmer the sauce over low heat for about 5 minutes.

4 Serve the chicken warm over rice, and garnish with the coconut, peanuts, chutney, scallions, and bacon.

EXTRA! EXTRA!

For a spicier curry flavor, use red curry powder instead of the usual supermarket yellow curry powder. Or, use garam masala, which has a unique and more pronounced spice flavor than yellow curry powder. Instead of chicken thighs you could use legs or wings or breasts that have been split in half.

Dairy-Free:
This Country Captain Chicken recipe is dairy-free.

Martha's Baked Chicken

SERVES: 4 TO 6 | PREP: 15 MINUTES
COOK: 1 HOUR, 30 MINUTES TO 1 HOUR, 45 MINUTES IN AN OVEN
OR 4 HOURS IN A SLOW COOKER

THANKS TO MY FRIEND MARTHA BOWDEN, HERE IS AN incredibly delicious and efficient way to roast a chicken. It's perfect as is and it will give you plenty of meat for Martha's Chicken and Dumplings, Gluten-Free Chicken Potpie, Chicken and Biscuit Pie, Artichoke Chicken Casserole, or Clay's Chicken Enchiladas. You will also get about two cups of homemade chicken broth to use in any recipe as needed. If a recipe calls for more than two cups of broth, use canned broth to make up the difference.

Vegetable oil spray, for misting the roasting pan or slow cooker

1 whole chicken (3 to 5 pounds; see Note)

½ cup low-sodium chicken broth (see *Extra! Extra!*)

1 teaspoon dried basil

½ teaspoon dried thyme leaves, or 1 tablespoon fresh thyme

½ teaspoon garlic powder, or 1 to 2 cloves garlic, crushed in a garlic press

¼ teaspoon salt

¼ teaspoon ground white pepper

4 to 5 ribs celery, rinsed and cut into 3-inch pieces

1 large onion, peeled and cut into quarters

1 Mist a roasting pan or slow cooker with vegetable oil spray. If you are baking the chicken preheat the oven to 325°F.

2 Rinse the chicken under cold running water and pat it dry with paper towels. Using a sharp knife,

trim all of the visible fat from the chicken and discard it.

3 Place the chicken in the prepared roasting pan or slow cooker. Gently pull the skin away from the breast meat but leave it attached. Pour the chicken broth over the chicken. Sprinkle the basil, thyme, garlic powder, salt, and white pepper over the breast meat and inside the cavity. Place half of the celery and 2 onion quarters inside the chicken cavity. Pull the chicken skin back securely over the breast meat and seasonings. Place the remaining pieces of celery and onion around the chicken and on top of the chicken breast.

4 Cover the roasting pan or place the lid on the slow cooker. Bake the chicken for 1 hour, 30 minutes to 1 hour, 45 minutes, or cook the chicken in the slow cooker on high heat for about 4 hours. The chicken is done when the juices run clear and an instant-read meat thermometer inserted in the thick part of a thigh, but not touching a bone, registers 190°F.

5 Using a large pair of tongs, remove the chicken from the roasting pan or slow cooker, holding it with the cavity facing down, let the juices drip from the chicken into the roasting pan or slow cooker for about 15 seconds. Transfer the chicken to a platter and let it rest for 15 to 20 minutes.

6 Place a wire sieve or a colander over a glass bowl and pour the cooking juices from the roasting pan or slow cooker into the bowl. You will have about 2 cups of broth if the chicken was baked and about 2⅓ cups of broth if the chicken was cooked in a slow cooker. Set the bowl of broth aside to cool for about 30 minutes so that the fat rises to the surface. Then, using a ladle, skim off as much fat as you can. Or refrigerate the broth overnight and you will be able to remove the hardened fat from the surface of the broth.

7 While the broth cools, skin and debone the chicken. Depending on the size of the chicken, you will have 4 to 5 cups of chopped or

shredded cooked chicken. Store the chicken and broth separately in airtight containers for up to 3 days.

Note: Martha prefers a "roasting" chicken, a little larger than a broiler-fryer and with more flavor, too. I prefer an organic chicken for its full flavor.

EXTRA! EXTRA!

This recipe works because its broth comes from the juices of the chicken, making it very well flavored. Add ¼ cup of white wine in addition to the ½ cup of broth when you cook the chicken and your kitchen will smell like heaven! Feel free to add a bay leaf or whatever combination of herbs suits you when cooking the chicken.

Dairy-Free:
This chicken recipe is dairy-free.

An Unbelievably Gluten-Free Meal

WHERE EATEN:

WHEN EATEN:

WHO WAS THERE:

TIPS FOR MAKING AT HOME:

NEW INSPIRATIONS:

Gluten-Free Chicken Potpie

MAKES: 6 SERVINGS
PREP: 15 TO 20 MINUTES
BAKE: 27 TO 33 MINUTES | REST: 10 MINUTES

ADAPTED FROM MY SISTER SUSAN'S FABULOUS POTPIE, this gluten-free version uses homemade pie crusts (page 318) or two of your favorite store-bought frozen gluten-free pie crusts. Unlike Susan's recipe, in which she thickens the broth with flour, I just sprinkle a little cornstarch onto the sautéed vegetables and chicken, add the chicken broth, then pour this filling with its lightly thickened sauce into the crust. In summer you can make this with garden veggies; in the winter use veggies straight from the freezer. While potpies often have just a top crust, this glorious potpie is the real deal with a crust on the top *and* a crust on the bottom.

2 unbaked gluten-free pie crusts (9 to 10 inches) homemade (page 318) or store bought, thawed if frozen

2 tablespoons butter or olive oil

1½ cups fresh or frozen vegetables (see Note), chopped if large

2 cups shredded or chopped cooked chicken, homemade (see Martha's Baked Chicken, page 159) or store-bought rotisserie chicken

2 tablespoons cornstarch

Salt and freshly ground black pepper

2 cups low-sodium chicken broth

1 Place a rack in the center of the oven and preheat the oven to 450°F.

2 Set one pie crust aside. Press the other crust into a 9-inch pie pan that is 2 inches deep. Crimp the edge

of the crust with a fork, then prick the bottom a few times. Bake the crust until it is well browned, 7 to 8 minutes. Remove the pie pan from the oven and set it aside. Reduce the oven temperature to 350°F.

3 Melt the butter or heat the olive oil in a large frying pan over medium heat. Add the vegetables and cook, stirring, for 1 to 2 minutes, depending on whether they need to be heated through or cooked. Add the chicken and cook, stirring, until warmed through, about 1 minute. Sprinkle the cornstarch over the vegetables and chicken, then season them with salt and pepper to taste. Pour the chicken broth into the pan, increase the heat to medium-high, and cook, stirring, until the mixture thickens slightly, 1 to 2 minutes. Set the chicken mixture aside.

4 Place a piece of waxed paper that is about 12 inches long on a work surface and place the remaining pie crust on top of it. Place a second piece of waxed paper on top of the pie crust. Using a rolling pin, roll out the pie crust until it is large enough to cover the top of the pie.

5 Pour the chicken mixture into the baked pie crust. Cover the top with the rolled-out pie crust. Using your fingertips, turn the edge of the top crust under the crimped edge of the bottom crust. Press around the edge of the crust with a fork to seal the two edges together. Using a sharp knife, make several vents in the top crust.

6 Place the potpie on a baking sheet and place it in the oven. Bake the potpie until the crust is golden brown and the juices bubble, 20 to 25 minutes. If the top has not browned sufficiently, place the potpie under the broiler until it turns golden. Let the potpie rest for about 10 minutes, then slice it and serve.

Note: From the freezer, I use peas, green beans, lima beans, and mixed veggies like peas and carrots or corn, peas, and carrots. In the spring, I use asparagus tips, fresh peas, and carrots. In the summer,

try zucchini and yellow summer squash, fresh green beans and crowder peas (a fresh pea cousin of blackeyed peas). In the fall, opt for late summer red bell peppers, zucchini, and mushrooms.

EXTRA! EXTRA!

To make the potpie ahead, you can assemble it through step 5, then cover and refrigerate it. The next day remove the potpie from the fridge, let it sit for about 15 minutes, then bake it as directed in step 6 in an oven pre-heated to 350°F.

Dairy-Free:

Because of the cream cheese in the pie crust this recipe cannot be made dairy-free.

An Unbelievably Gluten-Free Meal

WHERE EATEN: _____

_____

WHEN EATEN: _____

_____

WHO WAS THERE: _____

_____

_____

TIPS FOR MAKING AT HOME: _____

_____

_____

_____

NEW INSPIRATIONS: _____

_____

_____

Chicken and Biscuit Pie

SERVES: 6 TO 8
PREP: 45 TO 50 MINUTES
BAKE: 18 TO 20 MINUTES

AS A CHILD I PREFERRED CHICKEN AND BISCUIT PIE TO potpie because I got my very own biscuit. I remember that feeling of ownership as the biscuit was served onto my plate along with a big spoonful of the delicious broth, chicken, and vegetables hidden underneath. Here is a gluten-free version of that nostalgic recipe. You can easily cut the recipe in half, or you can go ahead and bake a big pan knowing you'll have leftovers for day two.

Vegetable oil spray, for misting the pan

Double recipe gluten-free Buttermilk Biscuits, 12 biscuits (page 128)

2 cups water

3 cups (12 ounces) frozen peas and carrots

4 cups chopped cooked chicken, homemade (see Martha's Baked Chicken, page 159) or store-bought rotisserie chicken

3 cups low-sodium chicken broth (homemade or store-bought)

½ cup milk

Salt and freshly ground black pepper

3 tablespoons cornstarch

1 Preheat the oven to 425°F. Mist a 13 by 9-inch glass baking dish with vegetable oil spray and set it aside.

2 Make the biscuit dough and set the 12 biscuits aside.

3 Place the water in a medium-size saucepan and let come to a boil over medium-high heat. Add the frozen peas and carrots and cook them until warmed through, about 2 minutes, then drain well. Add the chicken to the peas and carrots and spoon the mixture into the prepared baking dish in an even layer.

4 Set aside ¼ cup of the chicken broth. Place the remaining 2¾ cups of chicken broth and the milk in the same saucepan you used to cook the peas and carrots. Season with salt and pepper to taste. Heat over medium-high heat until the liquid comes to a boil, 3 to 4 minutes. While you are waiting for the liquid to boil, place the reserved ¼ cup of chicken broth in a small bowl and whisk in the cornstarch. Slowly pour the cornstarch mixture into the boiling liquid, stirring. Let the mixture return to a boil and cook, stirring, until it thickens, about 1 minute. Pour the hot broth mixture over the chicken and vegetables in the baking dish. Immediately arrange the biscuits on top, making 3 rows of 4 biscuits.

5 Place the baking dish in the oven and bake until the biscuits are lightly browned and the sauce is bubbling, 18 to 20 minutes. Serve the biscuit pie at once.

EXTRA! EXTRA!

Don't add frozen veggies right from the package to the baking dish. They will cool down the sauce and make the biscuits bake less quickly. Feel free to season the broth with cayenne pepper or a little nutmeg, or any of your favorite seasonings. And don't be confined to frozen veggies, either. Use 3 cups of your favorite chopped fresh vegetables in this recipe. If they are raw, lightly sauté them in a little butter or canola oil until soft.

Dairy-Free:

For a dairy-free biscuit pie substitute water for the milk in the filling and make the biscuits with plain soy yogurt.

Chicken Choices

You can use your favorite store-bought rotisserie chicken in recipes that call for cooked chicken. A large chicken will yield between 4 and 5 cups of shredded chicken. Or, cook your own chicken using Martha's Baked Chicken (page 159), or by simmering four large skinless boneless chicken breasts in seasoned water until cooked through, 20 to 25 minutes.

Martha's Chicken and Dumplings

SERVES: 4 TO 8
PREP: 30 MINUTES
COOK: 20 TO 25 MINUTES

MARTHA BOWDEN IS KNOWN FOR HER CHICKEN AND dumplings. In this version her dumplings are gluten-free and the chicken broth is thickened a bit with cornstarch. What you will have are soft, velvety dumplings, simmered in that broth with fresh, tender chicken—the ultimate comfort food. This recipe makes a lot, serving anywhere from four to eight people, depending on how hungry everyone is. Reheat leftovers in the microwave.

2¾ cups gluten-free baking mix, such as Bisquick

¼ teaspoon salt

¼ teaspon freshly ground black pepper

Dash of cayenne pepper

7½ teaspoons solid vegetable shortening, cut into small pieces

1 large egg, beaten

1 scant cup (about ⅞ cup) cold water (see Note)

Vegetable oil spray for spraying the waxed paper

6 cups low-sodium chicken broth, homemade or store-bought, or more as needed

4 tablespoons cornstarch

4 cups bite-size cooked chicken pieces, homemade (see Martha's Baked Chicken, page 159) or store-bought rotisserie chicken

Chopped flat-leaf parsley, for garnish

1 Place the baking mix, salt, black pepper, and cayenne pepper in a medium-size bowl and stir to combine. Place the pieces of shortening around the edge of the bowl and, using a pastry blender or 2 knives, cut it into the dry ingredients.

Add the egg and water, starting with ⅞ cup of water and stirring with a wooden spoon until the dough comes together. Add more water a tablespoon at a time if needed. Wrap the dough tightly in plastic wrap and refrigerate it until well chilled, at least 1 hour.

2 Tear off two 14-inch-long pieces of waxed paper. Spray one side of each piece with vegetable oil spray. Remove the chilled dough from the fridge. Place one piece of waxed paper, sprayed side up, on a work surface and place the dough in the center. Press the dough with your fingers to make a small disk. Place the second piece of waxed paper on top, sprayed side down. Using a rolling pin, gently roll the dough out into a flat circle, 12 to 13 inches in diameter and ¼ inch thick.

3 Measure ½ cup of the chicken broth and set it aside. Place the remaining 5½ cups of chicken broth in a large pot over medium heat and let come to a simmer. Stir the cornstarch into the reserved ½ cup of chicken broth. Stir the cornstarch

and broth mixture into the pot of broth, whisking until the mixture boils and is smooth, 1 to 2 minutes.

4 Remove the top piece of waxed paper from the dough. Using a sharp knife, cut the dough into long strips 1 to 1¼ inches wide. Cut these strips into 2- to 3-inch–long pieces. Place your fingers underneath the waxed paper and gently peel off the strips of dough. Working quickly, gently drop the dumplings into the

simmering thickened broth, placing them around the edge of the pot. Cover the pot and adjust the heat to keep the broth at a slow boil. Stir the dumplings every 3 minutes so they don't stick to the bottom of the pot but don't stir too hard because the dumplings are fragile until they are done. Cook the dumplings until they are tender when pierced with a fork, 18 to 22 minutes.

5 Add the chicken to the pot, stir, and cook until the chicken is just heated through, 2 to 3 minutes. You don't want the dumplings to overcook. If the broth gets too thick, thin it with a bit more broth. Ladle the chicken and dumplings into shallow bowls, garnish with the parsley, and serve. The chicken and dumplings can be refrigerated, covered, for 2 days.

Note: It's important to get the amount of water used in the dumplings right. If you use too much, the dumplings don't hold together when dropped in the hot broth. If you don't use enough, the dumpling dough doesn't come together in a ball that you can roll out. Start with about ⅞ of a cup, and if the dough seems dry, add a little more water. Chilling the dumpling dough in plastic wrap helps bind it together and makes it easier to roll out and cut.

EXTRA! EXTRA!

For the quickest method, use the meat from a rotisserie-cooked chicken from the supermarket and store-bought chicken broth. But for the best chicken and dumplings ever follow the directions for Martha's Baked Chicken on page 159 to cook the chicken and make broth. You will still need about 4 more cups of chicken broth to cook the dumplings.

Dairy-Free:
The chicken and dumplings are dairy-free.

Artichoke Chicken Casserole

SERVES: 8
PREP: 15 MINUTES
BAKE: 25 TO 30 MINUTES

CHICKEN CASSEROLES ARE AS MUCH A PART OF THE SOUTH as magnolia blossoms. They have been the food to feed company for generations. And the combination of canned artichoke hearts, chicken, and curry powder is a favorite in our family. This recipe is a wonderful combination of several recipes, a layering of rice and chicken and artichokes onto which you pour a blend of sour cream and cream of mushroom soup, then add a crunchy cracker and butter topping.

2½ cups cooked rice

3 cups shredded cooked chicken, homemade (see Martha's Baked Chicken, page 159) or store-bought rotisserie chicken

1 can (14 ounces) artichoke hearts packed in water, drained

1½ cups gluten-free cream of mushroom soup (see Notes)

1 cup reduced-fat sour cream

1 teaspoon curry powder

4 tablespoons (½ stick) butter

32 gluten-free buttery crackers, about 4 ounces (see Notes)

1 teaspoon poppy seeds (optional)

1 Place a rack in the center of the oven and preheat the oven to 375°F.

2 Place the rice in the bottom of a 2-quart baking dish. Scatter the chicken on top of the rice. Cut the artichoke hearts into ½-inch pieces and scatter these on top of the chicken.

3 Place the mushroom soup, sour cream, and curry powder in a small bowl and stir to mix. Pour the soup mixture on top of the artichoke hearts and smooth the top with a rubber spatula.

4 Melt the butter in a small saucepan over low heat or in a microwave-safe glass bowl in the microwave on high power for 45 seconds. Place the crackers in a food processor and pulse to form crumbs. Or place the crackers in a resealable plastic bag and crush them by pressing down on the bag with a heavy rolling pin. Toss the cracker crumbs with the melted butter and stir in the poppy seeds, if using. Spoon the cracker topping evenly over the chicken casserole. Place the baking dish in the oven.

5 Bake the chicken casserole until it bubbles around the edges and the crackers turn golden brown, 25 to 30 minutes. Serve the chicken casserole warm.

Notes: Progresso makes a gluten-free cream of mushroom soup. Glutino makes gluten-free buttery round crackers, and they come in a 4.4-ounce box, which contains 32 crackers.

EXTRA! EXTRA!

No artichoke hearts? Substitute 1½ cups of chopped fresh green beans. The baking time will be the same.

Dairy-Free:
You need canned soup to make this casserole creamy as well as quick and easy to prepare, so a dairy-free version is not an option.

Clay's Chicken Enchiladas

SERVES: 6
PREP: 45 MINUTES
BAKE: 25 TO 30 MINUTES | REST: 20 MINUTES

FAMILY FRIEND CLAY SCHAFFNER OF NASHVILLE IS KNOWN for her enchiladas, which she makes with flour tortillas. I love her recipe and have made it with corn tortillas as well, just right for the gluten-free kitchen. For a perfect presentation, serve the enchiladas with shredded lettuce, sliced avocado, fresh cilantro, salsa or chopped tomatoes, pinto beans, and shredded cheese.

FOR THE ENCHILADAS

4 tablespoons olive oil or vegetable oil

1 small onion, thinly sliced, plus ½ cup finely chopped onion

1 green bell pepper, stemmed, seeded, and thinly sliced

2 cans (about 4 ounces each) chopped green chiles, drained

1½ cups low-sodium chicken broth

1 can (10 ounces) chopped tomatoes with green chiles (see Notes), with their juice

1 teaspoon ground cumin

1½ cups reduced-fat sour cream

12 corn tortillas, 8- to 9-inches in diameter (see Notes)

4 to 5 cups shredded cooked chicken, homemade (see Martha's Baked Chicken, page 159) or store-bought rotisserie chicken

1 cup (4 ounces) shredded cheddar cheese

1 cup (4 ounces) shredded Monterey Jack cheese

FOR SERVING

Shredded lettuce

Sliced avocado

Fresh cilantro

Salsa or chopped tomatoes

Pinto beans

Shredded cheese

Cinco de Mayo

Clay's Chicken Enchiladas
and toppings

Crisp Cornmeal Cookies, page 357

Chocolate and dulce de
leche ice cream

1 Place a rack in the center of the oven and preheat the oven to 350°F.

2 Place 2 tablespoons of the olive or vegetable oil in a large frying pan over medium heat. When the oil is hot add the sliced onion and bell pepper and cook, stirring, until soft, 3 to 4 minutes. Remove the onion and pepper mixture and set it aside.

3 Place the remaining 2 tablespoons of oil in the same pan over medium heat. Add the chopped onion and cook, stirring, until soft, 3 to 4 minutes. Add the drained chiles, chicken broth, canned tomatoes and chiles with their juice, and cumin. Cook, stirring, uncovered, until slightly thickened, about 15 minutes.

Remove the sauce from the heat and stir in the sour cream.

4 Arrange the tortillas flat on a large work surface. Divide the chicken, reserved onion and pepper mixture, and cheddar and Monterey Jack cheeses evenly among the tortillas. Roll up the tortillas and place them side by side in a 13 by 9-inch glass baking dish, then pour the sauce over them. Bake the enchiladas, uncovered, until the sauce bubbles and the tortillas are heated through, 25 to 30 minutes. Or you can assemble the enchiladas a day ahead of time and bake them the next day. If the enchiladas have been refrigerated they may take 5 to 10 minutes longer to heat through.

5 Remove the baking dish from the oven and let the enchiladas rest for about 20 minutes before serving. Serve the enchiladas with lettuce, avocado, cilantro, salsa or chopped tomatoes, pinto beans, and shredded cheese.

Notes: There are several brands of the canned tomato and chiles

An Unbelievably Gluten-Free Meal

WHERE EATEN: _____

_____

WHEN EATEN: _____

_____

WHO WAS THERE: _____

_____

_____

TIPS FOR MAKING AT HOME: _____

_____

_____

_____

NEW INSPIRATIONS: _____

_____

_____

mixture but my favorite is Ro-Tel. I use the mild Ro-Tel version or, occasionally, the one with lime and cilantro.

If your corn tortillas are smaller than 8 inches in diameter you can make up to 18 enchiladas. Just use a smaller amount of the filling for each.

EXTRA! EXTRA!

Make this a vegetarian enchilada recipe by omitting the chicken and adding a mixture of pinto beans, black beans, and sautéed squash, eggplant, or mushrooms—as long as it comes to 4 to 5 cups of veggies. Use vegetable broth instead of the chicken broth.

Dairy-Free:

For enchiladas that are dairy-free, use soy yogurt or unsweetened coconut milk instead of the sour cream. Omit all the cheese.

Country-Fried Steak with Gravy

SERVES: 4
PREP: 25 TO 30 MINUTES
COOK: 12 TO 15 MINUTES TOTAL

COUNTRY-FRIED OR CHICKEN-FRIED STEAK, DEPENDING on where you live, is legendary comfort food, and is one of the recipes people most frequently request for me to turn gluten-free. In the traditional recipe you would pound a steak to tender thinness, dredge it in seasoned flour before frying, and then serve it with a cream gravy thickened with flour. But this gluten-free version uses cornstarch for dredging the meat, and you never miss the seasoned flour. The gravy is thickened with sweet rice flour. Enjoy every bite!

FOR THE STEAKS

4 boneless round steaks (6 to 8 ounces each; see Notes)

1 cup vegetable oil

½ cup cornstarch

1 teaspoon paprika

½ teaspoon salt

½ teaspoon freshly ground black pepper

2 large eggs, beaten

½ cup buttermilk

½ cup club soda (optional; see Notes)

FOR THE MILK GRAVY

¼ cup browned sweet rice flour (see *Extra! Extra!*)

2 cups whole milk

Salt and freshly ground black pepper

Steamed rice or cooked grits, for serving

1 Cook the steaks: Place the steaks in resealable plastic bags or between two pieces of plastic wrap. Pound them with a mallet meat tenderizer

until ¼ inch thick and tender (or let the butcher tenderize the steaks for you). Set the steaks aside.

2 Heat the oil in a large cast-iron frying pan over medium-high heat until the oil registers 360° to 370°F on a candy thermometer.

3 Combine the cornstarch, paprika, salt, and black pepper in a shallow bowl. Make an egg wash by combining the eggs, buttermilk, and club soda (if using). Dredge the steaks on both sides in the cornstarch mixture. Then, dunk the dredged steaks in the egg wash. Repeat the process, dredging the steaks in the cornstarch mixture a second time and dunking them in the egg wash.

{ *Be sure to spoon plenty of milk gravy over your steak and grits or rice.* }

4 Line a platter with paper towels. When ready to cook, slide 2 of the battered steaks into the hot oil. Cook until browned on one side, about 3 minutes. Turn the steaks and cook until browned on the second side, 2 to 3 minutes longer. Transfer the steaks to the paper towel–lined platter. Repeat with the remaining 2 steaks. Set aside the pan with the cooking oil. Season the steaks with salt and black pepper and cover them with aluminum foil to keep them warm.

5 Make the milk gravy: Discard all but ¼ cup of the cooking oil and place the pan with the oil over medium heat. Stir in the browned sweet rice flour until well combined, about 1 minute. Pour in the milk and whisk to combine. Cook, stirring, until the gravy thickens, 2 to 3 minutes. Remove the gravy from the heat and season it with salt and black pepper to taste.

6 Serve the steaks with rice or grits and the milk gravy.

Notes: I've called for round steaks here, but you can use whatever boneless steaks you like, such as rib eye. You will need to use a tenderizing mallet for the round steaks, whereas the more tender steaks just need to be flattened to a ¼ inch thickness.

The club soda lightens the egg wash. If you don't have any on hand, just use ½ to ¾ cup of buttermilk.

EXTRA! EXTRA!

This recipe for browning sweet rice flour comes from Glenn Brault and Bev Lieven of the Milwaukee Celiac Sprue Crew. Browning sweet rice flour gives it a nutty flavor and aroma. It also helps color the gravy an attractive light brown. Heat 1 cup of sweet rice flour in a heavy frying pan over medium heat. Cook, stirring, until the flour turns a light golden brown and has a mild nutty aroma, 4 to 5 minutes. Remove the pan from the heat. Spread the flour out on a rimmed baking sheet to stop the cooking and cool it. When the flour is cool, store it in a sealed jar and use it as you would wheat flour in gravy recipes.

Dairy-Free:
Omit the buttermilk from the egg wash and use 1 cup of club soda or 1 cup of water. Serve the steaks without the milk gravy.

Braised Pot Roast with Vidalia Onions

SERVES: 6 TO 8
PREP: 15 MINUTES
BAKE: 3 HOURS

THIS IS A RECIPE I SHARED IN *THE DINNER DOCTOR*. THE exceptional flavor comes from the roast cooking in its own juices, not swimming in water and tomatoes and all the other things people add to pot roast. You do need to dredge the beef in a little cornstarch to help thicken the pan juices. Add carrots, potatoes, turnips—any root vegetable you have on hand. It's a delicious one-pot meal.

1 boneless beef chuck roast
 (about 4 pounds)

Salt and freshly ground black pepper

3 tablespoons cornstarch

2 tablespoons vegetable oil

3 large sweet onions, such as Vidalia,
 peeled and cut in half crosswise

4 cups chopped carrots

4 cups chopped peeled potatoes,
 parsnips, or turnips, or
 combination of them

1 Place a rack in the center of the oven and preheat the oven to 300°F.

2 Pat the roast dry with paper towels and season it with salt and pepper to taste. Place the cornstarch in a shallow bowl. Dredge the roast in the cornstarch and shake off any excess.

3 Heat the oil in a 5- to 6-quart heavy casserole or Dutch oven over medium-high heat. Add the roast and brown it on both sides,

New Year's Eve Dinner with Friends

Cold Pimento Soup, page 79

Braised Pot Roast with Vidalia Onions

Best Caesar Salad with
Gluten-Free Croutons, page 251

Flourless Chocolate Cakes, page 295

3 to 4 minutes per side. Remove the casserole from the heat and transfer the roast to a plate. Place the onion halves, cut-side down, in the bottom of the casserole. Place the roast on top of the onions and cover the casserole.

4 Bake the roast until it is tender and the juices have thickened, about 3 hours. One hour before the beef is done, add the carrots and potatoes or other root vegetables to the casserole. Spoon the juices over the vegetables to baste them, replace the casserole lid, and return the casserole to the oven.

5 To serve, carefully remove the roast from the casserole and slice it. Arrange the slices of beef on plates with the carrots, onions, and potatoes. Spoon the pan juices over the top.

EXTRA! EXTRA!

Chuck roast is the typical cut for pot roast. But if tri-tip roast is available, use this as it has less fat but all the flavor of a chuck roast. Turn leftovers into a beef stew by chopping the leftover roast and adding it, the pan juices, and the cooked vegetables to a saucepan along with a little beef broth. Heat until bubbling and serve.

Dairy-Free:

The pot roast is dairy-free.

The Best GF Meat Loaf

SERVES: 8
PREP: 20 MINUTES
BAKE: 45 TO 50 MINUTES | REST: 20 MINUTES

MY FAVORITE MEAT LOAF RECIPE IS ONE GIVEN TO ME by my friend Judy Wright. But as Judy's recipe contains dried onion soup mix, and onion soup mix contains gluten, I had to create a meat loaf that was as moist and delicious as Judy's but didn't call for the soup mix. And it needed to use gluten-free sandwich bread. Here is the recipe. I used Udi's sandwich bread and fresh onion in this recipe. Fortunately ketchup and Worcestershire sauce are gluten-free. This recipe makes a lot but leftover meat loaf sandwiches are one of life's delights!

5 slices gluten-free white sandwich bread

½ cup milk or water

⅓ cup finely chopped onion

2 large eggs, lightly beaten

1 cup ketchup (see Notes)

2 tablespoons Dijon mustard

1 tablespoon Worcestershire sauce (see Notes)

2 teaspoons light brown sugar

½ teaspoon salt

Freshly ground black pepper

1 tablespoon minced fresh flat-leaf parsley (optional)

2 pounds lean ground beef (see Notes)

1 Place a rack in the center of the oven and preheat the oven to 375°F.

2 Trim the crusts from the sandwich bread and cut the bread into ½-inch cubes. You need 2 cups of bread cubes. Place these in a large

bowl and stir in the milk. Add the onion, eggs, ½ cup of the ketchup, and the mustard, Worcestershire sauce, brown sugar, and salt. Season with pepper to taste. Stir to combine and let the mixture rest at room temperature until the bread absorbs the milk, about 10 minutes.

3 Add the parsley, if using. Crumble the ground beef over the top of the bread mixture. Using clean hands or a large spoon, fold the beef into the bread mixture until just combined. Transfer the meat loaf mixture to a 13 by 9-inch glass baking dish. Using a spoon or your hands, form the mixture into a large oval, mounded in the center. Spoon the remaining ½ cup of ketchup over the top of the meat loaf and place the baking dish in the oven.

4 Bake the meat loaf until it tests done when sliced in the center with a knife, 45 to 50 minutes. If you would like the top more browned, place the baking dish under the broiler for about 1 minute once the meat loaf is done. Let the meat loaf rest for 20 minutes before slicing.

Notes: Most ketchup is gluten-free, but make sure and read the label to guarantee this. Worcestershire sauce is gluten-free, but check by reading the label.

For a nice upgrade, use half ground beef and half ground veal.

EXTRA! EXTRA!

How to make a perfect meat loaf sandwich? Choose soft gluten-free white sandwich bread and spread it with a little mayonnaise and ketchup. Add a slice of cold meat loaf. Top it with sweet pickles and a leaf of crunchy lettuce followed by a second slice of bread, and enjoy.

Or make a meat loaf patty melt. Omit the mayonnaise, ketchup, pickles, and lettuce and add a slice or two of your favorite Swiss or mozzarella cheese. Brush the bread with olive oil and cook the sandwich in a frying pan or on a griddle until it is lightly browned on both sides and the cheese has melted. Serve the melt with ketchup, lettuce leaves, and pickles.

Dairy-Free:

Make the meat loaf dairy-free by using water instead of milk for soaking the bread cubes.

Mexican Lasagna

SERVES: 6 TO 8
PREP: 20 TO 25 MINUTES
BAKE: 30 TO 35 MINUTES | REST: 20 MINUTES

DON'T THINK LASAGNA IS JUST AN ITALIAN RECIPE. LAYER corn tortillas with seasoned ground beef, salsa, and cheese and you have the beginning of a Mexican-inspired lasagna. And thanks to corn tortillas, this recipe is gluten-free!

Vegetable oil spray, for misting the baking dish

1 pound lean ground beef

Olive oil (optional)

2 cups frozen, canned, or fresh corn kernels

1 can (15 ounces) tomato sauce

1 cup salsa

1 tablespoon chili powder

2 teaspoons ground cumin

1 container (16 ounces) low-fat, small-curd cottage cheese

2 large eggs, lightly beaten

¼ cup (1 ounce) grated Parmesan cheese

1 teaspoon dried oregano

1 clove garlic, crushed in a garlic press

12 corn tortillas (8 inches in diameter)

1 cup shredded cheddar cheese

1 Place a rack in the center of the oven and preheat the oven to 375°F. Mist a 13 by 9-inch glass baking dish with vegetable oil spray and set it aside.

2 Crumble the beef into a large nonstick frying pan and place it over medium heat. If the beef is so lean it sticks to the pan, add a little olive oil. Cook the beef, stirring, until it is cooked through and browned,

5 to 6 minutes. Drain off any fat from the pan. Add the corn, tomato sauce, salsa, chili powder, and cumin to the pan. Stir to combine. Let the beef mixture simmer over medium-low heat until the flavors come together, 2 to 3 minutes.

3 Meanwhile, place the cottage cheese, eggs, Parmesan cheese, oregano, and garlic in a medium-size bowl and stir to combine.

4 To assemble the lasagna, overlap 6 corn tortillas in the prepared baking dish. Spread half of the beef mixture evenly onto the tortillas. Spoon all of the cottage cheese mixture on top of the beef and spread it out evenly. Layer the remaining corn tortillas over the beef. Top the tortillas with the remaining beef mixture. Cover the dish with aluminum foil and place it in the oven.

5 Bake the lasagna until it heats through, 30 to 35 minutes. Remove the baking dish from the oven, remove the foil, sprinkle the cheddar cheese over the top, replace the foil, and let the lasagna rest for 20 minutes before serving. Any leftover lasagna can be reheated in an oven preheated to 350°F; it will take 20 to 25 minutes.

EXTRA! EXTRA!

To make the lasagna lower in fat, you can replace the beef with 8 ounces of ground turkey and 1 cup of pinto beans.

Dairy-Free:

For a dairy-free lasagna, substitute dairy-free cream cheese, such as Better Than Cream Cheese, for the cottage cheese and omit the Parmesan and cheddar cheeses.

Hartley's Mexican Rice Supper

SERVES: 6 TO 8
PREP: 20 MINUTES
COOK: 30 TO 35 MINUTES

HARTLEY STEINER IS A BUSY MOM, FOOD BLOGGER, AND gluten-free cook who began communicating with me before I wrote *The Cake Mix Doctor Bakes Gluten-Free*. Hartley tipped me off that many gluten-free cooks cannot eat dairy so I needed to have dairy substitutes in my recipes. When I told Hartley I was working on a gluten-free dinner book, she quickly e-mailed this recipe. Her sons eat this dish on top of corn tortilla chips like nachos, she says. Or they wrap the beans, cheese, and rice in a corn tortilla, burrito style. Gluten-free never had it so good!

1 tablespoon olive oil

1 pound lean ground beef

1 medium-size onion, finely chopped

1 clove garlic, minced

1 can (14½ ounces) diced tomatoes, with their juices

1 can (about 15 ounces) black beans, rinsed and drained

1½ cups water

¾ cup raw long-grain rice

½ cup tomato sauce

1 to 2 teaspoons chili powder

½ teaspoon ground cumin

Dash of Worcestershire sauce

Salt and freshly ground black pepper

Shredded Mexican-blend cheese, shredded lettuce, chopped tomatoes, salsa, and/or sour cream, for serving

1 Heat the olive oil in a large frying pan over medium heat. Crumble the ground beef into the pan and

cook, stirring to break up the larger clumps, until the beef has browned all over and is cooked through, 4 to 5 minutes. Add the onion and garlic, and cook, stirring, until the onion is soft, 3 to 4 minutes. Add the tomatoes with their juices, and the black beans, water, rice, tomato sauce, chili powder, cumin, and Worcestershire sauce. Season with salt and black pepper to taste. Stir to mix well and let the mixture come to a boil. Reduce the heat, cover the pan, and let simmer until the rice is cooked through and tender, 25 to 30 minutes.

2 Serve with your choice of shredded cheese, lettuce, tomatoes, salsa, and sour cream.

EXTRA! EXTRA!

For fun, create a Mexican rice supper, setting out bowls of tortilla chips, lime wedges, sliced avocado, and all the rest of the suggested toppings so people can serve themselves.

Dairy-Free:

Serve the dish without the cheese and sour cream and it will be dairy-free.

Super Bowl Party

Good Old Nuts and Bolts, page 37

Hartley's Mexican Rice Supper

Hearty Vegetarian Chili, page 87, or Texas Tortilla Soup, page 100

Gluten-Free Saucepan Brownies, page 349

French Baked Pork Chops with Mustard Sauce

SERVES: 4
PREP: 15 MINUTES
BAKE: 25 TO 30 MINUTES

I T IS COMMON TO USE FLOUR TO THICKEN THE SAUCE WHEN braising meat. And that's what I did when I prepared this recipe in France many years ago as a student at La Varenne. This gluten-free rendition is a little lighter, not calling for the flour, but the seasoned pork chops have the same wonderful mustard and cream sauce. As Dijon mustard is a natural thickener and emulsifier, it pulls the sauce together nicely.

2 tablespoons vegetable oil

1 small onion, thinly sliced

4 bone-in pork loin chops
    (1½ to 2 pounds total)

Salt and freshly ground black pepper

1 cup low-sodium chicken broth

½ cup dry white wine

1 bay leaf

¼ cup heavy (whipping) cream

2 tablespoons Dijon mustard

1 tablespoon chopped fresh parsley,
    for garnish

1 Place a rack in the center of the oven and preheat the oven to 350°F.

2 Place the oil in a large heavy Dutch oven over medium heat. Add the onion and cook, stirring, until lightly browned, 4 to 5 minutes. Remove the onion and set it aside.

3 Place the pot back over medium heat. Season the pork chops with salt and pepper to taste on both sides. Place 2 pork chops in the hot oil and

brown them on both sides, 3 to 4 minutes per side. Remove the pork chops and set them aside. Repeat with the remaining 2 pork chops, removing them from the pot. Add the chicken broth, white wine, and bay leaf to the pot, stir to combine, scraping up any browned bits from the bottom of the pot. Return the pork and onion to the pot, cover it, and place it in the oven.

4 Bake the pork chops until they are tender, 25 to 30 minutes. Remove the pot from the oven, transfer the pork chops to a plate, and cover them with aluminum foil to keep warm.

5 Place the pot over medium heat. Add the cream and cook, stirring, until it comes to a boil. Remove the pot from the heat and stir in the mustard. Remove and discard the bay leaf. Taste for seasoning, adding more salt and/or pepper as necessary.

6 To serve place the pork chops on plates and pour the mustard sauce over them. Sprinkle the chops with the chopped parsley.

EXTRA! EXTRA!

This sauce works well with any cut of pork or veal. You can grill pork tenderloin and serve it with the mustard sauce on the side. To make the sauce by itself, brown the onion in a pan, add the chicken broth, white wine, and bay leaf. Let the sauce simmer, uncovered, until the liquid is reduced by half. Pour in the cream and let the sauce reduce by half again. Whisk in the mustard and season the sauce with salt and pepper to taste before serving. The mustard and onion sauce can be prepared up to a day ahead and reheated over low heat.

Dairy-Free:
Use unsweetened coconut milk instead of the heavy cream in the sauce for the pork chops.

Golden-Brown Ham and Cheese Impossible Pie

SERVES: 6 TO 8
PREP: 15 MINUTES
BAKE: 25 TO 30 MINUTES

A FUN RETRO RECIPE, MY CHILDREN LOVE THIS DISH because it is something they can assemble and bake on their own. Layer ham and cheese in a pie pan, cover it with a batter, bake, and voilà!— you have this wonderful crustless quiche. For an easy gluten-free dinner, this can't be beat.

Vegetable oil spray, for misting the pie pan

1½ cups chopped ham

1 cup (4 ounces) shredded sharp cheddar cheese

½ cup gluten-free baking mix (see Note)

1 cup milk

2 large eggs

2 tablespoons chopped scallion, both white and green parts, or fresh parsley

1 Place a rack in the center of the oven and preheat the oven to 400°F. Mist a 9-inch glass pie pan with vegetable oil spray.

2 Sprinkle the ham and then the cheese over the bottom of the prepared pie pan.

3 Whisk together the baking mix, milk, and eggs in a small bowl, then pour this batter evenly over the ham and cheese. Scatter the scallion or parsley over the top.

4 Place the pie pan in the oven. Bake the pie until it is golden brown and firm to the touch, 25 to 30 minutes. Remove the pie from the oven and let it cool for about 5 minutes, then cut it into wedges and serve. Any leftover pie can be reheated covered in aluminum foil in an oven preheated to 350°F.

Note: I used gluten-free Bisquick in this recipe.

EXTRA! EXTRA!

Bake 8 mini impossible pies in muffin tins. Mist the muffin cups with vegetable oil spray. Layer in the ham and cheese, then pour the batter on top, dividing it evenly among the cups. Add a sprinkle of scallions and bake the mini pies until golden brown, 18 to 22 minutes.

Dairy-Free:
You can omit the cheese and use rice milk instead of the cow's milk for a dairy-free pie.

{ OTHER NOT-SO-IMPOSSIBLE COMBOS }

Broccoli and cheese impossible pie: In place of the ham, add 1 cup of chopped briefly cooked fresh broccoli or thawed and drained frozen broccoli pieces along with the cheese and a dash of nutmeg in step 2, if desired, then proceed with step 3.

Taco cheese impossible pie: Brown 6 ounces of ground beef or turkey with taco seasoning and substitute it for the ham in Step 2, sprinkling the cheese over it. Then scatter scallions over the top. Serve the pie with chopped fresh tomatoes and cilantro.

New Orleans
Red Beans and Rice

SERVES: 8

SOAK: 2 HOURS

PREP: 20 MINUTES | COOK: 2 HOURS TO 2 HOURS, 30 MINUTES

Beans and rice offer so many possibilities for the gluten-free diet. One of the best is the classic red beans and rice as cooked in New Orleans. This is a recipe I have enjoyed for more than twenty years as it was first published in *The Atlanta Journal-Constitution* when I was food editor. If you are in a hurry, my quick-cook method for soaking beans is faster than soaking overnight. Then, mash about two cups of cooked beans and add them back to the pot as a way of thickening and creating a sauce with the beans.

1 pound small dry red beans

Boiling water, for soaking the beans

2 tablespoons olive oil

2 medium-size onions, chopped

2 ribs celery, chopped

1 large green bell pepper, stemmed, seeded, and chopped

4 cloves garlic, minced

1 cup chopped smoked ham

2 bay leaves

About 2 quarts water

Salt and freshly ground black pepper

4 cups cooked rice, for serving

1 Place the red beans in a large stainless steel bowl and cover them with boiling water. Let the beans sit for at least 2 hours to soak up the water.

2 Drain the water off the beans and discard it. Set the beans aside.

{ *Another favorite comfort dish—accompany red beans and rice with a green salad and you're set.* }

3 Place the olive oil in a large soup pot over medium heat. Stir in the onions, celery, bell pepper, garlic, and ham. Cook, stirring, until the onion and pepper are soft, 5 to 6 minutes. Remove the pot from the heat.

4 Add the drained beans and bay leaves to the pot along with enough water to cover the beans. Place the pot over medium-high heat and bring the liquid to a boil. Cover the pot and reduce the heat so the beans simmer until tender, 2 to 2½ hours, adding more water as needed to keep the beans from sticking.

5 Remove 2 cups of cooked beans from the pot and mash them

with a potato masher or pulse them in a food processor. When the beans are mashed, return them to the pot and stir to combine. Season the beans with salt and pepper to taste. Serve the beans with the cooked rice. Any leftover beans can be refrigerated, covered, for up to 3 days.

EXTRA! EXTRA!

These beans are a blank canvas, so add whatever ham or bacon or sausage you have in the fridge. Use what peppers you have on hand, increase the amount of garlic, and by all means top the finished beans with chopped parsley or scallions.

Dairy-Free:
These beans are dairy-free.

Old-Fashioned Pigs in Blankets

SERVES: 8
PREP: 40 MINUTES
BAKE: 12 TO 14 MINUTES

W HAT COULD BE SIMPLER AND MORE DELICIOUS THAN warm, yeasty bread wrapped around a hot dog? These are a meal in one, a meal on the run, a fun after-school snack, or a party food. Make the pigs in blankets healthier by using turkey hot dogs, which are lower in fat. For a version to serve with predinner drinks, use small cocktail franks (see *Extra! Extra!*).

1⅝ cups gluten-free all-purpose flour blend (see Notes)

1 teaspoon instant dry yeast (half a ¼-ounce package)

½ teaspoon salt

½ teaspoon cider vinegar

7½ teaspoons vegetable oil, plus oil for assembling the pigs in blankets

1 large egg, at room temperature

1 tablespoon honey or granulated sugar

½ cup warm milk (see Notes)

8 hot dogs of your choice

Mustard and ketchup, for serving

1 Preheat the oven to 400°F. Set aside a baking sheet.

2 Place the flour, yeast, and salt in a large bowl and stir to combine well. Set the flour mixture aside.

3 Place the cider vinegar, oil, egg, and honey in a medium-size bowl and whisk to combine. Add the warm milk and whisk until smooth. Pour the liquid mixture into the flour mixture. Beat at medium-high speed with an electric mixer fitted with a dough

hook or process in a food processor for about 3 minutes. The dough will be very thick but smooth.

4 Dip your fingers into a little vegetable oil. Divide the dough into 8 equal pieces. Using your fingers, flatten the pieces of dough into 3- to 4-inch rounds. Wrap each dough round around a hot dog and place it seam side down on the baking sheet. Place the baking sheet in a warm place in the kitchen and let the dough rise for about 15 minutes. The dough on the hot dogs will not quite double in size.

5 Place the baking sheet in the oven and bake the pigs in blankets until the dough is lightly browned on top, 12 to 14 minutes. Remove the baking sheet from the oven and serve the pigs in blankets warm with mustard and ketchup for dipping.

Notes: I used half of a 16-ounce box of Gluten Free Pantry all-purpose flour for testing this recipe.

If your milk is cold, warm it in a microwave oven on high for 30 seconds.

EXTRA! EXTRA!

For parties, make bite-size pigs in blankets. Use the same dough but break off 32 pieces. Cut each hot dog into 4 pieces, or use 32 cocktail franks. Wrap each small dough round around a quarter of a hot dog. Then let the dough rise for about 15 minutes. The smaller pigs in blankets will be ready to serve after baking for 8 to 10 minutes.

Dairy-Free:

Use water or rice milk instead of the cow's milk when making the dough for the pigs in blankets.

Cornmeal-Crusted Fried Fish

SERVES: 4
PREP: 10 TO 15 MINUTES
COOK: 12 TO 16 MINUTES TOTAL

L EAVE THE BATTERS FOR DEEP-FRYING. USE A LIGHT AND simple cornmeal dredge when frying the fish of your choice in a shallow pan. This is gluten-free cooking at its best, letting cornmeal be the crunchy exterior for fresh fish. Serve the fish with tartar sauce and fresh lemon wedges, or take a cue from Italian chicken piccata and serve it with lemon, chopped flat-leaf parsley, and capers.

FOR THE TARTAR SAUCE (OPTIONAL)

1 cup mayonnaise (preferably Hellmann's)

2 tablespoons finely chopped shallot (from 1 medium-size shallot)

¼ cup sweet pickle relish

2 tablespoons chopped drained capers

2 tablespoons chopped fresh flat-leaf parsley

Hot pepper sauce

FOR THE FISH

1½ to 2 pounds fish fillets, such as cod, flounder, snapper, halibut, or catfish

⅔ cup yellow cornmeal

1 tablespoon cornstarch

1 teaspoon seasoned salt, such as Lawry's

Freshly ground black pepper

4 cups vegetable oil, for frying

Lemon wedges, for serving

Chopped fresh flat-leaf parsley and capers (optional), for garnish

1 Make the tartar sauce, if using: Place the mayonnaise, shallot, pickle relish, chopped capers, and 2 tablespoons of parsley in a bowl and stir to mix. Season with hot pepper

{ WHY NOT PECAN- }
{ CRUST YOUR FISH? }

When making gluten-free bread crumbs by pulsing toasted gluten-free sandwich bread in a food processor, add a handful of chopped pecans to the processor and you have pecan crumbs that are delicious pressed onto fish or chicken fillets for frying.

sauce to taste. Place the tartar sauce in the refrigerator to chill. The tartar sauce will keep covered in the refrigerator for up to 4 days.

2 Prepare the fish fillets: Rinse the fish fillets under cold running water and pat them dry with paper towels. Cut the fillets into thirds and set them aside.

3 Place the cornmeal, cornstarch, and seasoned salt in a shallow bowl. Season with black pepper to taste and set the bowl aside.

4 Preheat the oven to 300°F. Line a baking sheet with paper towels.

An Unbelievably Gluten-Free Meal

WHERE EATEN:

WHEN EATEN:

WHO WAS THERE:

TIPS FOR MAKING AT HOME:

NEW INSPIRATIONS:

5 When ready to cook, place the oil in a large frying pan that is at least 3 inches deep. Heat over medium-high heat until the oil registers 360°F on a candy thermometer.

6 Dredge the pieces of fish on both sides in the cornmeal mixture. Slide the pieces of fish into the hot oil, adding 5 or 6 pieces to the pan at a time, being careful not to crowd it. Cook the fish until golden brown, 3 to 4 minutes. Using a slotted spoon, transfer the fish to the prepared baking sheet to drain. Place the baking sheet in the oven to keep the fish warm. Repeat with the remaining pieces of fish.

7 Serve the fish with lemon wedges, garnished with the parsley and capers, if desired. Or, serve the fish with the tartar sauce.

EXTRA! EXTRA!

Make mine fish tacos: Fry your favorite fish as instructed in this recipe, then pile the fish along with thin onion slices, chopped cilantro, sliced avocado, lime juice, and salsa or slaw in small warmed corn tortillas (wrap the tortillas in aluminum foil and warm them in a low oven). For an easy slaw, combine shredded coleslaw mix with 2 tablespoons of pickle relish and 2 tablespoons of your favorite salsa. Add enough mayonnaise to pull the slaw together.

Dairy-Free:

No changes are necessary—the fried fish recipe is dairy-free.

Fried Shrimp and Tempura Veggies

SERVES: 4
PREP: 15 TO 20 MINUTES
COOK: 12 TO 16 MINUTES

POTATO STARCH MAKES THE BEST BATTER FOR TEMPURA-style fried shrimp and vegetables. It is light and lets the flavor of the food come through: But you need to add eggs to the batter to give it body. Season the batter as you like, adding seasoned salt or just salt and pepper. The best vegetables for frying are bell pepper strips and whole mushrooms, thin strips of butternut or acorn squash, and green beans, as well as zucchini, thin slices of potato, and broccoli or cauliflower florets. Serve the shrimp and vegetables with soy sauce and the Sweet Chile Sauce, if desired.

2 pounds large shrimp in their shells

¾ cup potato starch

3 large eggs

Salt and freshly ground black pepper

6 cups (48 ounces) vegetable oil, for frying

½ cup sweet rice flour

4 cups assorted fresh vegetables, such as small whole mushrooms; red or green bell pepper, cut into ¼-inch strips; fresh green beans; thinly sliced butternut or acorn squash

Soy sauce, for serving

Sweet Chile Sauce (optional; recipe follows), for serving

1 Peel and devein the shrimp, leaving the tail ends on.

2 Place the potato starch and eggs in a medium-size bowl and beat until smooth. Season with salt and black pepper to taste and set aside.

3 Preheat the oven to 300°F. Line a baking sheet with paper towels.

4 Heat the oil in a large deep frying pan or wok over medium-high heat until the oil registers 360°F.

5 Place the rice flour in a shallow bowl and dredge the shrimp in it. Dip the shrimp into the batter then, working in batches of 6, place them in the hot oil and cook until golden brown, 3 to 4 minutes. Using a slotted spoon, transfer each batch to the prepared baking sheet and place it in the oven to keep the shrimp warm.

6 After you have cooked the shrimp, cook the vegetables. Dredge the vegetables in the rice flour and dip them into the batter. Working in batches so as not to overcrowd the pan, slide the vegetables into the hot oil and cook until golden brown, 2 to 3 minutes. Transfer each batch of vegetables to the baking sheet and return it to the oven to keep warm.

7 Serve the warm shrimp and veggies with soy sauce and the Sweet Chile Sauce, if desired.

EXTRA! EXTRA!

Instead of shrimp, fry battered fish. One of my favorites is the "fish kebab" at Whole Foods. You get an assortment, all delicious.

Dairy-Free:
This recipe is dairy-free.

Sweet Chile Sauce

Sweet and spicy simplicity best describes this recipe for the perfect tempura dipping sauce. Use the whole hot red peppers—seeds and veins—but not the stem ends.

MAKES: ABOUT ½ CUP

¾ cup water

¾ cup sugar

4 fresh hot red chile peppers, chopped with their seeds

Place the water in a small saucepan and bring to a boil over medium-high heat. Add the sugar and stir until it dissolves. Add the chile peppers. Reduce the heat to medium and let the mixture boil until slightly reduced, 7 to 8 minutes. Let the sauce cool slightly, then puree it in a blender or food processor. The chile sauce can be refrigerated, covered, for up to 2 weeks.

An Unbelievably Gluten-Free Meal

WHERE EATEN:

WHEN EATEN:

WHO WAS THERE:

TIPS FOR MAKING AT HOME:

NEW INSPIRATIONS:

Baked Eggplant and Zucchini Parmesan

SERVES: 4 TO 6
PREP: 25 MINUTES
BAKE: 30 TO 35 MINUTES

THERE REALLY ARE TIMES—ESPECIALLY IN THE HEAT OF August when fresh glossy purple eggplants pour into the local produce stand—that I swear I could be a vegetarian. Who needs meat when you have eggplant? And who needs eggplant any other way than fried (okay, maybe grilled, too). I fry eggplant by dipping it in egg that has been beaten with a teaspoon or two of water and seasoned with salt and pepper. That's it. No fussy batters or breadings, just egg. And I learned this method years ago when I came across my favorite recipe ever for Eggplant Parmesan. The egg batter helps bind the eggplant, sauce, and cheese together as one. I have tweaked that recipe recently to make it even more summery and vegetarian. My latest rendition includes zucchini—enjoy!

1 jar (26 ounces) tomato-based pasta sauce

2 tablespoons red wine

2 cloves garlic, minced

1 teaspoon dried basil, or ¼ cup torn fresh basil leaves

½ cup vegetable or olive oil, or more as needed

2 or 3 large eggs

Salt and freshly ground black pepper

1 large eggplant (1 to 1½ pounds), peeled and sliced crosswise ¼ inch thick

1 large zucchini (6 to 8 ounces), trimmed and sliced on the diagonal ¼ inch thick

3 cups blend of shredded mozzarella and Parmesan cheeses

An Unbelievably Gluten-Free Meal

WHERE EATEN:

_____

WHEN EATEN:

_____

WHO WAS THERE:

_____

_____

TIPS FOR MAKING AT HOME:

_____

_____

_____

NEW INSPIRATIONS:

_____

_____

_____

1 Place a rack in the center of the oven and preheat the oven to 375°F.

2 Place the pasta sauce, red wine, garlic, and basil in a medium-size saucepan over medium heat. Let simmer, stirring occasionally, while you cook the eggplant and zucchini.

3 Heat the oil in a heavy frying pan over medium-high heat. Beat 2 eggs in a wide, shallow bowl and season them with salt and pepper to taste. Arrange a double thickness of paper towels on the counter near the frying pan. Place 2 to 3 slices of eggplant in the beaten egg and turn them to coat. Using a fork, slide the eggplant slices into the hot oil and cook until golden brown and puffy but not cooked through, about 1 minute per side. Using a slotted spoon, transfer the eggplant slices to the paper towels to drain. Repeat with the remaining eggplant and zucchini slices, adding more oil as needed and beating another egg if needed for dipping.

August Garden
Supper

Chilled Cucumber and Tomato Soup,
page 77

Baked Eggplant and Zucchini
Parmesan or Spaghetti with Fresh
Tomatoes, Basil, and Mozzarella,
page 221

Blackberry and Raspberry
Cobbler, page 340

EXTRA! EXTRA!

Add smashed chicken (page 149) and you
have an elaborate chicken and eggplant
Parmesan. Fry only half as much eggplant
and zucchini as called for in this recipe. Place
2 cooked chicken breasts on the bottom of
the baking dish. Top these with half of the
sauce, then half of the cheese. Arrange the
fried eggplant or fried eggplant and zucchini
over the cheese, then top it with the rest of
the sauce and the rest of the cheese. Bake
the dish a little longer, 40 to 45 minutes.

4 Place half of the eggplant and
zucchini slices in the bottom
of a 2-quart baking dish. Pour half
of the pasta sauce mixture over the
veggies, spreading it out evenly.
Scatter 1½ cups of the cheese blend
over the sauce. Repeat with the
remaining eggplant and zucchini,
sauce, and cheese blend. Cover the
baking dish with aluminum foil and
bake until the casserole is bubbling
and the cheese has melted, 30 to
35 minutes. Remove the aluminum
foil and let the eggplant and zucchini
rest for about 5 minutes before
serving.

Dairy-Free:
It is not possible to make this recipe
dairy-free. But you can fry the
eggplant and zucchini in the egg
batter and serve it topped with warm
pasta sauce.

Cheese Grits Soufflé

SERVES: 6
PREP: 18 TO 22 MINUTES
BAKE: 32 TO 37 MINUTES

SOME SOUTHERNERS LOVE GRITS ANY WAY THEY ARE served. I like mine cooked with garlic, cayenne pepper, and cheddar. Here is a recipe everyone will love, and it's just right for a gluten-free diet, too. This is grits casserole meets cheese soufflé. Serve it as a vegetarian main dish or a side for steaks, chicken kebabs, pork chops, or grilled salmon.

1 teaspoon butter, plus 4 tablespoons
(½ stick) butter at room temperature

1 cup whole milk

1 cup water

1 teaspoon salt

½ cup grits, stone-ground, if possible

1 clove garlic, minced

Dash of cayenne pepper

1 cup (4 ounces) shredded sharp cheddar
cheese

Freshly ground black pepper

3 egg yolks, lightly beaten

9 egg whites

¼ teaspoon cream of tartar

1 Place a rack in the center of the oven and preheat the oven to 350°F. Rub a 2-quart baking dish with the 1 teaspoon of butter and set it aside.

2 Place the milk, water, and salt in a medium-size saucepan over medium-high heat. When the mixture comes almost to a boil, stir in the grits. Reduce the heat to low and let the grits simmer until they thicken, 4 to 5 minutes. Remove the pan from the heat. Stir in the 4 tablespoons of butter, the garlic, cayenne pepper, and cheese and season with black pepper to

taste. Stir until the butter and cheese have melted. Stir in the egg yolks and set aside.

3 Place the egg whites in a large clean stainless steel or glass bowl and beat with an electric mixer on high power until the egg whites are foamy, about 1 minute. Add the cream of tartar. Continue beating until the egg whites form stiff peaks, 1 to 2 minutes longer.

4 Spoon about one third of the beaten egg whites into the grits mixture, folding them in gently. Dump the remaining egg whites on top of the grits and fold them in until well combined. Pour the batter into the prepared baking dish and place the dish on a baking sheet in the oven.

5 Bake the soufflé until it is golden brown and puffed up, 32 to 37 minutes. Serve at once.

Dairy-Free:

To make dairy-free, use unsweetened coconut milk instead of whole milk and margarine instead of the butter. Omit the cheddar cheese.

EXTRA! EXTRA!

This soufflé recipe is just a blueprint for possible combinations of cheeses and seasonings. Try more hot pepper, adding some crushed red pepper flakes, or try a pinch of nutmeg. Instead of cheddar, try the nutty Spanish cheese Manchego or Comté, the wonderful full-flavored Swiss-type cheese from France's Jura region.

Thirteen Unbelievably Gluten-Free Ideas for Pasta and Pizza Night

1. *Fettuccine Alfredo with Mushrooms*
2. *Homestyle Spaghetti Carbonara*
3. *Spaghetti with Pecorino and Pepper*
4. *Spaghetti with Fresh Tomatoes, Basil, and Mozzarella*
5. *Unbelievable Spaghetti and Meatballs*
6. *Pasta with Fresh Pesto Sauce*
7. *The Best Skillet Lasagna*
8. *Meaty Macaroni*
9. *Stir-Fried Broccoli and Veggies over Rice Noodles*
10. *Classic Gluten-Free Pizza*
11. *Gluten-Free Thin-Crust Pepperoni Pizza*
12. *Grilled Chicken and Pesto Pizza*
13. *Greek Salad Pizza*

Pasta and Pizza Night

'll admit, I was doubtful at first about creating gluten-free pasta and pizza recipes. But so many of you told me you wanted to make a great pasta dish at home. And that you craved homemade pizza. So, I spent some time in the kitchen getting to know the ingredients that go into these recipes.

Let's Begin with Pasta

There are rows of pastas that cater to the gluten-free shopper on supermarket shelves. I tried as many as I could get my hands on here in Nashville. What an eye-opener! I found that pasta didn't have to be made from wheat to taste good. And in fact, the varieties available took the same-old, same-old feeling off of making a pot of spaghetti. As a general rule I learned to follow the cooking directions on the box as these cooking times were always right. Don't overcook gluten-free pasta. And to prevent noodles from clumping together after draining, rinse them with cold water and then proceed with the recipe.

Pasta made from brown rice flour has a nice bite to it when cooked. Corn pasta is a little more difficult to find, but I love how tender it is and have paired it with delicate sauces. Some pastas are made from a mixture of flours such as corn and quinoa, and these take well to heavier sauces. It is amazing the varities of "flours" pasta can be made from—so many gluten-free options.

{ PASTA SERVINGS }

If a pasta sauce is heavy with ingredients, for example ground meat or meatballs, olives, bell pepper, onion, and other vegetables, then 2 ounces of pasta per person is usually enough. Figure on 4 ounces of pasta per person if the sauce is clingy with few ingredients. Of course, it never hurts to err on the side of too much pasta. So, if you're not sure of the appetites of certain family members or friends, be sure to have extra on hand.

For weeknight meals, try the Homestyle Spaghetti Carbonara or Spaghetti with Fresh Tomatoes, Basil, and Mozzarella. For weekend company, bake The Best Skillet Lasagna, and Unbelievable Spaghetti and Meatballs.

And Now for Gluten-Free Pizza

With gluten-free pizza you can either buy a frozen crust and add the toppings, or you can make your own crust. To take the guesswork out of making the crust, I started with a pizza crust mix that I adapted to my own ingredients and then added my choice of toppings. The homemade crust was chewy, crusty, and flavorful—worth the effort for pizza night.

I share two pizza crust recipes in this chapter, one for a chewy classic style of pizza crust and another that is thinner and more crackerlike in texture. Suit yourself, and feel free to add your own sauces and toppings, for that is what is fun about making pizza at home!

Grilled Chicken and Pesto Pizza, or serve the Greek Salad Pizza as a fun appetizer. Anyway you fork into them or slice them, they are good!

Fettuccine Alfredo with Mushrooms

SERVES: 3 OR 4
PREP: 15 MINUTES
COOK: 12 TO 14 MINUTES

ONE OF MY KIDS' FAVORITE WEEKNIGHT MEALS IS MY easy fettuccine that I make using whatever ingredients are on hand in the fridge—mushrooms, onions, Parmesan cheese, often a smidgen of ham. Unlike the classic recipe for Alfredo sauce, this one begins with a sauté of the veggies, to which you add a little cornstarch for thickening and then add cream and fresh thyme. Serve the sauce atop or mixed into your favorite gluten-free fettuccine. I liked the Tinkyáda brown rice fettuccine with this recipe.

½ teaspoon salt, for cooking the pasta

8 ounces brown rice fettuccine or linguine

2 tablespoons olive oil

8 ounces sliced cremini or small portobello mushrooms

½ cup finely chopped white onion or scallions

1 tablespoon cornstarch

1 cup heavy (whipping) cream

1 tablespoon fresh thyme leaves

1 cup (4 ounces) grated Parmesan cheese

1 Bring a large pot of water to a boil over high heat and add the salt. When the water is boiling add the pasta and cook, stirring occasionally, until the pasta is just done, 12 to 14 minutes.

2 Meanwhile, place the olive oil in a large heavy frying pan over medium heat. Add the mushrooms and onion and cook, stirring, until the onion is soft and the mushrooms begin to give up their liquid, 4 to 5 minutes.

An Unbelievably Gluten-Free Meal

....

WHERE EATEN:

_____

_____

WHEN EATEN:

_____

_____

WHO WAS THERE:

_____

_____

TIPS FOR MAKING AT HOME:

_____

_____

_____

_____

NEW INSPIRATIONS:

_____

_____

_____

Sprinkle the cornstarch over all and stir to coat well. Pour in the cream and cook, stirring, until thickened, 2 minutes. If the sauce needs thinning, spoon in some of the water from the cooking pasta. Stir in the thyme and Parmesan cheese. Remove the pan from the heat and cover it to keep the sauce warm.

3 When the pasta is done, firm and not mushy, drain it well. Rinse it briefly with cold water to stop the cooking process and drain it again. Return the pasta to the pot and pour the warm mushroom sauce over it. Toss the pasta with the sauce, then serve.

EXTRA! EXTRA!

Add 1 cup of diced ham, smoked turkey, or smoked salmon to the sauce along with the Parmesan cheese and thyme. If you add smoked salmon garnish the pasta with capers and chopped chives.

Dairy-Free:

It is not possible to make this pasta recipe dairy-free.

Homestyle Spaghetti Carbonara

SERVES: 4
PREP: 20 MINUTES
COOK: 8 TO 10 MINUTES

H ARDLY A CLASSIC RECIPE BY ANY MEANS, THIS IS MY homestyle version of spaghetti carbonara, made with the Parmesan and bacon I have on hand, a few eggs, and gluten-free spaghetti. It's all in the prep—having the bowl of eggs and cheese ready, cooking the pasta, frying up crisp pieces of bacon or Italian pancetta. Then with just the right temperature the hot pasta meets the eggs and the most luxurious and yet rustic sauce forms. Serve it pronto!

3 large eggs

1½ cups (6 ounces) grated Parmesan cheese

6 ounces thick-sliced bacon or pancetta, cut crosswise into ½-inch strips

½ teaspoon salt

1 pound gluten-free spaghetti, such as corn spaghetti or brown rice spaghetti

Freshly ground black pepper

Chopped fresh flat-leaf parsley (optional), for garnish

1 Place the eggs and Parmesan cheese in a medium-size bowl and whisk to mix. Set the egg mixture aside.

2 Place the bacon in a large heavy frying pan over medium heat and cook until the bacon is browned and crisp, 7 to 8 minutes. Transfer the bacon to paper towels to drain.

3 Bring a large pot of water to a boil over high heat and add the salt. When the water is boiling add

{ *It's hard to believe that this lavish tasting dish is created from so few simple ingredients.* }

the spaghetti and cook, stirring occasionally, until the spaghetti is just done, 8 to 10 minutes. Do not overcook.

4 Drain the pasta, setting aside a scant 1 cup of the cooking water. Rinse the pasta briefly with cold water to stop the cooking process and drain it again. When the reserved 1 cup of pasta cooking water has cooled to warm to the touch, whisk ½ cup into the egg and Parmesan mixture. Set aside the remaining ½ cup of pasta cooking water.

5 Place the cooked bacon in the pasta cooking pot over medium heat. Stir in the pasta and a little of the reserved cooking water and heat until the pasta is hot, 1 to 2 minutes. Remove the pot from the heat and immediately pour in the egg mixture, tossing to combine it well with the pasta so that it cooks the eggs. Season the pasta with pepper to taste and serve at once with chopped parsley, if desired.

EXTRA! EXTRA!

Serve this spaghetti with a green salad and more Parmesan cheese for sprinkling on top of the salad and pasta. You can top the spaghetti with chopped ripe tomatoes in the summertime or with kalamata olives in the dead of winter. Use whatever gluten-free pasta you can find—made with corn or from brown rice.

Dairy-Free:
As the Parmesan cheese is critical to the taste of this dish, there is no dairy-free option.

Spaghetti with Pecorino and Pepper

SERVES: 4
PREP: 10 MINUTES
COOK: 8 TO 10 MINUTES

ITALY HAS TO BE THE WORLD'S FOOD TREASURE, FOR EACH and every region has its own recipes, all delicious and different. The foods of Rome are some of my favorites, and this easy pasta recipe is one of them. Called *cacio e pepe* in Rome, it is similar to carbonara but is just spaghetti tossed with good pecorino romano cheese, cream, olive oil, and a little freshly ground black pepper—that's it.

6 ounces pecorino romano cheese

½ teaspoon salt

1 pound gluten-free spaghetti, such as corn spaghetti or brown rice spaghetti

2 tablespoons heavy (whipping) cream

2 teaspoons olive oil

Freshly ground black pepper

1 Finely grate 4 ounces of the pecorino romano cheese into a medium-size bowl (you will have 1 cup of finely grated cheese). Set the finely grated cheese aside. Coarsely grate the remaining cheese and set this aside for topping the pasta.

2 Bring a large pot of water to a boil over high heat and add the salt. When the water is boiling, add the spaghetti and cook, stirring occasionally, until the spaghetti is just done, 8 to 10 minutes.

3 Drain the pasta, setting aside 1½ cups of the cooking water. Rinse the pasta briefly with cold water

to stop the cooking process, drain it again, and place it in a large bowl.

4 Slowly whisk 1 cup of the reserved pasta cooking water into the finely grated pecorino romano cheese until smooth. Whisk in the cream and olive oil and season the cheese mixture with plenty of black pepper to taste. Gradually pour the cheese sauce over the spaghetti, tossing it to coat. Add more of the reserved cooking water to thin the sauce, if needed. Serve the spaghetti with the coarsely grated pecorino romano cheese.

EXTRA! EXTRA!

In summertime this is the perfect main dish to serve alongside sliced ripe tomatoes or sautéed fresh zucchini. In cooler weather, serve grilled sausages or steaks and wilted spinach on the side.

Dairy-Free:
Cheese is the essential ingredient of this recipe, so you cannot make it dairy-free.

An Unbelievably Gluten-Free Meal

WHERE EATEN:

WHEN EATEN:

WHO WAS THERE:

TIPS FOR MAKING AT HOME:

NEW INSPIRATIONS:

Spaghetti with Fresh Tomatoes, Basil, and Mozzarella

SERVES: 4 TO 6
PREP: 20 TO 25 MINUTES
COOK: 8 TO 10 MINUTES

Years ago my friend Kren passed along an easy weeknight pasta recipe. Put ripe summertime tomatoes and basil in a large bowl and toss them with olive oil, salt, and pepper. Add cubes of fresh mozzarella cheese and hot cooked spaghetti. When you toss the spaghetti, the cheese begins to melt and, along with the tomatoes and basil, becomes the sauce. I have varied this recipe through the years, adding pressed garlic and pitted kalamata olives and often toasted pine nuts. But the core ingredients always stay the same. And now, I've changed the recipe once more. Gluten-free corn spaghetti is a delicious substitution for wheat spaghetti. You'll never miss it!

4 cups chopped ripe tomatoes (see Note)

1 to 2 cloves garlic, crushed in a garlic press

2 tablespoons olive oil, plus oil, for tossing with the spaghetti

Salt and freshly ground black pepper

1 pound corn spaghetti

2 cups (8 ounces) cubed fresh mozzarella cheese

1 cup packed fresh basil leaves, cut into slivers

1 Place the tomatoes, garlic, and olive oil in a large mixing bowl and toss to combine. Season with salt and pepper to taste. Set the tomato mixture aside.

2 Bring a large pot of water to a boil over high heat and add ½ teaspoon salt. When the water is boiling add the spaghetti and cook, stirring occasionally, until the spaghetti is just done, 8 to 10 minutes. Do not overcook.

3 Meanwhile, toss the mozzarella with the tomato mixture. Drain the spaghetti well and toss it with a little olive oil to prevent it from sticking. While it is still hot add the spaghetti to the bowl with the tomatoes and mozzarella and toss to combine well. Before serving, garnish the spaghetti with the basil and drizzle more olive oil on top.

Note: Use the best tomatoes you can find. In the wintertime use cherry or grape tomatoes, rinsed and cut in half. In the summertime use ripe red and yellow tomatoes. Peel these before chopping.

EXTRA! EXTRA!

To give the spaghetti a decidedly *arrabiata* flavor, sauté slices of garlic in olive oil until they darken but do not burn. Add a crumbled dried hot pepper. When tossing the spaghetti with the tomatoes and mozzarella, stir in the garlic and pepper oil.

Dairy-Free:
To make the spaghetti dairy-free omit the mozzarella cheese.

Unbelievable Spaghetti and Meatballs

SERVES: 8
PREP: 35 MINUTES
COOK: 38 TO 45 MINUTES

HOMEMADE MEATBALLS MIGHT SEEM TO BE OFF THE gluten-free recipe list, what with the need for bread crumbs to bind them, but you can get away with another binder—toasted gluten-free bread. Toasting improves the texture of gluten-free bread, making it taste better in sandwiches, and in this recipe it makes the bread crumbs more absorbent so they soak in all the milk, which keeps the meatballs moist. The spaghetti and meatballs feed a crowd—about eight—so cut the recipe in half if you need to serve four.

4 slices gluten-free bread

½ cup milk

1 pound lean ground beef

1 pound lean ground pork

2 ounces finely chopped prosciutto (optional; see Notes)

2 large eggs, beaten

1 cup (4 ounces) grated Parmesan cheese

⅓ cup chopped fresh parsley

½ teaspoon dried oregano

½ teaspoon dried basil

3 cloves garlic, finely chopped

Salt and freshly ground black pepper

Olive oil, for frying the meatballs

2 jars (24 to 26 ounces each) gluten-free pasta sauce

1 pound gluten-free spaghetti (see Notes)

1 Toast the bread, then let it cool. Break the bread into fine crumbs with your fingers. Place the crumbs in a small bowl and stir in the milk. Let the bread crumbs soak up the milk, 8 to 10 minutes.

2 Meanwhile, place the ground beef and pork, prosciutto, if using, eggs, ½ cup of the Parmesan cheese, and the parsley, oregano, basil, garlic, and 1 teaspoon of salt in a large bowl. Season with black pepper to taste. Using clean hands, gently combine the meat mixture to distribute the herbs and incorporate the eggs. Add the soaked bread crumbs and, using your hands, gently work the soaked crumbs into the meatball mixture. Don't overwork. Divide the meat mixture into approximately ¼ cup–size meatballs; you will have 16 to 20 meatballs. You can make smaller meatballs, if desired. The meatballs can be frozen for later use; see *Extra! Extra!*

3 Line a platter with paper towels. Place 2 to 3 tablespoons of olive oil in a large, deep frying pan over medium heat. When the oil is hot, place half of the meatballs in the pan and brown them on all sides, using a large spoon to turn them as they brown, 7 to 8 minutes. Transfer the browned meatballs to the paper towel–lined platter to drain. Cook

the second batch of meatballs the same way, adding more olive oil to the pan first, if needed.

4 Discard the cooking oil from the pan and wipe out the pan. Pour the gluten-free pasta sauce into the pan and let it come to a simmer over low heat, 4 to 5 minutes. Add the meatballs to the pan, spoon the sauce over them, and let them simmer until they are cooked through, 20 to 25 minutes.

5 Meanwhile, bring a large pot of water to a boil over high heat and add ½ teaspoon salt. When the water is boiling add the spaghetti and cook, stirring occasionally, until the spaghetti is just done 8 to 10 minutes. Drain the spaghetti and rinse it briefly with cold water to stop the cooking process. Drain the spaghetti again and return it to the pot. Toss the spaghetti with 1 tablespoon of olive oil.

6 Serve the spaghetti on the side of the sauce and meatballs, passing the remaining ½ cup of Parmesan cheese for spooning on top.

Notes: Prosciutto is thinly sliced Italian ham. You can omit it, if desired, although it does lend a more authentic Italian flavor to the meatballs. And as far as choosing the right gluten-free spaghetti, use the best you can find; one made of brown rice, or a mix of rice and corn, is fine.

EXTRA! EXTRA!

You can use any combination of herbs you like, adding fresh herbs in the summertime—a tablespoon each of fresh basil and oregano.

Make the meatballs ahead of time through step 2 and freeze them in plastic tubs or resealable bags. Then when you are in need of a last-minute dinner, pour as many frozen meatballs as needed into a pan of simmering pasta sauce, let them cook through, and as soon as the spaghetti cooks, dinner will be ready.

Dairy-Free:

Use rice milk in place of the milk when making the meatballs and omit the Parmesan cheese to make the spaghetti and meatballs dairy-free.

An Unbelievably Gluten-Free Meal

WHERE EATEN:

WHEN EATEN:

WHO WAS THERE:

TIPS FOR MAKING AT HOME:

NEW INSPIRATIONS:

Pasta with Fresh Pesto Sauce

SERVES: 4
PREP: 15 MINUTES
COOK: 8 TO 10 MINUTES

LINGUINE IS TRADITIONALLY THE PASTA OF CHOICE FOR pesto, but I have always bent that rule, serving pesto atop penne and spaghetti, and grilled chicken and fish, and of course, sliced ripe tomatoes. So use the pasta that is in your pantry for this recipe. You will need eight ounces to serve four modestly, and up to one pound if there are teenagers and hungry boys! Double the recipe for pesto if you are using a pound of pasta.

FOR THE FRESH PESTO SAUCE

2 cloves garlic, peeled

2 tablespoons pine nuts

⅓ cup grated Parmesan cheese

1 cup fresh basil leaves, rinsed and patted dry

½ cup fresh parsley leaves, rinsed and patted dry (see Notes)

½ cup good olive oil, or more as needed

Salt and freshly ground black pepper

FOR THE PASTA

½ teaspoon salt

8 ounces gluten-free pasta (see Notes)

⅓ cup grated Parmesan cheese, or more as needed, for serving

1 Make the fresh pesto sauce:
Place the garlic cloves in a food processor and process until minced, 5 or 6 pulses. Add the pine nuts and Parmesan cheese and pulse until finely chopped, 7 or 8 pulses. Add the basil and parsley and pulse until the herbs

are finely chopped, 7 or 8 pulses. With the motor running, pour in the olive oil until the pesto reaches the desired consistency. (Some people like a runny pesto and others like a thick pesto—suit yourself—but ½ cup of oil is a good start.) Season the pesto with salt and pepper to taste and set it aside.

2 Cook the pasta: Bring a large pot of water to a boil over high heat and add ½ teaspoon of salt. When the water is boiling, add the pasta and cook, stirring occasionally, until the pasta is just done, 8 to 10 minutes. Do not overcook. Drain the pasta, setting aside a little of the cooking water, and return the pasta to the pot. Stir in the pesto sauce, adding a little cooking water to thin the pesto, if desired; this makes it easier to blend pasta and sauce. Serve the pasta at once with Parmesan cheese.

Notes: I use parsley in my pesto sauce to keep it bright green in color.

I recommend brown rice spaghetti or the corn and quinoa elbow macaroni for serving with the fresh pesto sauce.

EXTRA! EXTRA!

I like a bright green pesto sauce because it looks fresh. So I use a mix of basil and parsley. I like pestos made from other herbs, too, such as dill or cilantro. Substitute an equal amount of one of these herbs for the basil, but keep the parsley. Serve these pestos over grilled chicken or fish, atop pizza, or just spoon a couple tablespoons into good mayonnaise for topping a turkey sandwich on gluten-free bread.

Dairy-Free:

Omit the Parmesan cheese and the pesto and pasta will be dairy-free. Be sure to taste for salt, adding more if necessary.

The Best Skillet Lasagna

SERVES: 8

PREP: 30 MINUTES

BAKE: 45 TO 50 MINUTES | REST: 15 MINUTES

I HAVE BEEN INTRIGUED BY SKILLET LASAGNAS EVER SINCE I saw a recipe for one in a Williams-Sonoma catalog. Such a great way to make the dish, I thought, although I never seemed to give it a try. So when testing recipes for this book, and thinking pasta and lasagna, I thought back to the skillet method and concocted my own delicious version. It is based around a very simple red sauce with turkey, onion, carrot, and garlic, which you layer in a large oven-proof skillet along with uncooked brown rice lasagna noodles, ricotta, and other cheeses. In about an hour you have the most yummy lasagna imaginable.

2 tablespoons olive oil

1 cup finely chopped onion

2 cloves garlic, minced

1 carrot, peeled and finely chopped

1 pound ground turkey

4 cups (32 ounces) good gluten-free marinara (pasta) sauce

2 tablespoons red wine (optional)

1 container (15 ounces) part-skim ricotta cheese

1 large egg

½ cup (2 ounces) grated Parmesan cheese

9 brown rice lasagna noodles (see Note)

3 cups (12 ounces) shredded mozzarella cheese

1 Place the olive oil in a large oven-proof skillet that is 12 inches in diameter, at least 3 inches deep, and has a lid that fits securely. Heat the oil over medium heat and add the onion, garlic, and carrot and cook, stirring,

Welcome Home Holiday Dinner

The Best Skillet Lasagna or Martha's Chicken and Dumplings, page 168

Green beans or braised kale

Quick-Cook Rice Pudding, page 288

until the onion softens and begins to brown, 4 to 5 minutes. Crumble the turkey into the skillet and cook, stirring, until the turkey is cooked through, 5 to 6 minutes. Add the marinara sauce and red wine, if using. Reduce the heat to low and let simmer, stirring occasionally, until the flavors come together, 5 minutes.

2 Place a rack in the center of the oven and preheat the oven to 400°F.

3 Leave about a third of the sauce in the skillet, transfer the remaining two thirds to a bowl, and set it aside. Place the ricotta, egg, and Parmesan cheese in a medium-size bowl and stir to combine. Break 3 of the lasagna noodles into 3-inch pieces and distribute them over the

sauce in the skillet. Spoon a third of the ricotta mixture on top of the lasagna noodles and spread it out thinly to nearly cover them. Sprinkle 1 cup of the mozzarella cheese evenly over the ricotta mixture. Repeat the layers of sauce, noodles, and cheese 2 times, ending with the mozzarella.

4 Place the lid on the skillet and carefully place the skillet in the oven. Bake the lasagna until the noodles have cooked through, the

An Unbelievably Gluten-Free Meal

WHERE EATEN:
_____

_____

WHEN EATEN:
_____

_____

WHO WAS THERE:
_____

_____

TIPS FOR MAKING AT HOME:
_____

_____

_____

_____

NEW INSPIRATIONS:
_____

_____

_____

_____

sauce bubbles, and the cheese has melted, 45 to 50 minutes. Remove the skillet from the oven and let the lasagna rest, covered, for 15 minutes before slicing and serving.

Note: I used the DeBoles gluten-free rice lasagna noodles, made from rice flour and rice bran extract. I did not preboil the noodles, but I did break them into 3-inch pieces to distribute them more evenly around the pan.

EXTRA! EXTRA!

I love lasagna made with ground turkey because it is lighter than beef. Use this recipe as a basic plan and add sliced mushrooms to the sauce or a layer of lightly steamed fresh spinach in the middle. Or change up the cheeses, adding a little feta to the mozzarella—so many possibilities.

Dairy-Free:
It is not possible to make this lasagna dairy-free.

Meaty Macaroni

SERVES: 6 TO 8
PREP: 25 MINUTES
BAKE: 35 TO 40 MINUTES | REST: 10 MINUTES

HERE IS A TAKE-OFF ON THE MEATY ZITI I INCLUDED IN *The Dinner Doctor,* minus the frozen creamed spinach. You make your own gluten-free creamed spinach by first sautéing fresh spinach in a large pot and then stirring in cream cheese and Parmesan cheese at the end. For the pasta, use whatever gluten-free pasta shape you can find—brown rice penne or elbow macaroni made with corn and quinoa are both good. The pasta only needs to cook briefly on top of the stove; it finishes cooking with the meat sauce in the oven. Pair this with a green salad and you have an easy and complete meal.

1 tablespoon olive oil

1 bag (10 ounces) fresh spinach

2 ounces cream cheese (¼ package), cubed

½ cup (2 ounces) grated Parmesan cheese

1 pound lean ground beef or turkey

1 can (28 ounces) crushed tomatoes,
 or 1 jar (26 ounces) gluten-free
 pasta sauce

1 to 2 cloves garlic, crushed in a garlic press

1 teaspoon dried oregano

1 teaspoon dried basil

½ teaspoon salt

8 ounces gluten-free macaroni
 or penne pasta

2 cups (8 ounces) shredded
 mozzarella cheese

1 Place the olive oil in a large heavy saucepan or frying pan over medium heat. Add the spinach and cook, stirring, until the spinach wilts and is tender, 2 to 3 minutes. Remove

the pan from the heat and stir in the cream cheese and Parmesan cheese until the cream cheese melts. Place the spinach mixture in a medium-size microwave-safe bowl and set it aside.

2 Place a rack in the center of the oven and preheat the oven to 375°F.

3 Wipe out the pan used for cooking the spinach. Crumble the ground beef or turkey into the pan. Cook, stirring and breaking up the lumps with a wooden spoon, over medium-high heat until the meat browns all over and is cooked through, 4 to 5 minutes. Stir in the tomatoes or pasta sauce, garlic, oregano, and basil. Set the meat sauce aside.

4 Bring a large pot filled with water to a boil over high heat and add the salt. When the water is boiling, add the pasta and cook, stirring occasionally, just 2 minutes. Drain the pasta and set it aside.

5 To assemble the casserole, spoon about 1 cup of the meat sauce in the bottom of a 3-quart glass or ceramic casserole dish. Arrange the drained pasta on top of the sauce. Pour the remaining meat sauce over the pasta. Heat the spinach mixture in a microwave oven on high power for 15 to 20 seconds to make it easier to spread. Spread the spinach mixture on top of the meat sauce. Cover the casserole with aluminum foil and place it in the oven.

6 Bake the casserole until it bubbles, 35 to 40 minutes. Remove the casserole from the oven, carefully remove the foil, and set it aside. Scatter the mozzarella cheese over the top, and recover the casserole with the foil. Let the casserole rest until the mozzarella melts, about 10 minutes, returning it to the warm oven if needed so cheese melts completely before serving.

This casserole can be made up to one day in advance. After you layer the ingredients in the casserole dish and cover it with aluminum foil, refrigerate it until baking time. The casserole may take a little longer to bake if it goes straight from the refrigerator to the oven.

Dairy-Free:

Use Tofutti's Better Than Cream Cheese instead of the regular cream cheese and omit the Parmesan and mozzarella cheeses. For a topping, crumble enough gluten-free crackers to measure ½ cup. Toss the cracker crumbs with 2 tablespoons of melted margarine and scatter them over the spinach mixture before baking the casserole.

An Unbelievably Gluten-Free Meal

WHERE EATEN:

_____

_____

WHEN EATEN:

_____

_____

WHO WAS THERE:

_____

_____

_____

TIPS FOR MAKING AT HOME:

_____

_____

_____

_____

NEW INSPIRATIONS:

_____

_____

_____

Stir-Fried Broccoli and Veggies over Rice Noodles

SERVES: 4
PREP: 20 MINUTES
COOK: 4 TO 5 MINUTES

A STIR-FRY IS A GREAT WAY TO GET YOUR VEGGIES IN ONE sitting. May I also mention it's a great way to clean out the fridge? Serve this stir-fry over rice vermicelli. These thin translucent noodles are made of ground white rice and water. They cook very quickly, so just pour boiling water over them and let them soak.

12 ounces rice vermicelli (see Notes)

2 teaspoons plus a dash of Asian (dark) sesame oil (see Notes)

2 tablespoons vegetable oil

4 cloves garlic, coarsely chopped

1 tablespoon grated fresh ginger

2 cups broccoli florets

1 red bell pepper, stemmed, seeded, and sliced

1 medium-size carrot, peeled and sliced into matchsticks

1 cup yellow squash, cubed

¼ cup low-sodium vegetable or chicken broth

1 to 2 tablespoons gluten-free soy sauce

1 tablespoon gluten-free hoisin sauce (see Notes) or teriyaki sauce

1 Place the vermicelli in a large bowl. Bring a tea kettle filled with water to a boil and, when the water has boiled, pour it over the noodles to cover them. Let the noodles soak until soft, 10 to 15 minutes. Drain the noodles and toss them with the 2 teaspoons of sesame oil. Set the vermicelli aside.

2 Place the vegetable oil in a large wok or heavy frying pan over medium-high heat. When the oil is hot, add the garlic and ginger. Cook, stirring, until the garlic takes on color, 30 to 45 seconds. Using a slotted spoon, remove the garlic and ginger from the wok or frying pan and set them aside. Add the broccoli, red pepper, carrot, and squash to the wok or frying pan over medium-high heat and cook, stirring, until the vegetables soften, 1 to 2 minutes. Add the broth, soy sauce, hoisin sauce, and a dash of sesame oil. Return the garlic and ginger to the wok or pan and cook, stirring, until the broccoli is tender, 1 minute longer. Don't let the sauce evaporate.

3 Serve the vegetables at once over the vermicelli.

Notes: Rice vermicelli is found in Asian markets and in stores that carry gluten-free ingredients. You can find it in sizes up to the width of fettuccine if you like a larger noodle.

Dark, or toasted, sesame oil is found with Asian ingredients in the supermarket. It is added at the end of cooking, as a condiment.

Hoisin sauce is a soybean-based sauce that contains sugar, vinegar, coloring, and often star anise and other flavorings.

EXTRA! EXTRA!

To add protein to this dish, add 4 to 6 ounces of sliced boneless chicken breast tenders to the pan before you add the broccoli and other veggies. Cook the chicken slices, stirring, until they cook through, 2 to 3 minutes, then add the veggies. You could also add peeled and deveined shrimp instead of chicken.

Dairy-Free:
This recipe is dairy-free.

Classic Gluten-Free Pizza

MAKES: TWO 12- TO 14-INCH ROUND OR TWO 13 BY 9-INCH PAN PIZZAS

SERVES: 8 | PREP: 1 HOUR

BAKE: 8 TO 10 MINUTES

PIZZA NIGHT IS APPEALING BECAUSE IT FOSTERS A REAL togetherness and also allows you to exercise your individualism, creating a pizza with the ingredients you like. If you have a place to buy fresh gluten-free pizza dough in your town, by all means make use of it. But if you don't, here is a simple, spongy, yeasty pizza crust to make at home on pizza night. This very basic recipe begins with a gluten-free French bread mix that jumpstarts a pretty decent crust, but be forewarned—the dough is light, airy, and wet. It does not have the stretch of conventional pizza dough (with gluten), so it may stick to your fingers and you will not be able to toss it in the air like they do on TV. Just lightly oil your fingertips and press the dough onto the pan.

FOR THE CLASSIC GLUTEN-FREE PIZZA CRUST

1 package (22 ounces) gluten-free French bread and pizza mix with yeast (see Note)

5 tablespoons plus 2 teaspoons olive oil, and oil for shaping the crusts

1 teaspoon cider vinegar

1 tablespoon granulated sugar

½ teaspoon salt

2 large eggs, at room temperature

2 egg whites, at room temperature

1¾ cups hot tap water

FOR THE TOPPING

1⅓ cups store-bought pizza sauce

1 cup fresh basil leaves (optional)

4 cups (16 ounces) shredded mozzarella cheese

1 Make the Classic Gluten-Free Pizza Crust: Place the flour from the pizza mix in a large bowl. Add the package of dry yeast from the mix and stir to combine. Set the bowl aside.

2 Place the 5 tablespoons of olive oil, and the cider vinegar, sugar, salt, eggs, and egg whites in a medium-size bowl. Whisk to combine. Slowly whisk in the hot tap water. Pour the egg mixture into the bowl with the flour and yeast mixture. Using an electric mixer fitted with a dough hook, beat on low speed until the ingredients are combined, about 15 seconds. Scrape down the side of the bowl with a rubber spatula. Beat on medium-high speed until the dough is smooth and well combined, 1½ to 2 minutes. (You can also use a food processor instead of an electric mixer to combine the dry ingredients with the wet.) Cover the bowl tightly with plastic wrap and place it in a warm place for the dough to double in size, about 40 minutes.

3 Place a rack in the bottom third of the oven and preheat the oven to 450°F. Lightly brush each of two 12- to 14-inch round pizza pans or two 13 by 9-inch baking sheets with 1 teaspoon of the olive oil.

4 Make the pizzas: After the dough has doubled in size, punch it down and divide it into 2 equal pieces. Place each piece of dough on a prepared pan. Oil your fingers with olive oil and press the dough to the edges of the pans. When you have pressed the dough to the edges and it is smooth, divide the pizza sauce evenly between the 2 crusts, leaving a 1-inch border of exposed crust. Place the basil leaves, if using, on top of the sauce. Scatter 2 cups of the mozzarella cheese on top of each pizza.

5 Place the pans, one at a time if necessary, in the oven and bake the pizzas until the cheese bubbles and the crust edges turn light golden brown, 8 to 10 minutes. Slice the pizzas to serve.

Note: Gluten Free Pantry French Bread and Pizza Mix is easy to find at Whole Foods and most large supermarkets.

EXTRA! EXTRA!

This recipe makes 2 large pizzas, enough to feed 8 generously. If you have a smaller crowd, make 1 pizza. When making the dough, go ahead and combine the yeast packet included in the pizza mix box with the dry ingredients. Measure out half of this mixture then whisk together the remaining ingredients for the crust, reducing each of them by half: 2½ tablespoons olive oil, ½ teaspoon cider vinegar, 1½ teaspoons sugar, ¼ teaspoon salt, 1 egg, and 1 egg white. Whisk in ¾ cup plus ⅛ cup hot tap water. Continue with the recipe starting from step 2, halving the amount of topping ingredients. Place the remaining half of the dry ingredients in a plastic bag to store in your pantry until ready to use.

Dairy-Free:

Omit the mozzarella cheese and scatter 1 cup of roasted vegetables on top of the pizza sauce on each pizza before baking it.

An Unbelievably Gluten-Free Meal

WHERE EATEN:

_____

WHEN EATEN:

_____

WHO WAS THERE:

_____

_____

TIPS FOR MAKING AT HOME:

_____

_____

_____

NEW INSPIRATIONS:

_____

_____

_____

Gluten-Free Thin Crust Pepperoni Pizza

MAKES: TWO 12-INCH ROUND OR TWO 17 BY 12-INCH PAN PIZZAS
SERVES: 8 | PREP: 1 HOUR, 5 MINUTES TO 1 HOUR, 10 MINUTES
BAKE: 14 TO 16 MINUTES

HERE IS ANOTHER EASY PIZZA CRUST, THIS ONE THINNER and crispier than the previous crust. Begin with a pizza crust mix, then add water, olive oil, and egg. I layered on the toppings before baking the crust. But if you like a crackerlike texture to your crust, prebake the crust for seven to eight minutes, then remove it from the oven, top it with the goodies, and return the pizza to the oven to bake until the cheese melts and the crust has browned, eight to ten minutes.

FOR THE THIN-CRUST PIZZA DOUGH

3½ cups gluten-free pizza crust mix with yeast, such as King Arthur brand

10 ounces hot tap water

2 large eggs

¼ cup olive oil, plus 2 tablespoons oil for shaping and brushing the crusts

FOR THE TOPPINGS

2 cups store-bought pizza sauce

½ packed cup pepperoni slices

4 cups (16 ounces) shredded mozzarella cheese

1 Make the thin-crust pizza dough: Place the flour from the pizza crust mix in a large bowl. Add the package of dry yeast from the mix and stir to combine. Set the bowl aside.

2 Place the water, eggs, and the ¼ cup of olive oil in a small bowl and whisk to combine. Pour the egg mixture into the bowl with the yeast and flour mixture. Using an electric mixer fitted with a dough hook, beat on low speed until just combined,

3 After the dough has risen by a third, punch it down lightly and divide it into 2 equal pieces. Oil your fingers with olive oil and press the dough into two 12-inch round pizza pans or two 17 by 12-inch jelly-roll pans. The dough will be wet. Let the dough rest, uncovered, in a warm place for 30 minutes.

4 Place an oven rack in its lowest position and preheat the oven to 400°F.

5 Make the pizzas: Brush each of the pans of pizza dough with 1 tablespoon of olive oil. Spread 1 cup of the pizza sauce on each pizza, leaving a 1-inch border of exposed crust and top it with half of the pepperoni. Top each pizza with 2 cups of mozzarella cheese.

6 Place the pans, one at a time if necessary, in the oven and bake the pizzas until the cheese bubbles and begins to brown, 14 to 16 minutes. Slice the pizzas to serve.

about 1 to 1½ minutes. Scrape down the side of the bowl with a rubber spatula. Increase the mixer speed to medium and beat for about 30 seconds. Increase the mixer speed to medium-high and beat until well combined, about 2 minutes. Scrape the dough to the center of the bowl. Cover the bowl tightly with plastic wrap and place it in a warm place for the dough to rise by a third, about 30 minutes.

An Unbelievably Gluten-Free Meal

WHERE EATEN:

_____

_____

WHEN EATEN:

_____

_____

WHO WAS THERE:

_____

_____

_____

TIPS FOR MAKING AT HOME:

_____

_____

_____

_____

NEW INSPIRATIONS:

_____

_____

_____

_____

EXTRA! EXTRA!

This recipe makes enough dough for 2 pizzas. If you would like to make enough dough for just 1 pizza, whisk half of the package of dry yeast from the pizza crust mix with 1¾ cups of the flour from the mix. Whisk together 5 ounces of hot tap water, 1 egg, and 2 tablespoons of olive oil and continue with the recipe as described in Step 2. Set the remaining pizza mix flour and dry yeast aside in a plastic bag for another use.

Flatbread Pizza

After the pizza dough has risen the second time, place an oven rack in its lowest position and preheat the oven to 400°F. Brush each pan of dough with 1 tablespoon of olive oil. Sprinkle each with 1 tablespoon of your favorite chopped fresh herbs—basil, oregano, chives, parsley, rosemary. Season the flatbreads with salt and pepper to taste. Lightly sprinkle each with grated Parmesan cheese, using about 1 tablespoon per flatbread. Drizzle 1 tablespoon of olive oil over each and bake until lightly browned, 10 to 12 minutes.

Dairy-Free:

Omit the mozzarella cheese and these pizzas are dairy-free.

Grilled Chicken and Pesto Pizza

MAKES: ONE 12- TO 14-INCH ROUND OR ONE 13 BY 9-INCH PAN PIZZA
SERVES: 3 TO 4 | PREP: 1 HOUR
BAKE: 10 TO 12 MINUTES

IF YOU HAVE LEFTOVER GRILLED CHICKEN IN THE HOUSE, some fresh basil, and the makings for a homemade pizza crust, you can create this fabulous grilled chicken pizza for an end of the work/school week Friday night dinner. It uses half of the recipe for the classic gluten-free crust and half a recipe of the fresh pesto sauce. Of course if you had a big chicken dinner on Sunday night, you might want to use the leftovers for pizza Monday. Pizza makes a great start to the week, too.

Half recipe Classic Gluten-Free Pizza Crust
  (see page 237)

1 teaspoon olive oil, plus oil for shaping
  the crusts

2 generous cups (8 ounces total) sliced
  grilled chicken

¼ cup thin strips roasted red peppers

Half recipe (about ¾ cup) Fresh Pesto
  Sauce (page 226)

2 cups (8 ounces) shredded mozzarella
  cheese

1 Prepare half a recipe of the Classic Gluten-Free Pizza Crust.

2 Place a rack in the bottom third of the oven and preheat the oven to 450°F. Lightly brush one 12- to 14-inch round pizza pan or one 13 by 9-inch baking sheet with the 1 teaspoon of olive oil.

3 After the dough has doubled in size, punch it down. Oil your fingers with olive oil and place the

An Unbelievably Gluten-Free Meal

WHERE EATEN:

WHEN EATEN:

WHO WAS THERE:

TIPS FOR MAKING AT HOME:

NEW INSPIRATIONS:

dough on the prepared pan. Press the dough to the edges of the pan. Arrange the chicken slices on top of the dough. Arrange the strips of roasted peppers alongside the chicken slices. Dollop the pesto over the chicken and roasted peppers. Scatter the mozzarella cheese on top.

4 Place the pan in the oven and bake the pizza until the cheese bubbles and begins to brown, 10 to 12 minutes. Slice the pizza to serve.

EXTRA! EXTRA!

If you are in a hurry, you can make this pizza using store-bought pesto sauce, not home-made. And, you can use a frozen gluten-free crust instead of making your own dough.

Dairy-Free:
Omit the mozzarella cheese and let the topping be dollops of the pesto sauce for a dairy-free version.

Greek Salad Pizza

MAKES: ONE 12-INCH ROUND OR ONE 13 BY 9-INCH PIZZA | SERVES: 4
PREP: 40 MINUTES | BAKE: 8 TO 10 MINUTES
COOL: 20 MINUTES

BEGIN WITH A CRISP CRACKERLIKE PIZZA CRUST, THEN top it with hummus, feta, tomatoes, cucumber, olives, red onion, and salad greens and you have a fun Greek Salad Pizza. Serve it for dinner during warm weather or as an appetizer anytime of the year. It's a pizza, but it's also a salad, a refreshing change from pizza sauce and pepperoni.

FOR THE CRUST

Half recipe Thin-Crust Pizza Dough (page 240)

2 teaspoons olive oil, plus oil for shaping the crust

1 teaspoon fresh rosemary or oregano (optional)

Salt and freshly ground black pepper

FOR THE TOPPINGS

1 cup hummus, homemade (page 42) or store-bought

1 cup (4 ounces) crumbled feta cheese

½ cup chopped cucumber

½ cup halved grape tomatoes

¼ cup pitted kalamata olives

2 tablespoons thinly sliced red onion

2 cups salad greens, such as arugula

2 teaspoons red wine vinegar

1 tablespoon olive oil

1 Make the thin-crust pizza dough: Prepare half a recipe and after the dough has risen for the first time, punch it down lightly. Oil your fingers with olive oil and press the dough into a 12-inch round pizza pan or a 13 by 9-inch jelly-roll pan. The dough will be wet. Let the dough rest,

As you can tell, this is a real knife and fork pizza.

uncovered, in a warm place for 30 minutes.

2 Place an oven rack in its lowest position and preheat the oven to 400°F.

3 Brush the pan of pizza dough with the 2 teaspoons of olive oil, sprinkle it with the rosemary, if using, and season it with salt and pepper to taste. Place the pan in the oven and bake the crust until it is lightly browned, 8 to 10 minutes. Remove the pan from the oven and let the crust cool for about 20 minutes.

4 Make the pizza: When the crust has cooled, spread the hummus evenly over it, leaving a 1-inch border of exposed crust. Scatter the feta over the hummus, then scatter the cucumber, tomatoes, olives, and red onion on top. Arrange the greens on top of the pizza and drizzle the vinegar and 1 tablespoon of olive oil over the salad greens. Slice the pizza and serve it to eat with knives and forks.

EXTRA! EXTRA!

Make a Mexican version of this pizza by substituting refried beans for the hummus. Add shredded mild cheddar or your favorite Mexican cheese blend instead of the feta. Omit the cucumber and olives, and add cubed avocado, chopped jalapeño peppers, and cilantro leaves. Instead of red wine vinegar, use fresh lime juice.

Dairy-Free:
Omit the feta cheese for a dairy-free pizza.

Fourteen Unbelievably Gluten-Free Salads and Sides

1. *Best Caesar Salad with Gluten-Free Croutons*
2. *Susan's Penne and Tomato Salad*
3. *Tomato Panzanella Salad*
4. *Tuna and White Bean Salad*
5. *Macho Nacho Taco Salad*
6. *Sesame Noodle Salad*
7. *Southern Squash Soufflé*
8. *Gluten-Free Baked Apricots*
9. *Delicious Dirty Rice*
10. *Easy Fried Rice*
11. *Curried Rice Pilaf*
12. *Gluten-Free Mac and Cheese*
13. *Cheryl's Corn Bread Dressing*
14. *Gluten-Free Broccoli Brag*

Salads and Sides

Unexpected is how I describe the recipes in this chapter. They are a mix of salads and sides and are suitable for so many meals throughout the year. They are delicious and unexpectedly at home on the gluten-free table.

Oh sure, rice dishes like the Delicious Dirty Rice and Easy Fried Rice may seem like no-brainers because rice contains no gluten. But what about a macaroni and cheese with not only gluten-free pasta but a sauce free of flour? And stuffing or dressing to go alongside the roasted holiday turkey? Not a smidgen of gluten in this recipe where cornbread is crumbled into the stuffing along with sautéed onion and celery, and sausage if you like.

Same goes for the casseroles like baked apricots where you use gluten-free crackers as the topper. But no crackers are needed in my version of the Southern Squash Casserole because you cook down the squash, letting the water evaporate so you don't need a thickener.

Ingredients that came in handy in this chapter are gluten-free sandwich breads, gluten-free penne and spaghetti, corn tortilla chips, gluten-free crackers, and white cornmeal. I especially would like you to try Cheryl's Corn Bread Dressing, Curried Rice Pilaf, Southern Squash Soufflé, Macho Nacho Taco Salad, and the Best Caesar Salad with Gluten-Free Croutons.

Best Caesar Salad with Gluten-Free Croutons

SERVES: 8

PREP: 35 MINUTES

YOU NEVER REALLY THINK ABOUT SALAD BEING GLUTEN-free until croutons are added. That changes it all. But a Caesar salad without croutons? Unthinkable! So here is an incredibly delicious Caesar salad where the croutons are not only fun to eat but they are gluten-free. Tote this to parties and share it with others—toss in the homemade croutons once you get to where you're going.

FOR THE SALAD DRESSING

1 large clove garlic, peeled

2 anchovy fillets (optional), chopped

1 tablespoon fresh lemon juice

2 teaspoons Dijon mustard

1 teaspoon Worcestershire sauce (see Note)

¼ cup (1 ounce) grated Parmesan cheese

⅓ cup olive oil

Salt and freshly ground black pepper

FOR THE SALAD

2 heads romaine lettuce, rinsed and dried

⅓ cup shredded Parmesan cheese, for sprinkling

Gluten-Free Croutons (recipe follows)

Freshly ground black pepper

1 Make the salad dressing: With the motor running, drop the garlic through the feed tube of a food processor and process until minced. Turn off the machine, scrape down the side of the bowl, and add the anchovy fillets, if using, and the lemon juice, mustard, Worcestershire sauce, and Parmesan cheese. Pulse until the mixture is smooth. With the motor running, slowly pour in

the olive oil and process until the dressing has thickened. Taste the dressing for seasoning, adding salt and/or pepper as necessary. Set the dressing aside.

2 Prepare the salad: Break the romaine into bite-size pieces and place it in a salad bowl. The romaine pieces can be refrigerated for up to 6 hours.

3 When ready to serve, add the dressing, Parmesan cheese, and the croutons to the romaine and toss to mix. Season with pepper to taste.

Note: Most Worcestershire sauce is gluten-free, but it still pays to read the labels.

EXTRA! EXTRA!

Add a little ground cumin and cayenne pepper to the salad dressing and you have the beginning of a Southwestern Caesar salad. Peel and cube an avocado, chop a small tomato, and thaw ½ cup of frozen roasted corn. Place these on top of the salad. If desired, omit the croutons, and make corn bread croutons instead. Let the Southern Skillet Corn Bread (see page 134) cool and

slice it into 1-inch-thick slices. Cut these slices into 1-inch cubes. Mist the corn bread cubes with vegetable oil and bake at 400°F until crisp on the edges, about 10 minutes. Remove the toasted corn bread cubes from the oven and scatter them over the salad.

Dairy-Free:

Omit the Parmesan cheese and you have dairy-free Caesar salad.

Gluten-Free Croutons

Once only the finishing touch on a bowl of pea soup, croutons' popularity has spread to salads, and not just the Caesar variety. Add these to the Tomato Panzanella Salad on page 258, and to any mixed greens that need some crunch.

MAKES: ABOUT 2 CUPS

6 to 8 slices firm gluten-free sandwich bread or French bread (see Note)

⅓ cup olive oil, or more as needed

Salt

1 Trim the crusts from the bread and stack the slices on top of each other. Cut the bread into 1-inch cubes. You need 2 cups of bread cubes.

2 Place ⅓ cup of olive oil in a large frying pan over medium-high heat. When the oil is hot, working in batches, add the bread cubes and cook, stirring, until they are browned all over, 3 to 4 minutes. Using a slotted spoon, transfer the croutons to paper towels to drain. Repeat with the remaining bread cubes, adding more olive oil as needed for frying. Sprinkle the croutons with salt to taste. The croutons will keep in an airtight container at room temperature for up to 4 days.

Note: Udi's makes good gluten-free sandwich bread and it is found in many supermarkets in the frozen food case. Or you might want to check with a local gluten-free bakery and see if they make a gluten-free French bread or multigrain bread.

{ *Leftover homemade croutons make a good crunchy snack, too.* }

Susan's Penne and Tomato Salad

SERVES: 6 TO 8
PREP: 10 MINUTES
COOK: 5 MINUTES

MY SISTER SUSAN IS A GREAT COOK, AND HERE IS ONE of her favorite potluck salad recipes. We've used this through the years, varying it with different shapes of pasta and types of vinaigrette. I couldn't wait to try it with gluten-free penne to see if the pasta would hold up to the add-ins and salad dressing. It does beautifully, and this is a great salad to take to an office party or neighborhood gathering.

Pinch of salt

1 pound gluten-free brown rice penne pasta

3 packed cups fresh spinach leaves

2 cups grape tomatoes

½ to 1 cup store-bought gluten-free balsamic vinaigrette or Easy Balsamic Vinaigrette (recipe follows) or more as needed (see Note)

1 cup (4 ounces) crumbled feta cheese

½ cup chopped fresh basil

8 ounces cooked shrimp (optional), for garnish

1 Bring a large pot of water to a boil over high heat. When the water is boiling add a pinch of salt, then add the penne and stir. Reduce the heat to medium and cook the penne, uncovered, until al dente, about 5 minutes.

2 While the penne is cooking, chop the spinach and cut the grape tomatoes in half. Drain the penne well in a colander. Transfer the penne to a serving bowl and pour ½ cup of balsamic vinaigrette over

it. Stir to combine. Fold in the chopped spinach, tomato halves, and feta cheese. Stir until all of the ingredients are coated with vinaigrette. Add more vinaigrette if needed to moisten the salad.

3 To serve, sprinkle the basil over the top of the salad. Add the shrimp, if desired. Or, cover the bowl with plastic wrap and place it in the refrigerator for up to 24 hours. Add more vinaigrette to the salad just before serving, along with the shrimp, if using, and the basil.

Note: If you serve this salad warm, right away, you will need about ½ cup of vinaigrette for it to pull together. But if you place the salad in the refrigerator to chill and then serve it, you will need more vinaigrette to moisten the ingredients.

EXTRA! EXTRA!

It's easier than ever to find gluten-free penne pasta. Choose multigrain pasta or one made with brown rice flour because these have more texture.

Just as you can top the salad with shrimp and turn this side into a main, you could also add crabmeat or smoked salmon.

Dairy-Free:
You can omit the feta cheese or choose a vegan feta, such as the one made by Sunergia. And if you can tolerate sheep's milk, feta is often made from this.

Summer Picnic with Friends

Parmesan Chicken Rolls, page 155
Susan's Penne and Tomato Salad
Cinnamon Plum Crostata, page 342

Easy Balsamic Vinaigrette

I used a bottled salad dressing for Susan's Penne and Tomato Salad— this is what makes it easy. Make sure the dressing is gluten-free or you can make this simple balsamic vinaigrette.

MAKES 1¼ CUPS

6 tablespoons balsamic vinegar
1 tablespoon Dijon mustard
1 large clove garlic, minced
1 cup olive oil
Salt and freshly ground black pepper

Place the vinegar, mustard, and garlic in a small bowl and stir to combine. Whisk in the olive oil until slightly thickened. Season with salt and pepper to taste. Refrigerate any leftover vinaigrette. It will keep for up to 3 days.

An Unbelievably Gluten-Free Meal

WHERE EATEN:

WHEN EATEN:

WHO WAS THERE:

TIPS FOR MAKING AT HOME:

NEW INSPIRATIONS:

Tomato Panzanella Salad

SERVES: 4

PREP: 20 MINUTES

THIS IS CLASSIC ITALIAN SALAD AT ITS BEST. WHEN YOU combine ripe tomatoes, fresh basil, good olive oil, and the best French or rustic gluten-free bread you can find, you have a meal. Make the croutons, then make the salad. Then pour a glass of wine and enjoy!

4 large ripe tomatoes, cut into 1-inch cubes (4 heaping cups)

½ cup thinly sliced red onion

½ cup pitted kalamata olives cut in half

1 clove garlic, crushed in a garlic press

2 tablespoons balsamic vinegar

2 tablespoons olive oil

¼ teaspoon salt, or more to taste

2 cups Gluten-Free Croutons (page 253)

1 cup torn fresh basil leaves

2 cups mixed greens (optional), for serving

1 Place the tomatoes, onion, olives, garlic, balsamic vinegar, olive oil, and salt in a large mixing bowl and stir to combine. Stir in the croutons and basil. Let the salad sit for about 5 minutes at room temperature. The salad can be made up to 1 hour ahead.

2 To serve, line a platter with the mixed greens, if desired. Spoon the bread salad over the greens.

EXTRA! EXTRA!

Use half red and half yellow tomatoes, and add a handful of cucumber slices, if desired.

Dairy-Free:

No dairy is in this salad.

Tuna and White Bean Salad

SERVES: 4 TO 6

PREP: 15 TO 20 MINUTES

NATURALLY GLUTEN-FREE, THIS SALAD IS DELICIOUS, and one I think you'll enjoy. I used to make it with dried beans and it made such a large amount that I would snack on the salad for days. But it's easier to begin with canned white beans and so I've adjusted the recipe to make enough salad for four to six. While you can serve the salad anytime of the year, it tastes best in spring and summer, when the weather is warm.

2 cans (15 ounces each) great northern beans, rinsed and drained

¼ cup olive oil, plus oil for drizzling

2 tablespoons fresh lemon juice (from 1 lemon)

Dash of hot pepper sauce

Salt and freshly ground black pepper

1 scallion, both white and green parts, chopped

2 tablespoons chopped fresh parsley

1 can (7 ounces) solid white albacore tuna, packed in water, drained

1 large ripe tomato

1 hard-cooked egg, peeled and chopped

8 pitted kalamata olives

1 Place the beans in a large mixing bowl and toss them with the olive oil and lemon juice. Season the beans with hot pepper sauce and salt and pepper to taste. Fold in the scallion and parsley.

2 Place the tuna and flake it. Spoon it onto the bean mixture.

3 Slice the tomato into wedges and arrange them around the edge of the bowl. Scatter the chopped egg over the top of the tuna. Scatter the olives around the egg.

An Unbelievably Gluten-Free Meal

....

WHERE EATEN:

_____

_____

WHEN EATEN:

_____

_____

WHO WAS THERE:

_____

_____

_____

TIPS FOR MAKING AT HOME:

_____

_____

_____

_____

NEW INSPIRATIONS:

_____

_____

_____

{ *This salad makes terrific picnic fare. Drizzle on the olive oil just before you're ready to dish it out.* }

4 Drizzle the top of the salad with olive oil (don't toss it). Serve the salad at the table.

EXTRA! EXTRA!

Instead of canned tuna, use 6 to 8 ounces of your favorite grilled fish—including fresh tuna, cod, and halibut.

Dairy-Free:
This salad is dairy-free!

Macho Nacho Taco Salad

SERVES: 6
PREP: 17 TO 20 MINUTES
COOK: 13 TO 14 MINUTES

THANKFULLY, GLUTEN-FREE CORN TORTILLA CHIPS ARE available, for they enliven a good Southwestern salad. This one is meaty and sure to appeal to the boys in your family, thus the name. Use either ground beef or turkey. It's all in the presentation, so if you have a big white platter or a big shallow bowl, pile everything on and let people serve themselves. If not, place the lettuce in a salad bowl and serve the toppings on the side. My family likes our taco salad with a little dressing on top—some like a buttermilk cilantro dressing and others ranch. Suit yourself or serve no dressing at all.

1 tablespoon olive oil

1 pound lean ground beef or turkey

1 package (1½ ounces) gluten-free taco seasoning, or 2 tablespoons chili powder, 2 teaspoons ground cumin, and ½ teaspoon salt

⅔ cup water

1 head iceberg lettuce, rinsed, drained, and shredded

2 large tomatoes, diced

1 can (about 15 ounces) kidney beans, rinsed and drained

1 avocado, peeled and diced

6 scallions, green parts only, chopped

½ cup loosely packed fresh cilantro leaves

8 ounces cheddar, Monterey Jack, or Cotija cheese, shredded or crumbled (2 cups)

1 cup gluten-free corn chips, crumbled

Tomato salsa or green chile salsa (optional), for garnish

Ranch or buttermilk salad dressing (optional)

1 Heat the olive oil in a large frying pan over medium-high heat. Crumble the ground beef or turkey into the pan and cook, stirring, until the meat browns and is cooked through, 3 to 4 minutes. Stir in the taco seasoning and water. Reduce the heat to low and let the meat mixture simmer until the juices cook down, about 10 minutes. Set the meat mixture aside. You can make the meat mixture up to 1 day ahead and refrigerate it, covered. Reheat the meat mixture before assembling the salad.

2 Place the lettuce in a large shallow bowl and top it with the tomatoes, followed by the kidney beans, avocado, scallions, cilantro, and cheese. Pour the hot meat mixture over the cheese. Scatter the crumbled corn chips on top. Serve with salsa as a garnish or with the salad dressing of your choice.

EXTRA! EXTRA!

Read the salad dressing bottle to make sure the dressing is gluten-free. The same goes for the taco seasoning packet. I find that I always have a little leftover salad dressing in the fridge or some ground cumin and chili powder, so there is no need to buy more dressing or a taco seasoning.

Dairy-Free:

Omit the cheese and the taco salad will still be macho and dairy-free. Serve the dairy-free salad with a vinaigrette.

Sesame Noodle Salad

SERVES: 4
PREP: 10 TO 15 MINUTES
COOL: 15 MINUTES

EVERY COOK NEEDS A BASIC ASIAN PASTA SALAD, READY when they are. It goes with so many entrées, such as grilled chicken and shrimp. It's even great with steak or a vegetarian meal of grilled vegetable kebabs. Doctor this salad up as you like, adding a little fresh grated ginger to the sesame oil dressing. Use the veggie substitutions noted in *Extra! Extra!* Just be sure to use gluten-free spaghetti or linguine, something that is becoming easier to find every day. Choose either a brown rice or an Asian white rice pasta. They tend to taste bland on their own but benefit from the garlic, sesame oil, and soy sauce in the recipe.

Pinch of salt

8 ounces gluten-free brown rice spaghetti

¼ cup Asian (dark) sesame oil

3 tablespoons gluten-free low-sodium soy sauce

¼ teaspoon freshly ground black pepper

1 clove garlic, minced

½ cup finely chopped red bell pepper

½ cup finely chopped fresh snow peas

1 Bring a large pot of water to a boil over high heat. When the water is boiling add a pinch of salt, if desired, then add the spaghetti, stirring to break up the strands. Let the spaghetti boil until it is just cooked al dente, 7 to 9 minutes. Do not overcook the spaghetti.

2 While the spaghetti is cooking, place the sesame oil, soy sauce,

black pepper, and garlic in a small bowl and whisk to combine. Set the sesame oil dressing aside.

3 Drain the spaghetti well in a colander. Transfer the spaghetti to a serving bowl and pour the sesame oil dressing over it. Toss the spaghetti to coat it with the dressing. Fold in the red pepper and snow peas. Let the salad cool to room temperature, about 15 minutes, or cover it with plastic wrap and refrigerate it until serving time. The salad can be refrigerated for 3 or 4 days.

EXTRA! EXTRA!

Serve the salad with grilled chicken, fried shrimp, or your favorite stir-fry. No snow peas? Substitute finely chopped steamed green beans or tiny broccoli florets.

Dairy-Free:
The Sesame Noodle Salad is dairy-free.

An Unbelievably Gluten-Free Meal

WHERE EATEN:

WHEN EATEN:

WHO WAS THERE:

TIPS FOR MAKING AT HOME:

NEW INSPIRATIONS:

Southern Squash Soufflé

SERVES: 6 TO 8
PREP: 25 TO 30 MINUTES
BAKE: 40 TO 45 MINUTES

I WAS TAUGHT BY MY MOTHER THAT IF YOU USE FRESH SUMMER squash and drain the cooked squash very well before adding it to other ingredients in a squash casserole, you don't need to thicken it with cracker or bread crumbs. My mother used to return the drained cooked squash to the pan to cook over low heat for a few minutes to let any moisture that still clung to the squash evaporate. If you want a topper for this casserole, sprinkle crumbled gluten-free crackers over it before baking. Squash soufflé is really squash casserole—soufflé just sounds more impressive!

3 pounds yellow summer squash, ends trimmed, squash sliced ½ inch thick

1 medium-size onion, peeled and cut in half

Salt and freshly ground black pepper

4 tablespoons (½ stick) butter

1 cup canned evaporated milk

2 large eggs, beaten

1 cup (4 ounces) shredded cheddar cheese

1 Place the squash in a large saucepan along with 1 onion half. Pour enough water into the pan to reach about one third of the way up the squash and season the squash with salt and pepper to taste. Let the water come to a boil over medium-high heat, then reduce the heat to low and let the squash simmer until tender, about 15 minutes. Drain the squash very well.

2 Place a rack in the center of the oven and preheat the oven to 350°F.

3 Return the squash to the saucepan and cook over low heat, stirring, until all of the moisture evaporates but the squash does not stick to the pan, about 2 minutes. Add the butter to the pan. Chop the remaining onion half into small dice and add it to the pan. Let simmer over low heat, stirring, until the diced onion softens, 3 to 4 minutes.

4 Remove the pan from the heat and stir in the milk, eggs, and ½ cup of the cheddar cheese. Pour the squash mixture into a 2-quart casserole dish and sprinkle the top with the remaining ½ cup of cheese. Bake the squash until the top is bubbly and browned around the edges and the cheese has melted, 40 to 45 minutes. The squash soufflé can be refrigerated, covered, for 2 or 3 days. To reheat the soufflé cover it with aluminum foil and bake it in an oven preheated to 350°F until heated through, 10 to 15 minutes.

EXTRA! EXTRA!

This is such a basic squash casserole recipe. You can use ½ cup of Parmesan cheese in addition to the cheddar. You can use zucchini instead of the yellow squash. You can use scallions for some or all of the onion. And, you can use cream or sour cream instead of the evaporated milk.

Dairy-Free:

Omit the butter and use margarine. Use unsweetened canned coconut milk instead of the evaporated milk. Omit the cheddar cheese. Add a handful of chopped fresh parsley or a mix of parsley and chives to the squash for additional color and flavor.

Gluten-Free Baked Apricots

SERVES: 8 TO 12
PREP: 10 MINUTES
BAKE: 48 TO 52 MINUTES

A YEAR-ROUND COMPLEMENT TO EVERYTHING—FROM THE first grilled salmon of spring, to summer barbecued ribs, to Thanksgiving roast turkey and Christmas ham—this side dish is classic. And the gluten-free version is delicious with crushed gluten-free crackers. I used the Glutino round crackers, from Italy, that are made of corn and rice. Who would know?

4 cans (about 15 ounces each) canned apricot halves in heavy syrup

¾ cup packed light brown sugar

¼ teaspoon cinnamon, or more to taste

1¼ cups crushed round gluten-free crackers (32 crackers)

5 tablespoons unsalted butter, at room temperature

1 Place a rack in the center of the oven and preheat the oven to 375°F.

2 Drain the apricot halves and set aside ¼ cup of the syrup. Place half of the apricots cut side up in the bottom of a 13 by 9-inch (3-quart) baking dish. Sprinkle half of the brown sugar over the apricots, then top the brown sugar with ⅛ teaspoon of cinnamon. Sprinkle half of the cracker crumbs evenly over the top. Repeat the layers with the remaining apricot

halves, brown sugar, ⅛ teaspoon of cinnamon, and cracker crumbs. Pour the reserved ¼ cup of apricot syrup evenly over the top and distribute the butter by teaspoonfuls on top. You can make the apricot casserole up to 5 hours ahead; leave it on the countertop before baking, do not refrigerate it.

3 Bake the apricots until they are bubbly and the top has lightly browned, 48 to 52 minutes. Remove the baking dish from the oven and let the apricots rest for about 10 minutes before serving. They are best served shortly after being baked because the topping will be crunchy. Any leftovers can be refrigerated covered for up to 3 days.

Thanksgiving Dinner

Roast turkey, page 283, and Cheryl's Corn Bread Dressing, page 281

Southern Squash Soufflé, page 266

Gluten-Free Baked Apricots

Roasted Brussels sprouts or green peas

Cranberry sauce

Classic Pumpkin Pie, page 327, or Our Favorite Pecan Pie, page 330

EXTRA! EXTRA!

The crackers are pretty crucial to the outcome of this recipe so look for the best-quality gluten-free crackers you can find. Whole Foods and stores that carry a variety of gluten-free products have some choices. Glutino crackers are delicious in this casserole and also with fresh fruit and cheese.

Dairy-Free:

You can substitute margarine for the butter in this recipe.

Delicious Dirty Rice

SERVES: 6 TO 8

PREP: 15 MINUTES

COOK: 20 TO 25 MINUTES

NOT ONLY IS RICE NATURALLY GLUTEN-FREE, IT IS A mainstay of diets around the world. But one of my favorite recipes using rice is this Texas version of dirty rice. Unlike other variations that might include chicken liver or sausage, this one has tomatoes, spices, and hot sauce. It is delicious served alongside roasted or fried chicken, grilled steaks or sausages, or on its own with a green salad.

FOR THE RICE

2 tablespoons vegetable oil

1 cup long-grain white rice

2 cups chopped fresh tomatoes

½ cup chopped onion

2 cloves garlic

1 teaspoon ground cumin

2½ cups low-sodium chicken broth

½ teaspoon salt

½ teaspoon hot pepper sauce

¼ teaspoon freshly ground black pepper

FOR GARNISH

2 tablespoons chopped fresh cilantro, parsley, or scallion

1 jalapeño pepper (optional), seeds and veins removed, pepper chopped

1 Place the oil in a large heavy pot over low heat. Add the rice and stir with a wooden spoon until lightly browned, 5 to 6 minutes. Remove the pot from the heat.

2 Place the tomatoes, onion, garlic, cumin, and ½ cup of the chicken

broth in a food processor and process until nearly smooth, 10 to 15 pulses. Place the pot with the rice over medium heat, add the tomato mixture, and stir to combine. Add the remaining 2 cups of chicken broth and the salt, hot pepper sauce, and black pepper. Let come to a boil, cover the pot, reduce the heat to low, and let simmer until the rice is nearly cooked through, about 15 minutes.

3 Remove the pot from the heat and let the rice rest for about 5 minutes, covered, then uncover the pot and fluff the rice with a fork. Serve the rice garnished with cilantro, parsley, or scallion, and jalapeño pepper, if desired. Any leftover rice will keep covered in the refrigerator for up to 3 days. To reheat the rice in the oven, cover the dish with aluminum foil and bake it in an oven preheated to 325°F until heated through, about 20 minutes. To reheat the rice on the stovetop, place it in a saucepan, add 2 to 3 tablespoons of water, and heat it over low heat, 4 to 5 minutes.

EXTRA! EXTRA!

For a complete meal, serve black beans alongside the rice. Or fold 1 cup of cooked black beans into the rice at the last moment for a very dirty rice.

Dairy-Free:

This dirty rice is dairy-free.

Easy Fried Rice

SERVES: 2 TO 4
PREP: 10 MINUTES
COOK: 7 TO 10 MINUTES

N O MATTER WHAT LEFTOVERS ARE IN OUR FRIDGE I CAN usually pull together a pretty impressive fried rice for my son. He loves the dish as a snack, meal, or even breakfast if I would serve it then! And the fried rice you make at home is a whole lot healthier than Chinese takeout. It has less oil, to begin with, and you are in control of the ingredients, so you can add more veggies. Naturally gluten-free, fried rice is often overlooked but is a mainstay in our kitchen.

2 tablespoons vegetable oil

½ cup chopped broccoli

¼ cup finely chopped purple or white onions or scallions

¼ cup finely chopped sweet or hot peppers

¼ cup finely chopped carrots

2 cups cold cooked rice (see *Extra! Extra!*)

1 cup chopped cooked chicken, pork tenderloin, steak, shrimp, or salmon

1 tablespoon gluten-free low-sodium soy sauce, or more to taste

1 large egg, lightly beaten

Hot pepper sauce (optional)

1 Place the oil in a large frying pan or wok and heat over medium-high heat. Add the broccoli, onion, peppers, and carrots and cook, stirring, until softened, 3 to 4 minutes. Add the rice and stir to break up clumps. Lower the heat a little to prevent sticking and add the meat or seafood and soy sauce. Cook, stirring, until heated through, about 3 minutes.

An Unbelievably Gluten-Free Meal

WHERE EATEN: _____

_____

WHEN EATEN: _____

_____

WHO WAS THERE: _____

_____

_____

TIPS FOR MAKING AT HOME: _____

_____

_____

_____

NEW INSPIRATIONS: _____

_____

_____

_____

2 Stir the beaten egg into the fried rice, and cook, stirring, until the egg turns opaque in color, about 1 minute. Taste for seasoning adding more soy sauce if necessssary and/or a little hot sauce, if using, then serve.

EXTRA! EXTRA!

There is no imperfect rice to use in this recipe—any rice will do. But I like the long grains of a rice like basmati because they don't stick and clump. You want the rice to distribute well and harmonize with all the other ingredients.

Dairy-Free:
Yes, this fried rice is dairy-free.

Curried Rice Pilaf

SERVES: 4
PREP: 20 MINUTES
COOK: 20 TO 25 MINUTES

WHAT IS THE ANSWER TO WHAT TO SERVE WITH A simple grilled chicken breast, a pan-fried steak, or a piece of broiled fish? A rice pilaf. It turns ordinary food into dinner party food very quickly. This naturally gluten-free recipe takes on exotic flavors with the curry powder, sweet raisins, and nutty toasted almonds.

2 tablespoons vegetable oil or butter

1 cup finely chopped onions

¼ cup shredded carrots

1 teaspoon curry powder (see *Extra! Extra!*)

1 cup basmati rice

2 cups low-sodium chicken broth

⅓ cup golden raisins

Salt and freshly ground black pepper

¼ cup finely chopped scallions, both white and green parts

1 tablespoon toasted sliced or slivered almonds (see Note)

1 Place the oil or butter in a medium-size saucepan over medium heat. Add the onions and carrots and cook, stirring, until the onion is soft, 4 to 5 minutes. Stir in the curry powder, rice, and chicken broth. Let the mixture come to a boil, then reduce the heat, cover the pan, and cook until the rice is just done, 18 to 20 minutes. Stir in the raisins and season with salt and pepper to taste.

2 To serve, spoon the pilaf onto a platter or serve it on plates.

An Unbelievably Gluten-Free Meal

....

WHERE EATEN:

_____

_____

WHEN EATEN:

_____

_____

WHO WAS THERE:

_____

_____

_____

TIPS FOR MAKING AT HOME:

_____

_____

_____

NEW INSPIRATIONS:

_____

_____

_____

Garnish the pilaf with the scallions and toasted almonds scattered generously across the top.

Note: To toast the almonds, place them in a small baking pan in a 350°F oven while the rice is cooking and bake them until aromatic and golden brown, 3 to 4 minutes. Watch the almonds carefully as they burn quickly.

EXTRA! EXTRA!

Use your favorite curry powder in this recipe. Or use garam masala, which has more cinnamon and less cumin. Or, add ¼ teaspoon of cinnamon, ¼ teaspoon of cayenne pepper, and ¼ teaspoon of ground cumin. The seasoning is up to you! And during the holidays, substitute dried cranberries for the raisins.

Dairy-Free:

Use oil for sautéing the onion and the rice pilaf will be dairy-free.

Gluten-Free Mac and Cheese

SERVES: 4
PREP: 10 MINUTES
COOK: 20 TO 26 MINUTES | BAKE: 8 TO 10 MINUTES (OPTIONAL)

MUCH OF THE MAC AND CHEESE LOVING WORLD HAS gotten used to a sauce that is thickened with flour. But one of my favorite pasta sauces is made just by reducing heavy cream over the heat and stirring in good cheese. The cream thickens on its own, and what results is a rich and velvety sauce that can enrobe macaroni in classic mac and cheese style or cling to fettuccine as in fettuccine Alfredo. Rice flour pastas and pastas made with corn flour tend to cook quickly so be careful not to overcook them. You can prepare this mac and cheese using only the stovetop or give it a cracker crumb topping and bake it.

Pinch of salt

8 ounces gluten-free elbow macaroni (see Note)

1 tablespoon olive oil or butter

3 cups heavy (whipping) cream

2 cups (8 ounces) shredded sharp cheddar cheese

½ cup (2 ounces) grated Parmesan cheese

Dash of ground nutmeg

Dash of paprika, for sprinkling on top

1 cup gluten-free cracker crumbs, for topping the casserole (optional)

1 tablespoon butter, melted (optional)

1 Fill a large pot two-thirds full with water and bring to a boil over medium-high heat. When the water is boiling add a pinch of salt and stir in the macaroni. Cook the macaroni until it is just done, 5 to 6 minutes.

Drain the macaroni in a colander and toss it with the olive oil or butter. Set the macaroni aside.

2 If you are baking the macaroni and cheese, preheat the oven to 400°F.

3 Add the cream to the pot in which you cooked the pasta and let come to a boil over medium heat, stirring. Let the cream cook until it has reduced to half its volume, about 1½ cups, 15 to 20 minutes. Turn off the heat and stir in the cheddar and Parmesan cheeses and nutmeg.

4 When the cheeses have melted completely, stir the cooked macaroni into the sauce. You can serve the macaroni and cheese at once sprinkled with paprika. Or to bake the dish transfer the macaroni and sauce to a 2-quart baking dish. Toss the cracker crumbs with the melted butter and scatter them over the top. Sprinkle the cracker crumbs with paprika. Bake until the macaroni and cheese is bubbly and the crumbs have browned, 8 to 10 minutes. The macaroni and cheese can be refrigerated, covered, for up to 3 days.

Note: I use macaroni made with a blend of corn and quinoa. Take care not to overcook the macaroni as it will cook in about 5 minutes. If you plan on baking the macaroni with sauce and cheese, you can slightly undercook it because it will finish cooking in the oven.

EXTRA! EXTRA!

Ordinary sharp cheddar is good in this recipe. But what is really great is a sharp English cheddar or Gruyère or Spanish Manchego cheese. Feel free to make the macaroni and cheese even more of a meal by folding in ½ cup of steamed frozen peas and ½ cup of chopped ham.

Dairy-Free:
It is not possible to make macaroni and cheese dairy-free.

Cheryl's
Corn Bread Dressing

SERVES: 8
PREP: 25 TO 30 MINUTES
BAKE: 1 HOUR, 15 MINUTES

CHERYL LESLIE AND HER FAMILY ORGANIZE AN ANNUAL fundraising walk in Rye, New York, to raise money for celiac disease research. They have been doing this since 2006 when Cheryl's son Colin was diagnosed with the disease at the age of fourteen. As of this writing, the Colin Leslie Walk for Celiac Disease has raised more than $300,000 to benefit the Celiac Disease Center at Columbia University. In addition to organizing fundraising events, mom Cheryl is a good cook. She shares this favorite Thanksgiving recipe for dressing, something that celiacs often have to go without during the holidays. If she's busy, Cheryl begins with a package of Gluten Free Pantry corn bread mix. But since that mix can be tough to find, and since cornmeal is naturally gluten-free, why not make your own corn bread? One skillet of corn bread yields enough crumbled corn bread for this recipe (you'll find the corn bread recipe on page 134). Stuffing or dressing? If a recipe goes into a turkey, I call it stuffing, and if it bakes alone in a casserole dish to serve alongside the turkey, I call it dressing. I think this works best as a dressing.

6 to 8 cups crumbled gluten-free corn bread (page 134)

1 pound breakfast sausage

5 tablespoons butter

¾ cup finely chopped onion

¾ cup finely chopped celery

1 teaspoon dried thyme

Pinch of powdered sage

Salt and freshly ground black pepper

2 large eggs, beaten

1 cup low-sodium chicken broth, or more as needed

1 Crumble bite-size pieces of corn bread into a large mixing bowl. It is best if you let the corn bread dry out overnight on the counter before baking the dressing.

2 Cook the sausage according to the package directions, crumble it, and drain it well on paper towels. Add the sausage to the crumbled corn bread. Set the pan aside.

3 Place a rack in the center of the oven and preheat the oven to 350°F.

4 Place the butter in the same pan you used to cook the sausage. Leave the browned bits and grease in the pan. Place the pan over medium heat and add the onion and celery. Cook, stirring, until the onion is soft, 4 to 5 minutes. Add the onion and celery mixture to the corn bread. Add the thyme and sage and season with salt and pepper to taste. Stir in the eggs and mix until well combined.

5 Spoon the corn bread mixture into a 13 by 9-inch glass or ceramic baking dish. Pour the chicken broth over the mixture. Cover the dish with aluminum foil and bake the dressing until cooked through, about 1 hour. Remove the foil from the baking dish and return it to the oven to brown the dressing, about 15 minutes longer. The dressing can be refrigerated, covered, for 2 or 3 days. To reheat the dressing, cover the baking dish with aluminum foil and bake the dressing in an oven preheated to 350°F until heated through, 15 to 20 minutes.

Cheryl says this is a forgiving recipe, and she is right. You can bake the dressing, tote it to another kitchen for Thanksgiving, and keep it covered and warm until serving. For a fresh sweet flavor you can add chopped apples when you sauté the onions and celery. And feel free to use a handful of chopped fresh parsley along with the dried thyme.

Dairy-Free:

Opt for soy margarine or the Earth Balance shortening sticks instead of the butter.

There's no such thing as too much dressing!

Note: Cheryl likes to use brown-and-serve breakfast sausage, which she cooks, drains, and dices, because it is less greasy than other sausage.

{ HOW TO ROAST A TURKEY }

1. Rinse a 16- to 18-pound turkey in cool running water, and remove the neck and giblets from the cavity. Pat the turkey dry with paper towels and season the cavity with salt and pepper. Place the turkey in a large roasting pan about 2½ inches deep. Fold the wing tips back underneath the turkey, and tie the legs together with kitchen twine. Place the turkey in the refrigerator while you prepare the turkey broth.

2. Place the turkey neck (discard the giblets) in a medium-size saucepan, and cover with 4 cups (1 quart) water. Add salt and pepper to taste, a bay leaf, and a handful of chopped onion. Add a rib of celery if you have it. Bring the water to a boil, then reduce the heat and let the broth simmer, covered, until the turkey neck has cooked through and the broth has taken on flavor, 30 minutes. Remove the broth from the heat, and set it aside, uncovered, to cool.

3. Preheat the oven to 325°F. Remove the turkey from the refrigerator and rub the skin with 8 tablespoons soft butter. Season with salt and pepper. Tent the turkey with aluminum foil.

4. Place the turkey in the oven, and with the door of the oven open, pour 2 cups of the turkey broth around the turkey in the roasting pan. Close the oven door and roast the turkey, basting it by spooning cooking juices over the top every 30 minutes. Add more stock as needed to the pan. Remove the foil from the turkey after 2 hours. Roast uncovered until the skin is golden and a meat thermometer inserted in the thigh reads 180°F, another 1½ to 2 hours for a total cooking time of 3½ to 4 hours.

5. Let the turkey rest in the pan for 15 minutes, then remove it carefully to a platter. Let it rest another 30 minutes before carving. Makes 18 to 24 servings.

Gluten-Free Broccoli Brag

SERVES: 12
PREP: 10 MINUTES
BAKE: 48 TO 52 MINUTES | COOL: 10 MINUTES

Broccoli Brag is a classic Thanksgiving casserole that hails from Chattanooga, Tennessee. I have my own version of this great side dish, using ricotta cheese instead of the cottage cheese called for in the original recipe. And now with this gluten-free version, we have another variation! What is important is that the broccoli, cheddar cheese, and eggs bake up into a puffy and flavorful soufflé and feed a lot of people—that you don't want to change.

Vegetable oil spray, for misting the baking dish

2 packages (10 ounces each) frozen chopped broccoli

4 tablespoons (½ stick) butter, melted

6 large eggs, beaten

1 container (15 ounces; 2 cups) part skim ricotta cheese

2 cups (8 ounces) shredded cheddar cheese

2 tablespoons cornstarch

1 teaspoon salt, or more to taste

¼ teaspoon hot pepper sauce

Freshly ground black pepper

1 Place a rack in the center of the oven and preheat the oven to 325°F. Lightly mist a 13 by 9-inch glass or ceramic baking dish with vegetable oil spray and set the dish aside.

2 Place the broccoli in a large microwave-safe glass bowl and microwave on high power until thawed, 1½ to 2 minutes. Leaving the broccoli in the bowl, drain it over the sink, pressing on it with a fork to extract as much liquid as possible.

3 Add the butter, eggs, ricotta, 1 cup of the cheddar cheese, and the cornstarch, salt, and hot pepper sauce. Season with black pepper to taste. Stir to combine well. Transfer the broccoli mixture to the prepared baking dish and scatter the remaining 1 cup of cheddar cheese evenly over the top.

4 Bake the casserole until it turns golden brown and bubbles around the edges, 48 to 52 minutes. Let the casserole cool for about 10 minutes before serving. Any leftovers can be refrigerated for up to 3 days.

EXTRA! EXTRA!

You can use small curd cottage cheese instead of ricotta. And you can use fresh broccoli instead of frozen. You will need 2 heaping cups of steamed chopped fresh broccoli.

Dairy-Free:
This casserole has so many dairy ingredients, it is not possible to make it dairy-free.

An Unbelievably Gluten-Free Meal

WHERE EATEN:

WHEN EATEN:

WHO WAS THERE:

TIPS FOR MAKING AT HOME:

NEW INSPIRATIONS:

Twenty-Seven Unbelievably Gluten-Free Sweets

1. Quick-Cook Rice Pudding

2. Indian Pudding with Pumpkin

3. Warm Lemon Pudding Cake

4. Flourless Chocolate Cakes

5. Slow Cooker Peanut Butter Brownie Pudding

6. Amazing Angel Food Cake

7. Red Velvet Cake with Cream Cheese Frosting

8. Fresh Orange Cupcakes

9. Gingerbread Cupcakes with Quick Lemon Buttercream Frosting

10. Cookies and Cream Cheesecake

11. Homemade Gluten-Free Pie Crust

12. Blueberry Glacé Pie

13. Easy Apple Tart

14. Classic Pumpkin Pie

15. Our Favorite Pecan Pie

16. Tennessee Chess Pie

17. Little Fudge Tarts

18. Old-Fashioned Peach and Blueberry Cobbler

19. Blackberry and Raspberry Cobbler

20. Cinnamon Plum Crostata

21. Pear and Cranberry Crostata

22. Fried Apple Pies

23. Gluten-Free Saucepan Brownies

24. Gluten-Free Chocolate Chip Cookies

25. Bev's Raisin Cookies

26. Crisp Cornmeal Cookies

27. Sweetened Whipped Cream

Sweets for Every Occasion

H ere are more than two dozen recipes that prove that you do not need wheat flour to bake great desserts. The proof? An incredible array of cakes, including: a Red Velvet Cake, an amazing Angel Food Cake, a slow-cooker brownie pudding, saucepan brownies, and tasty orange cupcakes.

Once you master a range of gluten-free cakes, it is time to take on pie crust. My basic recipe begins with a gluten-free pie crust mix, which I found gritty and tough when baked using package directions. I doctored it up with cream cheese to make it tender. If you'd rather not make your own you can substitute your favorite pre-made gluten-free crust in these recipes that include pies, cobblers, and even little fried pies.

An eclectic list of pantry items is needed for these yummy desserts—gluten-free pie crust mix, gluten-free cake mix, sweet rice flour, sorghum flour, gluten-free brownie mix, cornmeal, cornstarch, and rice—but you'll love the results. Not to forget a useful baking mix—gluten-free Bisquick—which jumpstarts cookies nicely. Quite possibly all these ingredients are already in your kitchen, so let's get baking!

Quick-Cook Rice Pudding

SERVES: 4 TO 6
PREP: 50 MINUTES, INCLUDING COOKING THE RICE
BAKE: 15 TO 20 MINUTES

WHEN THIS BOOK WAS IN ITS INFANCY, AND I WAS thinking of the naturally gluten-free desserts I should include in it, baked rice pudding came to mind. I have a soft spot in my heart for rice pudding because it has only a handful of ingredients, and is the best comfort food ever. The only caveat for a busy family is that rice pudding that begins with uncooked rice can take two hours or more to bake in the oven. So I came up with this faster method in which you let the rice cook in the milk mixture on top of the stove first and then bake it for twenty minutes in the oven.

3 tablespoons butter, plus 2 teaspoons butter, at room temperature, for greasing the casserole

4 cups (1 quart) whole milk

½ cup granulated sugar

1 teaspoon pure vanilla extract

⅛ teaspoon ground nutmeg

⅓ cup uncooked short-grain rice (see Note)

⅔ cup raisins (optional)

1 Rub the 2 teaspoons of butter in the bottom and on the sides of a 1-quart casserole. Set the casserole aside.

2 Place the milk, sugar, vanilla, nutmeg, and the 3 tablespoons of butter in the top of a double boiler over medium-high heat, stir to combine, and heat until the milk comes to a boil, 4 to 5 minutes. Stir in the rice and reduce the

{ *It takes only 10 minutes of real prep time to make this pudding.* }

heat to medium. Cook, stirring occasionally, until the mixture thickens and the rice has cooked, about 40 minutes. Stir in the raisins, if using.

3 Meanwhile, place a rack in the center of the oven and preheat the oven to 350°F.

4 Pour the rice mixture into the prepared casserole. Place the casserole in the oven and bake the rice pudding until it is lightly browned, 15 to 20 minutes. Serve warm. Rice pudding keeps for up to 3 days in the refrigerator. To reheat it, pour ¼ cup milk over the pudding. Tent it with waxed paper, and place it in the microwave on high power until the pudding is heated through, 30 seconds, or cover the rice pudding with aluminum foil and place it in a 325°F oven for 20 minutes.

Note: Be sure to use short-grain rice—which is starchy—in this recipe. Do not use such long-grain rice as basmati or converted rice.

EXTRA! EXTRA!

For a richer pudding, use 3 cups of milk and 1 cup of heavy (whipping) cream. And for a lemon-scented pudding, omit the nutmeg and fold in 2 teaspoons of grated lemon zest.

Dairy-Free:
Use rice milk and margarine in the rice pudding in place of the whole milk and butter.

Indian Pudding with Pumpkin

SERVES: 8

PREP: 30 TO 35 MINUTES

BAKE: 2 HOURS

THIS IS A NEW RENDITION OF INDIAN PUDDING, AN ALL-American classic dessert, which is naturally gluten-free. Scalding the milk and slowly whisking in the cornmeal over low heat is a necessary step in creating this velvety textured comfort food.

Vegetable oil spray, for misting the baking dish

3 cups whole milk

1 large egg

1 large egg yolk

3 tablespoons granulated sugar

1 teaspoon ground ginger

¾ teaspoon ground cinnamon

¾ teaspoon salt

5 tablespoons (about ⅓ heaping cup) yellow or white cornmeal

⅓ cup molasses

2 tablespoons (¼ stick) unsalted butter

1 cup canned 100% pure pumpkin

½ cup raisins

2 tablespoons very finely chopped walnuts (optional)

1 Place a rack in the center of the oven and preheat the oven to 300°F. Mist a 2-quart baking dish with vegetable oil spray and set it aside.

2 Pour the milk into a medium-size saucepan over medium heat and heat until scalding (you'll see tiny bubbles form around the edge of the pan and the milk will become very steamy—don't let it boil!), 8 to 10 minutes.

3 Meanwhile, beat the egg and yolk in a small bowl. Place the sugar, ginger, cinnamon, and salt in another small bowl and stir to mix.

4 Once the milk has reached the scalding point whisk in the cornmeal, adding about 1 teaspoon at a time and whisking constantly; keep the temperature on medium heat. When all of the cornmeal has been added, continue to stir the cornmeal mixture over medium heat for 13 to 15 minutes. It will slowly thicken. Reduce the heat to medium-low. Add the molasses and butter, continuing to stir until combined. Slowly pour the beaten egg into the hot cornmeal mixture while whisking. Continue to whisk for about 1 minute. Remove the cornmeal mixture from the heat and whisk in the pumpkin and the sugar mixture until well combined. Stir in the raisins and the walnuts, if using. Pour the cornmeal mixture into the prepared baking dish.

5 Bake the pudding until well browned and a bit jiggly in the center, about 2 hours. Serve the pudding warm. Indian pudding keeps for up to 3 days in the refrigerator. To reheat it, pour ¼ cup milk over the pudding. Tent it with waxed paper, and place it in the microwave on high power until the pudding is heated through, 30 seconds, or cover the pudding with aluminum foil and place it in a 325°F oven for 20 minutes.

EXTRA! EXTRA!

What makes this Indian pudding so appealing is that it has a real gingerbread favor. But if you prefer less ginger, reduce it to ½ teaspoon.

Dairy-Free:

It is not possible to make the Indian pudding dairy-free; you need the creaminess of the whole milk and butter.

Warm Lemon Pudding Cake

SERVES: 6 TO 8

PREP: 25 MINUTES

BAKE: 40 TO 45 MINUTES | COOL: 15 MINUTES

SORT OF A CAKE, SORT OF A PUDDING, THIS IS A WARM comfort food everyone will love. It never fails to amaze me that the batter separates out into a layer of moist pudding on the bottom and a layer of flavorful cake on the top as the cake bakes. Martha Bowden, who tests recipes with me, fondly remembers the lemon pudding cake her mother used to bake. So our goal was to create a gluten-free version. Here is the recipe—enjoy!

1 extra-large or 2 small lemons

3 large eggs

¾ cup whole milk

¾ cup granulated sugar

⅓ cup gluten-free baking mix,
    such as Bisquick

2 teaspoons confectioners' sugar,
    for garnish

1 cup fresh blueberries or raspberries,
    for garnish (optional)

1 Rinse and pat dry the lemon or lemons with paper towels. Grate enough of the lemon rind to produce 1 teaspoon of yellow lemon zest. Cut the lemon or lemons in half and squeeze the juice through a fine-mesh sieve to produce ¼ cup of lemon juice, discarding the seeds and pulp. Set the lemon zest and juice aside.

2 Place a rack in the center of the oven and preheat the oven to 350°F. Prepare a water bath in which to bake the pudding by pouring water to a depth of ½ inch into a 13 by 9-inch glass baking dish. Place the baking dish in the oven to warm.

3 Separate the eggs, placing the whites in a large mixing bowl and the yolks in a medium-size mixing

bowl. Beat the egg whites with an electric mixer on high speed until stiff peaks form, 4 to 5 minutes. Set the beaten whites aside.

4 Using the electric mixer (you don't need to wash the beaters), beat the egg yolks on medium speed until just blended, about 10 seconds. Add the milk, and lemon juice and zest and beat on medium speed until well combined, about 15 seconds. Add the sugar and baking mix and beat on medium speed until just incorporated, about 15 seconds. Pour the lemon batter on top of the beaten egg whites. Using a rubber spatula, fold the batter into the whites until just incorporated. Pour the mixture into a 2-quart casserole. Open the oven door and place the casserole in the water bath.

5 Bake the pudding cake until it is golden brown, 40 to 45 minutes. Carefully lift the casserole out of the water bath and place it on a wire rack to cool. Let the pudding cake cool for about 15 minutes, then serve it warm sprinkled with confectioners' sugar and topped with the berries, if

desired. The Warm Lemon Pudding Cake will keep for up to 3 days in the refrigerator. To reheat it, cover the cake with aluminum foil and place it in a 325°F oven for 15 to 20 minutes.

EXTRA! EXTRA!

The lemon cake is more puddinglike when it first comes out of the oven. As the cake cools it sets up and is more like cake. Suit yourself, but I prefer the cake warm and pudding-y.

Dairy-Free:
You can make the pudding cake with unsweetened coconut milk so it's dairy-free.

Spring Supper on the Porch

Simple Seafood Gumbo, page 104, with rice

Green salad

Warm Lemon Pudding Cake

Flourless Chocolate Cakes

SERVES: 8

PREP: 20 MINUTES

BAKE: 12 TO 15 MINUTES | COOL: 10 MINUTES

JODY LEHMAN, WHO OWNS A COOK'S PLACE GOURMET STORE in Tupelo, Mississippi, follows a gluten-free diet. One of her favorite desserts is this chocolate cake, which has no flour. The recipe was shared by local chef David Leathers in a cooking class at her store. I love this recipe, too, and baked it in eight small ramekins. It is amazing that a dessert with so much intense chocolate flavor and good texture can contain no flour.

8 tablespoons (1 stick) unsalted butter, plus 2 teaspoons butter, at room temperature, for greasing the ramekins

8 ounces semisweet chocolate, coarsely chopped

4 large eggs

¼ cup granulated sugar

½ teaspoon pure vanilla extract

¼ teaspoon sea salt

Confectioners' sugar and fresh berries, or peppermint or vanilla ice cream, for serving

1 Place a rack in the center of the oven and preheat the oven to 400°F. Rub eight 1-cup ceramic or glass ramekins or custard cups with the 2 teaspoons of butter. Place these on a baking sheet and set them aside.

2 Place the 8 tablespoons of butter and the chocolate in a heavy saucepan over low heat. Heat, stirring, until the chocolate has melted, 3 to 4 minutes, then remove it from the heat.

296 SWEETS FOR EVERY OCCASION

3 Place the eggs, sugar, vanilla, and salt in a large mixing bowl and beat with an electric mixer on medium-high speed until the eggs are frothy and have almost doubled in size, about 4 minutes. Add the chocolate mixture a little at a time, beating continuously on low speed or whisking with a wire whisk. (Do not add all the chocolate at one time or the heat of the chocolate will cook the eggs.) The batter will thicken as the chocolate is incorporated.

4 Divide the batter among the prepared ramekins, spooning about ¾ cup into each. Put the baking sheet with the ramekins in the oven. Bake the cakes until they have risen and the edges are set, 12 to 15 minutes. Remove the ramekins from the oven and let the cakes cool for 10 minutes.

5 To serve, run a knife around the edge of each cake and turn it out onto a dessert plate. Sift confectioners' sugar over the cakes and top them with berries. Or leave the cakes in their ramekins and spoon peppermint or vanilla ice cream on them before serving them warm.

EXTRA! EXTRA!

Use the best chocolate you have for these little cakes. I like bittersweet chocolate, and if you use bittersweet chocolate chips there is no need to chop the chocolate, an added bonus.

Dairy-Free:
Use margarine instead of butter in the chocolate cakes and serve them with fresh berries.

Slow Cooker Peanut Butter Brownie Pudding

SERVES: 8 TO 10
PREP: 15 TO 20 MINUTES
BAKE: 2 HOURS | COOL: 20 MINUTES

I HAVE SHARED VARIATIONS OF THIS RECIPE IN MY OTHER cookbooks, and it is a favorite because no one can ever believe you begin with a brownie mix. The outcome is ooey-gooey wonderfulness, and served warm with vanilla ice cream it is irresistible. Here is a gluten-free version, made simple and doable because it's based on a gluten-free brownie mix.

Vegetable oil spray, for misting the slow cooker

1¼ cups water

¾ cup packed light brown sugar

2 tablespoons unsweetened cocoa powder

1 package (16 to 17 ounces) gluten-free brownie mix

½ cup creamy peanut butter

2 tablespoons (¼ stick) butter, melted

2 large eggs

1 cup (6 ounces) semisweet chocolate chips

Vanilla ice cream, for serving

1 Mist the inside of a 5-quart slow cooker with vegetable oil spray and set it aside.

2 Place 1 cup of the water and the brown sugar and cocoa powder in a small saucepan over medium heat and stir until the brown sugar dissolves, 3 to 4 minutes. Set the pan aside.

3 Place the brownie mix, peanut butter, butter, eggs, and ¼ cup of water in a large mixing bowl and stir with a large wooden spoon until

{ *Peanut butter and chocolate— this pudding is a miracle in a microwave.* }

well combined, 40 to 50 strokes. The batter will be very thick. Fold in the chocolate chips. Spoon the batter into the slow cooker and spread it out evenly. Pour the brown sugar and cocoa powder mixture evenly over the batter. Place the lid on the slow cooker and set the power on high.

4 Bake the pudding for 1½ hours. Remove the lid and run a rubber spatula around the edge of the pudding, spreading out the liquid from the center to the edge so that all of the liquid will be absorbed. Replace the lid and continue cooking the pudding until it is nearly set, 30 minutes longer.

5 Turn off the cooker, remove the cover, and let the pudding cool for about 20 minutes before serving it warm with vanilla ice cream. Store the pudding, covered, in the refrigerator for up to 2 days. You can reheat individual portions by spooning them into microwave-safe serving bowls and heating these in the microwave oven on high power for 10 to 15 seconds.

EXTRA! EXTRA!

Use your favorite brownie mix. I like King Arthur gluten-free brownie mix. Also use whatever chocolate chips you have on hand. Nestlé are fine, but if you want a deeper, richer flavor use the Ghirardelli bittersweet chips.

Dairy-Free:
Use margarine instead of butter and carob chips instead of chocolate chips, which may contain milk. Serve the pudding with a dairy-free vanilla frozen dessert, such as Tofutti.

Amazing Angel Food Cake

SERVES: 10 TO 12

PREP: 40 MINUTES

BAKE: 30 TO 35 MINUTES | COOL: 1 HOUR

A S I HAVE MENTIONED BEFORE, THE IDEA FOR THIS cookbook took hold while I was on tour with my gluten-free cake cookbook. At a book signing in Austin, Texas, a woman asked why I had not included an angel food cake recipe. I apologized and said I would put one in my next book if only I knew how to bake one that was gluten-free. Up went another hand and a kind woman shared her method: "Use half sorghum flour and half sweet rice flour." And with this clue I headed straight into the kitchen once I returned home. This is one great gluten-free cake with amazing texture—you will never guess it is gluten-free. Thank you, Austin!

12 large eggs

1 cup confectioners' sugar

½ cup sorghum flour

½ cup sweet rice flour

¼ teaspoon salt

1½ teaspoons cream of tartar

2 teaspoons pure vanilla extract

1 cup granulated sugar

1 Place a rack in the center of the oven and preheat the oven to 350°F. Set aside an ungreased 10-inch tube pan.

2 Separate the eggs, placing the whites in a large stainless steel bowl and setting aside the yolks for another use. Let the whites come to room temperature, about 30 minutes.

Delicious with or without whipped cream and berries.

3 Meanwhile, place the confectioners' sugar, sorghum flour, sweet rice flour, and salt in a medium-size mixing bowl and set it aside.

4 When the egg whites have come to room temperature, add the cream of tartar and vanilla and beat with an electric mixer on medium speed until foamy, about 2 minutes. Add the granulated sugar 2 tablespoons at a time and beat on medium-high speed until the sugar dissolves and the whites are stiff and glossy, 6 to 8 minutes. Sprinkle the flour mixture, ¼ cup at a time, over the beaten egg whites and, using a rubber spatula, gently fold it into the whites just until the flour mixture disappears. Spoon the batter into the tube pan. Run a dinner knife through the batter to remove any air pockets. Place the tube pan in the oven.

5 Bake the angel food cake until it is golden brown, 30 to 35 minutes. Remove the tube pan from the oven and turn it upside down. If the pan does not have feet that support the pan upside down, prop it up on 3 custard cups or a wire rack. Let the cake cool in the pan to room temperature, about 1 hour.

6 Remove the cake from the tube pan: If your pan has a removable bottom, run a long sharp knife around the edge of the cake and gently lift the center tube with the cake on it from the side of the pan. Shake the cake loose from the tube and place it on a cake plate to serve. If your pan doesn't have a removable bottom, gently shake the cake loose and tip it out. This cake keeps in a cake saver at room temperature for up to 5 days.

{ TAKE THE CHILL OFF }

It is no myth that room temperature egg whites beat to a greater volume than those straight from the refrigerator. If you don't have time to let your egg whites come to room temperature as specified in step 2, try this shortcut: Place the refrigerated whole eggs in a large bowl and cover them with hot tap water for 5 minutes before separating the whites from the yolks.

EXTRA! EXTRA!

To add a nice faint almond flavor to this angel food cake, use 1½ teaspoons of vanilla extract and ½ teaspoon of pure almond extract instead of the 2 teaspoons of vanilla.

Dairy-Free:

The angel food cake is dairy-free.

An Unbelievably Gluten-Free Meal

WHERE EATEN:

WHEN EATEN:

WHO WAS THERE:

TIPS FOR MAKING AT HOME:

NEW INSPIRATIONS:

Red Velvet Cake with Cream Cheese Frosting

SERVES: 12
PREP: 20 TO 25 MINUTES
BAKE: 21 TO 25 MINUTES

WHEN I WAS TESTING RECIPES FOR MY GLUTEN-FREE cake book, I considered including a red velvet cake but thought, no, gluten-free cooks won't like a recipe that contains red food coloring. Boy, was I proven wrong once I hit the book tour. At each and every stop, once it was time for questions, someone would ask either how to make a red velvet cake using a gluten-free cake mix, or more to the point, why did I omit red velvet? So here it is, a luscious red velvet beginning with a cake mix, adding cocoa for flavor and butter for texture, and the de rigueur cream cheese frosting.

FOR THE RED VELVET CAKE

Vegetable oil spray, for misting the cake pans

Rice flour, for dusting the cake pans

1 package (15 ounces) gluten-free yellow cake mix (see *Extra! Extra!*)

1 package (3.4 ounces) vanilla instant pudding mix

2 tablespoons unsweetened cocoa powder

1 cup water

8 tablespoons (1 stick) unsalted butter, at room temperature

3 large eggs

1 tablespoon pure vanilla extract

3¼ teaspoons (from 1-ounce bottle) red food coloring (see Note)

FOR THE CREAM CHEESE FROSTING

1 package (8 ounces) cream cheese, at room temperature

4 tablespoons (½ stick) unsalted butter, at room temperature

3 cups confectioners' sugar, sifted

1 teaspoon pure vanilla extract

1 Make the red velvet cake: Place a rack in the center of the oven and preheat the oven to 350°F. Mist two 8-inch round cake pans with vegetable oil spray and dust them with rice flour. Shake out the excess rice flour and set the cake pans aside.

2 Place the cake mix, pudding mix, and cocoa in a large mixing bowl and whisk until well combined. Add the water, butter, eggs, vanilla, and food coloring and beat with an electric mixer on low speed until just combined, about 30 seconds. Stop the machine and scrape down the side of the bowl with a rubber spatula. Increase the mixer speed to medium and beat the batter until it is smooth and well combined, 1 to 1½ minutes longer, scraping down the side of the bowl again if needed.

3 Divide the batter evenly between the 2 prepared cake pans, smoothing the tops with the rubber spatula. Place the pans in the oven side by side. Bake the cake layers until the tops spring back when lightly pressed with a finger, 21 to 25 minutes. Transfer the cake pans to wire racks and let the cake layers cool for 15 minutes. Run a knife around the edge of each cake pan and shake the pans gently to loosen the cakes. Invert each layer onto a wire rack, then invert it again onto another rack so that the layers are right side up and let cool for at least 20 minutes longer.

4 Make the cream cheese frosting: Place the cream cheese and butter in a large mixing bowl and beat with an electric mixer on low speed until creamy, about 30 seconds. Stop the machine and add the confectioners' sugar and vanilla a little at a time, beating with the mixer on low speed just to incorporate the sugar. Increase the

Valentines for the Ones You Love

French Baked Pork Chops with Mustard Sauce, page 190

Roasted potatoes and asparagus

Red Velvet Cake with Cream Cheese Frosting

mixer speed to medium and beat the frosting until it is creamy and light, 1 to 2 minutes longer.

5 To frost the cake, place one layer, right side up, on a cake plate or stand. Spread the top of that layer with ¾ cup of frosting, spreading it evenly to the edges. Place the second layer, right side up, on top of the first and, using a long metal spatula, carefully spread a thin layer of frosting around the side of the cake just to seal the crumbs. Do not let the crumbs rub off into the frosting or they will turn the frosting pink. Spread a second thicker layer of frosting around the side of the cake. Spoon the remaining frosting on top of the cake and spread it evenly to the edge, adding a decorative pattern of swirls to the top with the metal spatula or the back of a spoon.

6 For easiest slicing, refrigerate the cake uncovered for 1 hour. To store the cake for longer than 6 hours, place it in a cake saver in the refrigerator. It's best eaten on the day it is baked.

Note: You can buy all-natural red food coloring made by India Tree. It is made from highly concentrated vegetable colors.

EXTRA! EXTRA!

Most gluten-free cake mixes are smaller (15 ounces) than regular cake mixes. (I used Betty Crocker's Gluten Free Yellow Cake Mix for this recipe.) Because of this, the yield is a little smaller and a layer cake needs to be baked in 8-inch pans. These smaller pans make the cake layers taller, making the cake look more impressive when frosted on your cake stand.

Dairy-Free:
Use margarine instead of butter in the cake. And for the frosting, use a dairy-free cream cheese, such as Better Than Cream Cheese, for the cream cheese, use margarine instead of butter, and increase the confectioners' sugar to 4 cups.

Fresh Orange Cupcakes

MAKES: 16 CUPCAKES
PREP: 30 MINUTES
BAKE: 15 TO 18 MINUTES

ORANGE AS A FAVORITE FLAVOR KNOWS NO AGE BOUND-aries and it's one to remember when you need to bake cupcakes for a party. Because many gluten-free folks follow dairy-free diets as well, I intentionally made them dairy-free. Orange juice is the perfect dairy-free liquid, and in the frosting I call for a cream cheese substitute, as well as margarine. Although I am not a big fan of margarine in baking, the orange zest is the flavor present in the frosting and you really don't taste the margarine at all.

FOR THE ORANGE CUPCAKES

1 package (15 ounces) gluten-free yellow
  cake mix

¼ cup granulated sugar

⅔ cup fresh orange juice
  (from 2 large oranges)

½ cup vegetable oil

3 large eggs

1 teaspoon pure vanilla extract

1 teaspoon grated orange zest

FOR THE DAIRY-FREE ORANGE CREAM CHEESE FROSTING

4 ounces dairy-free cream cheese,
  at room temperature (see Notes)

4 tablespoons margarine, at room
  temperature (see Notes)

3 cups confectioners' sugar, sifted

2 teaspoons grated fresh orange zest

1 Make the cupcakes: Place a rack in the center of the oven and preheat the oven to 350°F. Line 16 cupcake

cups with paper liners and set the pans aside.

2 Place the cake mix, granulated sugar, orange juice, oil, eggs, vanilla, and orange zest in a large mixing bowl and beat with an electric mixer on low speed until the ingredients are just combined, about 30 seconds. Stop the machine and scrape down the side of the bowl with a rubber spatula. Increase the mixer speed to medium and beat the batter until it is smooth, 1 to 1½ minutes. Scoop ¼ cup batter into each of the lined cupcake cups and place the pans in the oven side by side.

3 Bake the cupcakes until the tops spring back when lightly pressed with a finger, 15 to 18 minutes. Transfer the pans to wire racks and let the cupcakes cool in the pans for 1 to 2 minutes, then carefully transfer the cupcakes to the racks to cool completely before frosting, about 30 minutes longer.

4 Meanwhile make the dairy-free orange cream cheese frosting:

A favorite with tea—both hot and iced.

Place the dairy-free cream cheese and margarine in a large mixing bowl and beat with an electric mixer on low speed until creamy, about 30 seconds. Stop the machine and add the confectioners' sugar and orange zest a little bit at a time, beating on low speed until the confectioners' sugar is incorporated, about 30 seconds. Increase the mixer speed to medium and beat the frosting until fluffy, 1 to 2 minutes longer.

5 Frost the cupcakes generously with the frosting. As the frosting is soft, place the cupcakes in a cake saver and refrigerate them if not serving them in the next 4 hours. These cupcakes are best eaten on the day they are made.

An Unbelievably Gluten-Free Meal

WHERE EATEN: _____

_____

WHEN EATEN: _____

_____

WHO WAS THERE: _____

_____

_____

TIPS FOR MAKING AT HOME: _____

_____

_____

_____

_____

NEW INSPIRATIONS: _____

_____

_____

_____

Notes: Dairy-free cream cheese substitutes (like Better Than Cream Cheese) come in 8-ounce containers, so use half of a container. And if you don't want to make the frosting dairy-free use 4 ounces of cream cheese and 4 tablespoons (½ stick) of butter instead of the margarine.

EXTRA! EXTRA!

No fresh oranges? Just use orange juice from a carton in the cake and omit the orange zest in the cake and frosting. You will miss the intense orange flavor though, so even if you have just a small orange, grate the zest to use in the frosting.

Dairy-Free:
The orange cupcakes are dairy-free.

Gingerbread Cupcakes with Quick Lemon Buttercream Frosting

MAKES: 16 CUPCAKES
PREP: 40 MINUTES
BAKE: 15 TO 18 MINUTES

YOU REALLY DON'T NEED FROSTING AT ALL ON THESE incredibly moist cupcakes. But you will not regret frosting them with lemon buttercream, for lemon and the spices in the cupcakes are the perfect partners. It's suited to fall but also right for spring bake sales and summer picnics.

FOR THE GINGERBREAD CUPCAKES

1 package (15 ounces) gluten-free yellow cake mix

1 teaspoon ground ginger

1 teaspoon ground cinnamon

½ teaspoon ground nutmeg

¼ teaspoon ground cloves

8 tablespoons (1 stick) unsalted butter, at room temperature

3 large eggs

1 cup orange juice

2 tablespoons molasses

1 teaspoon pure vanilla extract

FOR THE LEMON BUTTERCREAM FROSTING

1 large lemon

4 tablespoons (½ stick) unsalted butter, at room temperature

2 cups confectioners' sugar, sifted

1 Make the gingerbread cupcakes: Place a rack in the center of the oven and preheat the oven to 350°F. Line 16 cupcake cups with paper liners and set the pans aside.

{ *To frost or not to frost— so good either way.* }

2 Place the cake mix, ginger, cinnamon, nutmeg, and cloves in a large mixing bowl and stir to combine the spices with the cake mix. Add the butter, eggs, orange juice, molasses, and vanilla and beat with an electric mixer on low speed until the ingredients are just combined, about 30 seconds. Increase the mixer speed to medium and beat until the batter is smooth, about 1½ minutes. Scoop ¼ cup of batter into each of the lined cupcake cups and place the pans in the oven side by side.

3 Bake the cupcakes until the tops spring back when lightly pressed with a finger, 15 to 18 minutes. Transfer the pans to wire racks, and let the cupcakes cool in the pans

for about 1 minute, then carefully transfer them to the racks to cool completely, about 30 minutes.

4 Make the lemon buttercream frosting: Rinse the lemon and pat it dry with a paper towel. Grate enough of the lemon rind to produce 1 teaspoon of yellow lemon zest. Place this in a medium-size mixing bowl. Cut the lemon in half and squeeze the juice through a fine-mesh sieve to produce 3 to 4 teaspoons of lemon juice, discarding the seeds and pulp. Pour this into the mixing bowl. Place the butter in the bowl along with the confectioners' sugar. Beat with an electric mixer on low speed until just combined, about 30 seconds. Stop the machine and scrape down the side of the bowl with a rubber spatula. Increase the mixer speed to medium-high and beat until creamy, 1 to 2 minutes longer.

5 Frost the cupcakes with the lemon frosting. These cupcakes are best eaten on the day they are made.

An Unbelievably Gluten-Free Meal

WHERE EATEN: _____

_____

_____

WHEN EATEN: _____

_____

_____

WHO WAS THERE: _____

_____

_____

TIPS FOR MAKING AT HOME: _____

_____

_____

_____

_____

NEW INSPIRATIONS: _____

_____

_____

_____

EXTRA! EXTRA!

Want to bake a cake? First, prep the pans: Mist two 8-inch cake pans with vegetable oil spray and dust them with rice flour. Shake out the excess rice flour and set the cake pans aside. Divide the batter between the 2 pans and bake the cake layers at 350°F for 20 to 25 minutes. Let the layers cool, then spread frosting on top of one layer, place the second layer on top, and frost the top of the cake. The sides will be frosting-free.

Dairy-Free:

Use ½ cup of vegetable oil in the cupcake batter instead of the butter. Use margarine instead of the butter in the buttercream frosting.

Cookies and Cream Cheesecake

SERVES: 12 | PREP: 30 MINUTES
BAKE: 45 MINUTES, PLUS 2 HOURS WITH THE OVEN TURNED OFF
COOL: 1 HOUR | CHILL: AT LEAST 4 HOURS

What's not to like about this cheesecake? Nothing! White chocolate is a key ingredient, and it is best to use bar chocolate instead of the white chocolate chips because it melts better. Then there are chocolate sandwich cookies in the crust. Use an entire eight-ounce bag of gluten-free chocolate sandwich cookies—any brand you choose. As with all cheesecakes, this dessert slices best when allowed to chill overnight.

21 gluten-free chocolate sandwich cookies
(from an 8-ounce package)

6 ounces white chocolate

32 ounces (four 8-ounce packages) cream cheese, at room temperature

1 cup granulated sugar

2 tablespoons cornstarch

1 cup sour cream

2 teaspoons pure vanilla extract

4 large eggs

1 Place a rack in the center of the oven and preheat the oven to 350°F. Set aside a 9-inch springform pan.

2 Break 9 of the cookies in half and place them in a food processor. Pulse the cookies until crumbly, about 15 times. You should have 1¼ cups of cookie crumbs. Place the cookie crumbs in the bottom of the springform pan and distribute them evenly with your fingers. The crumbs may thinly cover

the bottom of the pan. Set the pan with the chocolate crumb crust aside.

3 Break the white chocolate into 1-inch pieces and place them in an 8-ounce microwave-safe container. Microwave the chocolate on high power for 20 to 30 seconds, remove it from the microwave, and stir it until the chocolate has melted. If the chocolate has not melted, return the container to the microwave for another 5 to 10 seconds. Set the white chocolate aside to cool.

4 Place the cream cheese and sugar in a large mixing bowl and beat with an electric mixer on low speed until the sugar is incorporated, about 20 seconds. Increase the mixer speed to medium and beat the cream cheese mixture until creamy, about 1½ minutes. Stop the machine and add the cornstarch, sour cream, cooled white chocolate, and the vanilla. Beat on low speed until combined, about 30 seconds. Add the eggs, one at a time, beating on low speed until each is just combined. Set the cheesecake batter aside.

5 Place 11 of the cookies on a cutting board and coarsely chop them. You should have about 1½ cups of chopped cookies. Fold the chopped cookies into the cheesecake batter.

6 Place the springform pan on a baking sheet. Pour the cheesecake batter over the chocolate crumb crust and smooth the top with a rubber spatula. Place the pan in the oven and let the cheesecake bake until it is golden brown around the edges but still a little jiggly in the center, 45 minutes. Turn off the oven, leaving the cheesecake in the oven for 2 hours to set.

7 At the end of the 2 hours, remove the pan from the oven and let the cheesecake cool to room temperature for about 1 hour. Cover the top of the cheesecake pan with plastic wrap and place the pan in the refrigerator for the cheesecake to chill for at least 4 hours, or preferably overnight.

8 To serve, remove the side of the springform pan. Place the cheesecake, still attached to the bottom of the pan, on a serving plate. Divide the remaining chocolate sandwich cookie in half and garnish the center of the cheesecake with the cookie halves. Slice and serve.

EXTRA! EXTRA!

For a classic cheesecake, omit the chocolate sandwich cookies in the crust and filling. Substitute your choice of gluten-free vanilla cookies for the crust; you'll need 1¼ cups of finely chopped cookies. Serve the cheesecake with sliced sweetened strawberries.

Dairy-Free:

It is not possible to make the cheesecake dairy-free.

An Unbelievably Gluten-Free Meal

WHERE EATEN:
_____
_____

WHEN EATEN:
_____
_____

WHO WAS THERE:
_____
_____
_____

TIPS FOR MAKING AT HOME:
_____
_____
_____
_____

NEW INSPIRATIONS:
_____
_____
_____

Homemade Gluten-Free Pie Crust

MAKES: THREE 9-INCH PIE CRUSTS | PREP: 30 MINUTES
CHILL: 2 HOURS | PREBAKE (OPTIONAL; FOLLOW INSTRUCTIONS IN
WHATEVER PIE RECIPE YOU'RE USING): 12 TO 15 MINUTES

MY QUEST TO CREATE AN EASY, FLAWLESS, AND ABOVE all, delicious gluten-free pie crust began in Knoxville, Tennessee. I was there attending a springtime gluten-free fair and after talking about cakes I mentioned to the crowd that I was working on a dinner cookbook and wanted to create the best-ever gluten-free pie crust. An hour later a sweet woman and her husband came up to meet me. She said she had been baking gluten-free pies for twenty years and had mastered the crust recipe. She told me she began with the brand of pie crust mix that came in a green box to which she added her secret ingredient—cream cheese. Her husband gave it his nod of approval. "She's a great cook," he confirmed, with a twinkle in his eye.

Back home, I learned the green box was the Gluten Free Pantry brand of pie crust mix. I baked it following the package directions but thought it needed improvement. So, to reduce overbrowning, I omitted the sugar called for on the package and decided to try the cream cheese trick. I added a little baking powder, cold butter, and cold cream cheese, then eggs, cold water, and a little cider vinegar. Why vinegar? Acids seem to tenderize rice flour, making it less gritty. In the baked crust you don't get a vinegar taste at all; this pie crust tastes buttery and rich. Enjoy, and hats off to you, Knoxville!

2 large eggs, lightly beaten

3 tablespoons very cold water

1 tablespoon cider vinegar

1 package (16 ounces) pie crust mix (see Notes)

¼ teaspoon baking powder

10 tablespoons (1¼ sticks) cold butter (see Notes)

¾ package (6 ounces) cold cream cheese

1 Place the eggs, cold water, and cider vinegar in a small bowl and stir to combine. Place the egg mixture in the refrigerator to chill.

2 Place the pie crust mix and baking powder in a large bowl and stir to combine well.

3 You can either mix the pie dough by hand or use a food processor.

Bowl Method: Remove the butter and cream cheese from the refrigerator. Cut the butter into 10 pieces. Place the butter in the bowl with the pie crust mix. Cut the cream cheese into 10 pieces and place them in the bowl with butter. Using a pastry blender or 2 knives, cut the butter and cream cheese into the pie crust mix until the mixture is the size of small peas. This will take 2 to 3 minutes. Pour the chilled egg mixture into the large mixing bowl. Using a large spoon or your hands, mix until the egg mixture is incorporated into the dough.

Food Processor Method: Pour half of the pie crust mix into a food processor. Remove the butter and cream cheese from the refrigerator. Cut the butter into 10 pieces and place 5 of these on top of the pie crust mix in the food processor. Cut the cream cheese into 10 pieces. Place 5 of these on top of the butter in the food processor. Pour the remaining pie crust mix into the processor and place the remaining pieces of butter and cream cheese on top. Pulse until the mixture is well incorporated and looks like small peas, 20 to 22 times. Remove the lid and pour half of the pie crust mixture into the large mixing bowl. Pour half of the egg mixture over the crust mixture into the food processor. Return the rest of the crust mixture to the food processor and pour the remaining egg mixture on top. Pulse until all is well incorporated, about 15 times. Place the dough in a large bowl.

4 Tear off three 12-inch pieces of plastic wrap and place them on the counter. Using your hands, divide the dough into 3 equal balls. Place 1 ball of dough on each sheet of plastic wrap. Press the balls of dough into 6-inch disks and wrap the disks in the plastic wrap. Refrigerate the dough for at least 2 hours, or up to 3 days. Or wrap the individual disks in freezer paper, place them in freezer bags, and freeze for up to 6 months. Allow the dough to thaw in the refrigerator overnight or on a kitchen counter for 1 hour.

5 To roll out the dough, place a 12-inch piece of parchment paper on a work surface. Unwrap a refrigerated disk, place it on the parchment paper, and let it come to room temperature, about 10 minutes. Using your hands and working from the center, press down on the dough, pushing to the edge to form a 12-inch circle for a 9- to 10-inch pie (see Notes).

Or, to use a rolling pin, place a second piece of parchment paper on top of the dough. Roll out the disk from the center to the edge to form a 12-inch circle.

6 To fit the dough into the pie pan, if there is a top piece of parchment paper, carefully peel it off the dough. Trim the edges of the dough, if necessary. Using the remaining parchment, carefully flip the dough onto the pie pan, centering it, then peel off the paper. Using your fingers, mold the dough into the pie pan. (If the dough is too soft to mold, slide it in the pie pan and place it in the refrigerator to chill before for 5 to 10 minutes.) Press the dough to the edge of the pie pan. Using a knife, trim the crust so that it reaches about ¼ inch above the edge of the pan and then gently fold the edge of dough over and decoratively crimp or press it together with a fork to seal it.

7 To prebake the crust (bake it before filling) preheat the oven to 425°F oven.

8 Using a fork, prick the bottom and side of the crust. Bake the crust until light golden, 12 to

15 minutes. Let the crust cool, then proceed with the recipe.

Notes: I started with a Gluten Free Pantry pie crust mix for this recipe. I like the flavor of lightly salted butter in the crust. If you use unsalted butter, add ¼ teaspoon of salt.

An alternative and easy method for shaping the pie crust is to place the disk of dough in a pie pan and press the dough out to the edge of the pan with your fingers.

EXTRA! EXTRA!

You can use this crust for any pie recipe calling for a 9- to 10-inch pie crust—it's perfect with fruit pies, chocolate pies, even chicken potpie and pizza turnovers.

Dairy-Free:

Use margarine instead of the butter and use a dairy-free cream cheese, such as Tofutti's Better Than Cream Cheese, instead of the cream cheese. Make sure both are cold.

{ TO BAKE A PIE WITH A TOP CRUST }

When making a two-crust pie such as the Gluten-Free Chicken Potpie on page 162 or fruit pies like apple or peach, you do not prebake the bottom crust. Roll out and fit one circle of dough in a 9- to 10-inch pie pan as described in Steps 5 and 6 of the Homemade Gluten-Free Pie Crust recipe. Fill the crust with fruit or whatever the recipe directs. Roll out a second disk of dough to form a circle as you did for the bottom crust. Gently flip the top crust on top of the pie, making sure to center it. Trim the edge of the top crust so that it extends about ¼ inch beyond the rim of the pie pan. Fold the edge of the top crust under the edge of the bottom crust and press them together attractively. Cut 3 slits in the top crust to vent the pie. Bake the pie in a 425°F oven for 40 to 45 minutes, or as the recipe directs. For the last 20 minutes of baking, loosely cover the pie with aluminum foil so the crust will not overbrown. Or cover the pie with a crust cover, which will protect the outside crust from becoming too brown.

Blueberry Glacé Pie

SERVES: 8
PREP: 25 TO 30 MINUTES
COOL: 15 MINUTES | CHILL: 4 HOURS

I LOVED ADAPTING THIS BLUEBERRY LOVERS' PIE TO A GLUTEN-free pie crust. Cornstarch thickens the cooked blueberry portion of the pie, which is poured on top of fresh blueberries and cream cheese in the pie crust. The recipe comes from Martha Bowden's family recipe files, and it is a dandy for summertime.

1 gluten-free pie crust, homemade (9-inches; page 318) or store-bought, thawed if frozen

2 quarts (4 cups) fresh blueberries, rinsed and drained

1 cup water

1 cup granulated sugar

3 tablespoons cornstarch

¼ package (2 ounces) cream cheese, at room temperature

Sweetened Whipped Cream (page 359), for serving

1 Prebake the pie crust following the directions in steps 7 and 8 on page 320 and set it aside to cool.

2 Place 1 cup of the blueberries and ⅔ cup of the water in a medium-size saucepan over medium-high heat. Bring to a boil, stirring, then reduce the heat to low and let simmer until the berries begin to burst, about 3 minutes.

3 Place the sugar and cornstarch in a small bowl and stir to combine. Add the remaining ⅓ cup of water

{ *Save this pie for blueberry season— it's got just the right amount of cooked and uncooked berries.* }

and mix well until smooth. Slowly pour the sugar mixture into the hot berries, stirring gently. Continue to stir, letting the mixture come to a slow boil, 3 to 4 minutes. Stir the berry mixture until it thickens, 1 to 2 minutes. Remove the pan from the heat and let the berries cool for about 15 minutes.

4 Spread the cream cheese in the bottom of the cooled pie crust. Scatter the remaining 3 cups of fresh blueberries evenly over the cream cheese. Slowly ladle the warm blueberries and sauce over the fresh blueberries. Refrigerate the blueberry pie, uncovered, until it is cold, at least 4 hours. To serve, top the pie with Sweetened

Whipped Cream (page 359), slice it, and serve. The pie will keep in the refrigerator, covered with plastic wrap or aluminum foil, for up to 2 days.

EXTRA! EXTRA!

To make a Strawberry Glacé Pie, substitute 2 quarts (4 cups) of fresh strawberries, rinsed, drained, and sliced for the blueberries.

Dairy-Free:
Start with a dairy-free pie crust (see page 321). Substitute Tofutti's Better Than Cream Cheese for the cream cheese in the filling and use a nondairy whipped topping as a garnish.

Easy Apple Tart

SERVES: 8
PREP: 30 MINUTES
BAKE: 35 TO 40 MINUTES

THIS MAY BE THE BEST GLUTEN-FREE APPLE TART YOU have ever tasted. And it is also the simplest apple tart you will ever have baked. More a French tart than a deep-dish American pie, you simply layer thin slices of the best apples you have on hand in a pie crust, season them with sugar and a little cinnamon, and bake the tart in a hot oven. The heat of the oven causes the moisture of the apples to evaporate, cooking the tart more quickly. With a less watery filling, you don't need to thicken with flour, and I think you arrive at a tart with a more pronounced and condensed apple flavor. Plus it's dead simple, which means you can bake this apple tart often in the fall when the good apples are in season.

3 large apples (see *Extra! Extra!*), rinsed, cored, peeled, and thinly sliced

1 teaspoon lemon juice

Dough for 1 gluten-free pie crust, homemade (9-inches; page 318) or store-bought, thawed if frozen

¼ cup plus 2 tablespoons apricot preserves

½ cup granulated sugar

½ teaspoon ground cinnamon

2 tablespoons (¼ stick) butter, cold

Vanilla ice cream, for serving

1 Place a rack in the center of the oven and preheat the oven to 425°F.

2 Toss the apple slices with the lemon juice to prevent browning and set the apples aside.

3 Press the dough into a 9- to 10-inch tart or quiche pan that is 1¼ inches deep. Using a knife, trim the crust so that it reaches about ¼ inch above the edge of the pan and then gently fold the edge of dough under and decoratively crimp or press it together with a fork to seal it. Using a fork, gently poke holes in the crust. Place the crust in the oven to prebake until light golden, 8 to 10 minutes. Remove the crust from the oven and spread the ¼ cup of apricot preserves over the bottom of the crust.

4 Combine the sugar and cinnamon in a small bowl and set the cinnamon sugar aside.

5 Arrange half of the apple slices in a circular pattern, in the bottom of the crust, overlapping them just a bit. Sprinkle ¼ cup of the cinnamon sugar over the apples. Arrange the remaining apples in a second layer, overlapping them in a circular pattern. Sprinkle them with the remaining cinnamon sugar. Dot with the butter and place the tart pan in the oven.

6 Bake the tart until the crust is well browned and the apples are tender, 35 to 40 minutes. Remove the tart pan from the oven. Place the remaining 2 tablespoons of apricot preserves in a microwave-safe container and heat it in a microwave oven on low heat for 10 seconds. Brush the preserves over the cooling tart. Let the tart cool 45 minutes, then slice it and serve with vanilla ice cream.

EXTRA! EXTRA!

The best pie apples are Jonathan, Jonagold, pippin, Braeburn, Fuji, Gala, Pink Lady, Honeycrisp, and winesap. They are crisp and bold in flavor.

Dairy-Free:

Layer the apples in a dairy-free pie crust (see page 321) and dot the top of the tart with margarine instead of butter.

Classic Pumpkin Pie

SERVES: 8

PREP: 45 MINUTES

BAKE: 55 MINUTES | COOL: 2 HOURS

I TESTED THIS RECIPE IN THE HEAT OF SUMMER AND ATE chilled slices of it with whipped cream. It was so delicious, and much more appreciated than after a heavy Thanksgiving meal! So I urge you to bake this pie all year long because canned pumpkin is always on the store shelves, and you may agree that the pie is seasonless. You must prebake the cookielike crust for ten minutes because the traditional pumpkin and spice filling is heavy and moist, and by prebaking you give the crust a head start in the race to doneness.

Dough for 1 gluten-free pie crust, homemade (9-inches; page 318) or store-bought, thawed if frozen

1 can (15 ounces) 100% pure pumpkin

1 cup lightly packed light brown sugar

1 teaspoon ground cinnamon

½ teaspoon ground ginger

¼ teaspoon salt

¼ teaspoon ground nutmeg

⅛ teaspoon ground cloves

3 large eggs

1 cup heavy (whipping) cream

¼ cup whole milk

FOR GARNISH

Pie crust leaves (optional; see *Extra! Extra!*)

Sweetened Whipped Cream (page 359), for serving

1 Place a rack in the center of the oven and preheat the oven to 375°F.

2 Roll out the pie dough and fit it into a 9-inch pie pan following the instructions in steps 5 and 6 on page 320. Prick the bottom and sides

An Unbelievably Gluten-Free Meal

WHERE EATEN:

_____

_____

WHEN EATEN:

_____

_____

WHO WAS THERE:

_____

_____

_____

TIPS FOR MAKING AT HOME:

_____

_____

_____

_____

NEW INSPIRATIONS:

_____

_____

_____

_____

of the crust with a fork. Cover the edge of the crust with strips of aluminum foil and place the pie crust in the oven. Bake the crust until lightly browned, 10 to 12 minutes. Allow the crust to cool. Leave the oven on.

3 Place the pumpkin, brown sugar, cinnamon, ginger, salt, nutmeg, and cloves in a large mixing bowl and stir to combine. Add the eggs, cream, and milk and mix well with a wooden spoon until smooth. Pour the filling into the crust, cover the edges of the crust with aluminum foil, and place the pie pan in the oven.

4 Bake the pie for 45 minutes, then remove the foil covering the edge of the crust. Continue to bake the pie until a sharp knife inserted in the center comes out clean, about 10 minutes longer. Transfer the pie pan to a wire rack and let the pie cool to room temperature, up to 2 hours. If you need to store the pie longer, once it has cooled, cover it with plastic wrap or aluminum foil and refrigerate it

for up to 3 days. Serve the pumpkin pie topped with the decorative crust leaves, if desired, and with whipped cream.

If you are using a homemade pie crust and have pie crust scraps from rolling out a 9-inch crust, you can make leaves to decorate the baked pie. While the pie is baking, gather the scraps of dough together, roll them into a small ball, and refrigerate them for 30 minutes. Then roll out the dough between 2 pieces of waxed paper to a ⅛-inch thickness. Work quickly to keep the dough as cold as possible. Using small leaf-shaped cookie cutters, cut the dough into leaf shapes and transfer these to a baking sheet. Leave the oven on after the pie has baked and bake the leaves until lightly browned, 15 to 17 minutes. Let the leaves cool on the baking sheet and then arrange them on top of the pie to decorate it.

Dairy-Free:
Start with a dairy-free pie crust (see page 321) and use 1¼ cups of coconut milk instead of the heavy cream and whole milk. The texture of the pumpkin filling will not be as creamy or the flavor as rich.

Our Favorite Pecan Pie

SERVES: 8 TO 10
PREP: 10 MINUTES
BAKE: 55 TO 58 MINUTES | COOL: 1 HOUR

PECAN PIE IS A WORK OF ART IN THE MOUTH—SWEET, salty, crunchy, gooey. The star of the pie is the pecans, supported by the dark corn syrup and finally the crust. The homemade gluten-free pie crust is made tender with cream cheese. But you can just as easily pile the filling into a store-bought gluten-free crust. When pecans are in season in late fall in Texas and Georgia and throughout the South, this is a great way to make use of the harvest.

Dough for 1 gluten-free pie crust, homemade (9-inches; page 318) or store-bought, thawed if frozen (see Note)

3 large eggs

1 cup granulated sugar

1 cup dark corn syrup

2 teaspoons pure vanilla extract

3 tablespoons butter, melted and cooled

1½ cups chopped pecans

1 Place a rack in the center of the oven and preheat the oven to 350°F.

2 Roll out and fit the homemade pie dough into a 9-inch pie pan following the instructions in steps 5 and 6 on page 320 or place a thawed 9-inch pie crust in an aluminum foil pan. Place the pie pan on a baking sheet. You do not need to prebake the crust.

{ *Rich and delicious, a thin slice should do it, but it's hard to say no to seconds.* }

3 Place the eggs in a large mixing bowl and whisk to combine. Add the sugar and whisk until well combined. Add the corn syrup, vanilla, and butter and stir until combined and smooth. Fold in the pecans. Pour the batter into the pie crust. The crust will be quite full; don't worry as the pie will bake up but not over the side of the crust.

4 Place the pie pan in the oven and bake the pie until the pecans are well browned and the center of the pie jiggles a little when you shake the pan, 55 to 58 minutes. Transfer the pie pan to a wire rack and let the pie cool for 1 hour before slicing. Store the pecan pie, covered with plastic wrap or aluminum foil, at room temperature for up to 2 days.

Note: Read the label when selecting a frozen gluten-free crust. Look for the first ingredient, and if that ingredient is brown rice you will have a more nutritious crust with a hearty taste and texture that will go well with this hearty pecan filling.

EXTRA! EXTRA!

A trick to making even a frozen pie crust look homemade is to slip the frozen pie out of the aluminum pan and into your favorite 9-inch pie pan. When the crust softens as it thaws, you can use your fingers to crimp the edges for a homemade look.

Dairy-Free:

Start with a dairy-free pie crust (see page 321) and substitute margarine for the butter in the pecan filling.

Tennessee Chess Pie

SERVES: 8
PREP: 20 MINUTES
BAKE: 35 TO 40 MINUTES

THIS IS THE PIE MY SON BEGS ME TO BAKE. IT IS NATIVE to the South and a family favorite at our house. The natural thickener is eggs plus a little cornmeal. Chess pie is one of the best to serve during summertime, for picnics and potlucks, and for bake sales. If you feel the need to embellish the pie add a little coconut for a coconut chess or lemon for lemon chess pie. It's that easy.

Dough for 1 gluten-free pie crust, homemade (9-inches; page 318) or store-bought, thawed if frozen

1 cup granulated sugar

4 tablespoons (½ stick) butter, at room temperature

3 large eggs

3 tablespoons buttermilk

1 tablespoon yellow or white cornmeal

¼ teaspoon salt

½ teaspoon pure vanilla extract

1 Place a rack in the center of the oven and preheat the oven to 400°F.

2 Roll out and fit the homemade pie dough into a 9-inch pie pan following the instructions in steps 5 and 6 on page 320 or place a thawed 9-inch pie crust in an aluminum foil pan. Place the pan on a baking sheet. You do not need to prebake the crust.

3 Place the sugar and butter in a large bowl and beat with an

July 4 Neighborhood Potluck—What to Bring Suggestions

Real Deal Gluten-Free Fried Chicken, page 145

Tuna and White Bean Salad, page 259

Sesame Noodle Salad, page 264

Tennessee Chess Pie

electric mixer on medium-high speed until creamy, 1 minute. Add the eggs, one at a time, beating until each is incorporated, 45 seconds. Add the buttermilk, cornmeal, salt, and vanilla and beat on low speed until just combined, 30 seconds. Pour the filling into the crust. Reduce the oven temperature to 350°F and place the pie in the oven.

4 Bake the pie until the filling has just set, 35 to 40 minutes. Tent the pie with aluminum foil after the first 15 minutes to prevent the crust from overbrowning. Transfer the pie pan to a wire rack and let the pie rest at least 1 hour before slicing. Store the Tennessee Chess Pie, covered with plastic wrap or aluminum foil, at room temperature for up to 3 days.

EXTRA! EXTRA!

For a coconut chess pie use coconut extract instead of vanilla extract and fold ½ cup of shredded coconut into the filling before pouring it into the crust. Or, for a lemon chess pie, use 1 tablespoon of fresh lemon juice, reduce the buttermilk to 2 tablespoons, and fold in 1 teaspoon of grated lemon zest.

Dairy-Free:

Use margarine instead of the butter. Use 2 tablespoons of unsweetened coconut milk and 1 tablespoon of distilled white vinegar or cider vinegar instead of the buttermilk. And, use a dairy-free pie crust (see page 321).

Little Fudge Tarts

MAKES: 16 TO 18 TARTS
PREP: 45 MINUTES
BAKE: 16 TO 18 MINUTES

NO NEED FOR FANCY TART PANS OR ANY SPECIAL OCCASION to bake these chocolate tarts. They are an easy and everyday gluten-free dessert. You just press the dough into muffin pans and fill them with the fudge batter. The tarts are very easy to tote to parties and to sell at bake sales. A popular dessert for kids, I like the tarts both with and without nuts.

Dough for 1 gluten-free pie crust (9-inches; page 318), chilled

2 squares (1 ounce each) unsweetened chocolate

8 tablespoons (1 stick) unsalted butter, at room temperature

1 cup granulated sugar

2 large eggs

2 tablespoons cornstarch

1 teaspoon pure vanilla extract

¼ teaspoon salt

⅓ cup finely chopped pecans or walnuts (optional)

Ice cream or Sweetened Whipped Cream (page 359), for serving (optional)

1 Tear off a 12-inch piece of parchment paper and place it on a work surface. Place the pie crust dough in the center of the parchment paper. Using the heels of your hands and your fingers, press the dough out into a circle, 11 to 12 inches in diameter and ⅛ to ¼ inch thick. Work quickly to keep the dough as cold as possible. Using a 2½-inch biscuit cutter, cut out rounds and place each in a muffin cup. Press the dough up the side of each cup. The dough should come about halfway up the side of each cup. Gather the

scraps together and, again using your fingers, press the dough into a circle, cut out rounds, and press them in the muffin cups. You should have enough dough for 16 to 18 muffin cups. Set the muffin pans aside.

2 Place the chocolate in a small saucepan over low heat and cook, stirring, until melted, about 5 minutes. Remove the pan from the heat.

3 Place the butter and sugar in a large mixing bowl and beat with an electric mixer on medium-high speed until creamy, about 2 minutes. Add the melted chocolate and beat well. Add the eggs, cornstarch, vanilla, and salt and beat on medium speed until smooth, about 1 minute. The batter will be thick. Spoon about 2 generous tablespoons of batter into each tart, filling it quite full. If desired, scatter the chopped nuts over the tops of the filled tarts.

4 Place the muffin pans in the oven. Bake the tarts until the filling is set around the edge and the crusts are lightly brown, 16 to 18 minutes. The filling will rise above the tart crusts and it will fall slightly as the tarts cool. Transfer the pans to wire racks and let the tarts cool in the pans for about 10 minutes. Run a sharp knife around the edge of each tart. Carefully lift each tart out of the cup to the wire rack.

5 Serve the tarts, warm or cooled to your liking with ice cream or

An Unbelievably Gluten-Free Meal

WHERE EATEN:

_____

_____

WHEN EATEN:

_____

_____

WHO WAS THERE:

_____

_____

_____

TIPS FOR MAKING AT HOME:

_____

_____

_____

_____

NEW INSPIRATIONS:

_____

_____

_____

whipped cream or just as is. Store the Little Fudge Tarts in a cake saver or covered with plastic wrap at room temperature for up to 4 days.

EXTRA! EXTRA!

You can make savory tarts by baking just the crusts and then filling them with chicken salad. Prick the bottom of the tart crusts and bake them at 425°F for 12 to 15 minutes.

Dairy-Free:

Start with a dairy-free pie crust (see page 321) and substitute margarine for butter in the filling.

Pie in the Sky

Thinking a whole pie? Press the pie crust into a 9-inch pie pan. Prick the bottom with a fork. Spoon the chocolate filling into the pie crust and bake the pie at 325°F until the filling rises above the crust and the crust is golden brown, 25 to 30 minutes. Let the pie cool for about 1 hour before slicing.

Old-Fashioned Peach and Blueberry Cobbler

SERVES: 8

PREP: 40 MINUTES

BAKE: 35 TO 40 MINUTES | COOL: 30 MINUTES

ANY COMBINATION OF FRUIT CAN BE TURNED INTO A cobbler with just one gluten-free pie crust and a two-quart baking dish. You place part of the pie crust in the bottom of the baking dish, toss the fruit with sugar and cornstarch to thicken the juices, and then scatter pieces of any remaining crust across the top. It's easy, fresh, and perfect for the pie lovers in your house.

5 to 6 medium-size ripe peaches

1 cup fresh blueberries, rinsed and drained

¾ to 1 cup granulated sugar, plus
   1 tablespoon sugar for sprinkling
   over the cobbler

2 tablespoons cornstarch

¼ teaspoon ground cinnamon

Dough for 1 gluten-free pie crust
   (9-inches; page 318)

Vanilla ice cream, for serving

1 Rinse, peel, and pit the peaches, then cut them in ¼-inch slices and place them in a medium-size bowl. Add the blueberries and set the fruit aside.

2 Place ¾ to 1 cup of sugar, depending how sweet you like your cobbler, and the cornstarch and cinnamon in a small bowl. Stir to combine and then stir the sugar mixture into the peaches and blueberries. Set the fruit aside.

3 Place a rack in the center of the oven and preheat the oven to 425°F.

4 Pinch off about ⅓ cup of the pie crust dough, wrap it in plastic wrap, and set it aside in the refrigerator. Using your fingers, press the remaining pie crust into a 2-quart baking dish. Press the dough over the bottom and as far up the sides as you can. The crust will be ⅛ to ¼ inch thick. Cover the baking dish with aluminum foil, pressing it into the crust, and place the baking dish in the oven to prebake the crust for 8 to 10 minutes.

5 Remove the baking dish from the oven but leave the oven on. Pour the reserved fruit into the hot crust. Set the baking dish aside.

6 Remove the reserved piece of pie crust dough from the fridge and place it between 2 pieces of waxed paper. Using your hands or a rolling pin, press the dough to a ⅛-inch thickness. Carefully peel off the top layer of waxed paper and use a small cookie cutter or the top of a small juice glass to cut out pieces of dough. Scatter the dough pieces over the fruit and sprinkle the remaining tablespoon sugar over the top. Place the baking dish back in the oven.

7 Bake the cobbler until the fruit bubbles and the crust is lightly browned, 35 to 40 minutes. Remove the baking dish from the oven and let the cobbler cool for about 30 minutes, so the juices can thicken. Serve the cobbler warm with vanilla ice cream. Store the cobbler, covered, in the refrigerator for up to 4 days. (You can reheat individual portions by spooning them into microwave-safe serving bowls and heating them in the microwave oven on high power for 10 to 15 seconds.)

EXTRA! EXTRA!

Other great combinations of fruit for this cobbler are peaches and raspberries or blackberries and blueberries. If using all berries, you'll need 2½ cups.

Dairy-Free:

This cobbler is dairy-free if you use a dairy-free pie crust (see page 321).

Blackberry and Raspberry Cobbler

SERVES: 8
PREP: 30 MINUTES
BAKE: 35 TO 40 MINUTES | COOL: 20 MINUTES

IT IS POSSIBLE TO MAKE ALL SORTS OF GLUTEN-FREE cobblers as long as the pie crust is gluten-free and you use cornstarch for thickening. If you like a cobbler with juices that have a more natural juicy consistency, use two tablespoons of cornstarch, but if you prefer a firmer cobbler, go with three tablespoons cornstarch. Suit yourself!

2 tablespoons (¼ stick) cold butter, cut into ½-inch pieces, plus 1 tablespoon butter, at room temperature, for greasing the baking pan

3 cups (24 ounces) fresh blackberries

3 cups (24 ounces) fresh raspberries

1⅓ cups granulated sugar, plus 1 tablespoon sugar for sprinkling over the cobbler

2 to 3 tablespoons cornstarch

Dough for 1 gluten-free pie crust (9-inches; page 318), cold

Vanilla ice cream, for serving

1 Place a rack in the center of the oven and preheat the oven to 425°F. Rub the 1 tablespoon of soft butter in the bottom of a 13 by 9-inch glass baking dish. Set the dish aside.

2 Rinse, drain, and pat the berries dry. Place them in the prepared baking dish. Combine the 1⅓ cups of sugar and the cornstarch in a small bowl and sprinkle the mixture over the fruit. Toss to coat the fruit with the sugar. Dot the top of the fruit with the 2 tablespoons of butter. Set the dish aside.

3 Place the cold pie crust dough on a 14-inch piece of waxed paper. If the crust is already rolled out, slice it into ¾-inch-wide strips. If the dough has not been rolled out, using the heel of your hand, press the dough out to form a 12 by 9-inch rectangle. Transfer the waxed paper to a baking sheet and place it in the refrigerator to chill for about 15 minutes. Remove the dough from the refrigerator and flip it off the baking sheet onto a work surface, peeling the paper off the dough. Using a sharp knife, slice the dough into ¾-inch strips.

4 To make a lattice crust for the cobbler, gently pick up the dough strips (they're fragile), arranging half of them in a diagonal pattern over the fruit, ½ inch apart. Piece the strips together if needed to make longer strips. Arrange the remaining strips, in a diagonal pattern going the other direction, piecing strips together if needed. Using your fingertips, seal the ends of the strips at the point where they meet the bottom crust and press down gently to make sure they

adhere. Sprinkle the remaining tablespoon of sugar over the crust and place the baking pan in the oven.

5 Bake the cobbler until the berries bubble and the crust is golden brown, 35 to 40 minutes. Remove the dish from the oven and let the cobbler cool and set for about 20 minutes. Serve the cobbler warm with vanilla ice cream. Store the cobbler, covered, in the refrigerator for up to 4 days. You can reheat individual portions by spooning them into microwave-safe serving bowls and heating these in the microwave oven on high power for 10 to 15 seconds.

EXTRA! EXTRA!

Cobblers are a great way to feed a crowd. Make 2 cobblers and let both cool in the pan for about 1 hour, then serve.

Dairy-Free:
Start with a dairy-free pie crust (see page 321) and use margarine instead of butter in the filling and this cobbler is dairy-free.

Cinnamon Plum Crostata

SERVES: 6 TO 8
PREP: 1 HOUR
BAKE: 22 TO 25 MINUTES

SUMMER IS *CROSTATA* SEASON. THAT'S WHEN YOU CAN PILE whatever fruit is in season into a free-form pie crust on a baking sheet, bake it, then serve it with ice cream. I've made *crostatas* out of plums, peaches, blueberries, blackberries—you name it. Until this book I had not baked a gluten-free *crostata*. But once I got the pie crust perfected, I gave it a try, and it worked well in this version with plums and cinnamon. For best flavor, choose the black plums of late summer. Slice the *crostata* into sloppy wedges and serve it in shallow bowls with vanilla ice cream or whipped cream.

Dough for 1 gluten-free pie crust, homemade (9-inches; page 318), cold

5 to 6 large black plums

½ to ⅔ cup granulated sugar, plus 1 tablespoon sugar for sprinkling over the crostata

¼ teaspoon ground cinnamon

1 egg white, slightly beaten

1 tablespoon sugar

Ice cream or Sweetened Whipped Cream (page 359), for serving

1 Remove the pie crust dough from the refrigerator or freezer while preparing the plums. Place a rack in the center of the oven and preheat the oven to 425°F.

2 Rinse, pit, and slice the plums into 6 wedges each. Place the plums in a medium-size bowl and set aside. Place ½ to ⅔ cup of sugar, depending on how sweet you want the plums to be, and the cinnamon in a

small bowl and stir to combine. Set the cinnamon sugar aside.

3 Place a 16-inch piece of parchment paper on a baking sheet. Place the pie crust dough in the center of the parchment paper. Using the heels of your hands and your fingers, press the dough out into an 11- to 12-inch circle. Sprinkle half of the cinnamon-sugar mixture over the center of the pie crust, leaving a 1½-inch border. Attractively arrange the plum wedges on top of the sugar, leaving the border of the crust bare. Sprinkle the remaining cinnamon sugar on top of the plums.

4 Carefully pull the edges of the parchment paper up to lift the dough border over the fruit, pressing the dough with your fingers to form creases and seal the fruit in. The fruit in the center of the *crostata* remains uncovered by crust. Repair any tears by patching the dough with your fingers. Using a pastry brush, brush the egg white over the border edge of the crust. Sprinkle the border with the remaining

tablespoon of sugar. Place the baking sheet in the oven.

5 Bake the *crostata* until the crust is golden brown and the fruit and sugar are bubbling, 22 to 25 minutes. Tent the *crostata* with aluminum foil after 16 to 18 minutes to prevent it from overbrowning. Let the *crostata* cool for about 15 minutes, then slice it like a pizza and serve it in shallow bowls with vanilla or cinnamon ice cream, or whipped cream. It's best to eat the *crostata* on the day it's baked.

EXTRA! EXTRA!

For a multicolored *crostata,* use half plums and half peaches. Just before baking sprinkle a handful of fresh raspberries over the plums and peaches for a bright red pop of color.

Dairy-Free:

If you use a dairy-free pie crust (see page 321) and serve it without ice cream, this *crostata* is dairy-free.

Pear and Cranberry Crostata

SERVES: 6 TO 8

PREP: 1 HOUR

BAKE: 22 TO 25 MINUTES

L OOKING FOR AN UNUSUAL DESSERT TO BRING TO A FALL or winter dinner party? Something out of the ordinary for a family holiday dinner? Turn the gluten-free pie crust dough into a *crostata,* filling it with seasonal pears and a handful of fresh cranberries. Once baked the pears offer sweetness and the cranberries tang, and all you need to pull this delightful pastry together is a scoop of ice cream—try vanilla, dulce de leche, honey, or lemon.

Dough for 1 gluten-free pie crust, homemade (9-inches; page 318), cold

4 to 5 large pears

⅔ to ¾ cup granulated sugar, plus 1 tablespoon granulated sugar for sprinkling over the crostata

¼ teaspoon ground cinnamon

1 cup fresh cranberries

1 egg white, slightly beaten

Ice cream, for serving

1 Remove the pie crust dough from the refrigerator or freezer while preparing the fruit. Place a rack in the center of the oven and preheat the oven to 425°F.

2 Rinse, peel, core, and slice each pear into 8 to 10 slices. Place the pears in a medium-size bowl and set aside. Place ⅔ to ¾ cup of the sugar, depending on how sweet you want the fruit to be, and the cinnamon in a small bowl. Set the cinnamon sugar aside.

3 Place a 16-inch piece of parchment paper on a baking sheet. Place the pie crust dough in the center of the parchment paper. Using the heels of your hands and your fingers, press the dough out into an 11- to 12-inch circle. Sprinkle half of the cinnamon-sugar mixture in the center of the pie crust, leaving a 1½-inch border. Attractively arrange the pear slices on top of the sugar, leaving the border of crust bare. Sprinkle the cranberries on top of the pears. Sprinkle the remaining cinnamon sugar on top of the fruit.

4 Carefully pull the edges of the parchment paper up to lift the dough border over the fruit, pressing the dough with your fingers to form creases and seal the fruit in. The fruit in the center of the *crostata* remains uncovered by crust. Repair any tears by patching the dough with your fingers. Using a pastry brush, brush the egg white over the border edge of the crust. Sprinkle the border with the remaining 1 tablespoon of sugar. Place the baking sheet in the oven.

5 Bake the *crostata* until the crust is golden brown and the fruit and sugar are bubbling, 22 to 25 minutes. Tent the *crostata* with aluminum foil after 16 to 18 minutes to prevent it from overbrowning. Let the *crostata* cool for about 15 minutes, then slice it like a pizza and serve it in shallow bowls with ice cream. It's best to eat the *crostata* on the day it's baked.

EXTRA! EXTRA!

Not a fan of cranberries? Omit them, using ⅔ cup of sugar and adding ¼ cup of raisins instead.

Dairy-Free:
Use a dairy-free pie crust (see page 321) and serve without ice cream and this *crostata* is dairy-free.

Fried Apple Pies

MAKES: ABOUT 15 APPLE PIES
PREP: 1 HOUR, 15 MINUTES
COOK: 1 TO 2 MINUTES

WHEN I WAS IN COLLEGE I HAD A FRIEND WHO RECEIVED a box of fried apple and peach pies every other week as a care package from home. I would try to time when the shipment came in and hope that Helen would share one. To me, fried pies are an incredible delicacy because I know the work involved in making the pastry, rolling and cutting it, cooking down the fruit filling, then frying the pies. It is important to use dried fruit in these pies because the flavor is concentrated and you don't have all the liquid you would with fresh fruit. Liquid would make the pies soggy and not crisp. For the best-ever gluten-free fried pies, use the gluten-free pie crust recipe on page 318 rather than store-bought frozen pastry. My cream cheese pastry holds up well to frying.

1 cup dried apples

1 cup water

¼ cup granulated sugar

¼ teaspoon ground cinnamon

Dough for 1 gluten-free pie crust, homemade (9-inches; page 318), chilled

About 1½ cups vegetable oil, for frying

Confectioners' sugar, for dusting the pies

1 Place the dried apples in a medium-size saucepan and add the water, sugar, and cinnamon. Bring the water to a boil over medium heat, then reduce the heat to medium-low and let simmer until most of the liquid has evaporated, 35 to 40 minutes. If you want your apples to have a pureelike consistency without

chunks, strain them through a wire mesh sieve. Set the apple mixture aside.

2 Remove the pie crust dough from the refrigerator. Pinch off tablespoon-size pieces of dough and using your fingers, press them into 3-inch circles. You will get about 15 circles from 1 disk of pie crust dough. Spoon about 1 teaspoon of filling into the center of each dough circle and fold the circle in half to make a half moon shape. Press the edges together and seal them well by pressing down on them with a fork. Repeat the process until you have used all of the dough and all of the filling. Set the little pies aside.

3 Pour the oil to a depth of at least ½ inch into a deep heavy frying pan and heat over medium-high heat until the oil reaches a temperature of 365° to 375°F on a candy thermometer. Slide a few apple pies into the oil, being careful not to overcrowd the pan. Cook the pies until browned on both sides, about 1 minute per side, using a slotted spoon to turn them over in

the oil. Transfer the pies from the oil to paper towels to drain. Repeat with the remaining apple pies.

4 Dust the apple pies with confectioners' sugar and serve warm. Store the Fried Apple Pies in an airtight container at room temperature for up to 4 days.

EXTRA! EXTRA!

If you want to make fried pies from the entire recipe of Homemade Gluten-Free Pie Crust (page 318), the 3 crusts will yield about 45 pies. You will need to triple the recipe for the filling. And should you prefer peach pies, substitute dried peaches for the apples.

Dairy-Free:

Use a dairy-free pie crust (see page 321) and the Fried Apple Pies are dairy-free.

Gluten-Free Saucepan Brownies

MAKES: 16 SMALL OR 8 LARGE BROWNIES
PREP: 10 MINUTES
BAKE: 25 TO 30 MINUTES

NATURALLY GLUTEN-FREE, THESE BROWNIES ARE SO fudgy, chewy, and chocolaty, you'll never miss the flour. That's because the cocoa and cornstarch in the recipe give just the right amount of structure to the brownies. The flavor comes from the butter, cocoa, vanilla, and chocolate chips. And the ease comes from making them in one pan on top of the stove, then pouring into a square pan and baking.

Vegetable oil spray, for misting the baking pan

¼ cup cornstarch, plus cornstarch, for dusting the baking pan

8 tablespoons (1 stick) unsalted butter

¼ cup unsweetened cocoa powder (see Note)

½ cup firmly packed light brown sugar

½ cup granulated sugar

1 teaspoon pure vanilla extract

2 large eggs

½ teaspoon salt

½ cup semisweet chocolate chips

1 Place a rack in the center of the oven and preheat the oven to 350°F. Lightly mist an 8-inch square baking pan with vegetable oil spray, then dust it with cornstarch. Set the baking pan aside.

2 Place the butter in a medium-size saucepan over low heat and stir until melted. Add the cocoa powder and stir until thickened and smooth, about 15 to 20 seconds. Remove the pan from the heat and stir in the brown sugar, granulated sugar, and

vanilla until smooth. Break the eggs into the pan and stir to combine well. Add the ¼ cup of cornstarch and the salt and stir until the batter is smooth. Fold in the chocolate chips.

3 Pour the batter into the prepared baking pan and place the pan in the oven. Bake the brownies until the edges are firm, the top is shiny, and the center is just set, 25 to 30 minutes. If you like your brownies gooey, bake them for 25 minutes and if you like them more chewy, bake them for 30 minutes.

4 Remove the baking pan from the oven and let the brownies cool for 1 hour before slicing them into 1-inch squares, if desired. (Some people eat them straight from the pan!) Store the brownies, covered with plastic wrap or aluminum foil, at room temperature for up to 5 days.

Note: For the best flavor, use the best cocoa powder you have. I bake with Hershey's day-to-day, but when I want more flavor I use Ghirardelli cocoa.

EXTRA! EXTRA!

Instead of vanilla, use half almond extract and half vanilla extract. Or use a teaspoon of espresso powder instead of the vanilla.

To make brownie sundaes, bake the brownies ahead of time, let them cool, then cut them into large squares and cover the pan to keep the brownies fresh. To serve, place a brownie in the bottom of a shallow microwave-safe bowl and microwave on high power for 8 to 10 seconds. Remove the bowl from the microwave and top the brownie with a scoop of vanilla ice cream and a drizzle of your favorite chocolate sauce.

Dairy-Free:

Use margarine instead of butter and ½ cup of carob chips in place of the semisweet chocolate chips.

Gluten-Free Chocolate Chip Cookies

MAKES: ABOUT 3 DOZEN COOKIES
PREP: 10 MINUTES
BAKE: 8 TO 11 MINUTES PER BATCH

NOW YOU CAN HAVE A HOMEMADE GLUTEN-FREE CHOCOLATE chip cookie in a few simple steps. These buttery, chewy cookies begin with a gluten-free baking mix, and make a perfect treat dunked in a glass of milk, or a cup of tea or coffee. The rice flour in the baking mix makes these cookies crispy, too. Chocolate, chewiness, crispiness—who needs more?

12 tablespoons (1½ sticks) unsalted butter, at room temperature

1⅓ cups firmly packed light brown sugar

⅔ cup granulated sugar

3 large eggs

2 teaspoons vanilla extract

1 tablespoon cornstarch or vanilla instant pudding mix

2⅔ cups (16 ounces) gluten-free baking mix (see Note)

1 cup miniature semisweet chocolate chips

½ cup chopped pecans (optional)

1 Place a rack in the center of the oven and preheat the oven to 375°F. Set aside 2 ungreased baking sheets.

2 Place the butter, brown sugar, and granulated sugar in a large mixing bowl. Using a hand mixer, beat on medium-high speed until the mixture is creamy and comes together, 1 to 1½ minutes. Add the eggs and vanilla, and beat on medium speed until the batter is smooth, about 1 minute.

the cookies spread a lot. Place the baking sheets in the oven.

5 Bake the cookies until they are lightly golden, 8 to 9 minutes, or for a crunchier cookie with a more golden brown color, bake them 10 to 11 minutes. Transfer the baking sheets to wire racks and let the cookies cool for about 1 minute. Using a metal spatula transfer the cookies to wire racks to cool completely, about 10 minutes longer. Repeat with the remaining cookie dough. Store the cookies in an airtight container at room temperature for up to 5 days.

Note: In developing this recipe, I used gluten-free Bisquick and it took an entire box (16 ounces; 2⅔ cups). I added a little cornstarch or pudding mix to soften the texture and make the batter less gritty.

3 Stir the cornstarch or pudding mix into the baking mix. Add the baking mix to the batter in three batches, beating on low speed for about 30 seconds after each addition. Fold in the chocolate chips and the pecans, if using.

4 Drop the dough by teaspoons onto the baking sheets, spacing the dough about 3 inches apart as

An Unbelievably Gluten-Free Meal

WHERE EATEN:

_____

_____

WHEN EATEN:

_____

_____

WHO WAS THERE:

_____

_____

TIPS FOR MAKING AT HOME:

_____

_____

_____

_____

NEW INSPIRATIONS:

_____

_____

_____

EXTRA! EXTRA!

Use this chocolate chip cookie recipe as a starting point for all kinds of fun cookie combinations. Add ½ cup of Allison's Gluten-Free Granola (page 15). Add ¼ cup of chopped pistachios and ¼ cup of dried cherries. Or, substitute white chocolate chips for the chocolate chips, add ¼ cup of chopped macadamia nuts, and 2 tablespoons of shredded coconut.

Dairy-Free:

Substitute carob chips for the chocolate chips and use margarine instead of butter.

Back to School Party

Old-Fashioned Pigs in Blankets, page 196

Macho Nacho Taco Salad, page 261

Fresh fruit

Gluten-Free Chocolate Chip Cookies

Bev's Raisin Cookies

MAKES: ABOUT 30 COOKIES
PREP: 15 TO 20 MINUTES
BAKE: 10 TO 12 MINUTES PER BATCH

MILWAUKEE HAS A LOT OF GREAT GLUTEN-FREE COOKS, and one such cook is Bev Lieven who has lived gluten-free for more than thirty years. Bev's forte is to be able to take a regular wheat flour recipe and convert it to a gluten-free recipe, like these raisin cookies, based on a recipe she clipped years ago from a Chex recipe booklet. When General Mills reformulated Rice Chex and removed the malt, Bev pulled out this recipe and was eager to bake these cookies again.

Vegetable oil spray, for misting the
  baking pans

1 cup gluten-free all-purpose flour
  (see Note)

1 teaspoon baking powder

¼ teaspoon baking soda

¼ teaspoon salt

1 large egg

⅓ cup granulated sugar, plus sugar for
  flattening the cookies

⅓ cup firmly packed light brown sugar

1 teaspoon pure vanilla extract

⅓ cup vegetable oil

1 cup raisins

3 cups Rice Chex cereal, crushed to
  1½ cups

½ cup flaked coconut (optional)

1 Place a rack in the center of the oven and preheat the oven to 350°F. Lightly mist 2 baking sheets with vegetable oil spray and set them aside.

2 Place the flour, baking powder, baking soda, and salt in a small bowl and stir to combine well. Set the flour mixture aside.

3 Place the egg in a large mixing bowl and beat with an electric mixer on medium speed until it increases in volume, 2 to 3 minutes. Add the granulated sugar, brown sugar, and vanilla and beat to just combine. Add half of the flour mixture and beat until just combined. Add the oil and beat to combine. Add the remaining flour mixture and beat until the ingredients are well combined, 30 seconds. Stir in the raisins, Chex cereal, and the coconut, if using.

4 Drop the cookie dough by heaping teaspoons onto the prepared baking sheets 2 inches apart. Place some granulated sugar in a shallow bowl, dip a glass in the sugar, and use the glass to press down on the spoonfuls of dough to flatten them. Place the baking sheets in the oven.

5 Bake the cookies until they are lightly browned around the edges, 10 to 12 minutes. Transfer the baking sheets to wire racks and let the cookies cool for about 1 minute. Using a metal spatula, transfer the cookies to wire racks to cool completely, about 15 minutes longer. Repeat with the remaining cookie dough, if any. The cookies can be stored in an airtight container at room temperature for up to 5 days.

Note: I used King Arthur gluten-free all-purpose flour in this recipe.

EXTRA! EXTRA!

Bev says it is important to beat the egg until it thickens because this increases its ability to bind, helping the ingredients stay together in the dough.

Dairy-Free:
The raisin cookies are dairy-free.

Crisp Cornmeal Cookies

MAKES: 30 TO 32 COOKIES
PREP: 15 TO 20 MINUTES
BAKE: 8 TO 10 MINUTES PER BATCH

FLIP THROUGH OLD AMERICAN COOKBOOKS AND ALSO Italian cookbooks and you might find a recipe for cornmeal cookies. Cornmeal has long been a staple ingredient in both countries, although most people in the States tend to think of it in corn bread and not cookies. But when cornmeal is mixed with a gluten-free baking mix, sugar, butter, egg, and flavorings, it results in a crisp and delicious cookie.

1 large orange

8 tablespoons (1 stick) unsalted butter,
    at room temperature

3 tablespoons solid vegetable shortening

⅔ cup granulated sugar

1 large egg

1 teaspoon pure vanilla extract

1 cup gluten-free baking mix,
    such as Bisquick

½ cup white cornmeal

½ cup confectioners' sugar

1 Place a rack in the center of the oven and preheat the oven to 375°F.

2 Rinse the orange and pat it dry with a paper towel. Grate enough of the orange rind to produce about 1 tablespoon of orange zest. Cut the orange in half and juice it. You will need 2 tablespoons of juice. Set the orange zest and juice aside.

3 Place the butter, shortening, and granulated sugar in a large mixing bowl and beat with an electric mixer on medium-high speed until creamy, about 30 seconds. Add the egg, orange zest, 1 tablespoon of the orange juice, and the vanilla. Beat on medium speed until combined, about 20 seconds. Place the baking mix and cornmeal in a small bowl and stir to mix, then add it to the butter mixture and beat on low speed until just combined, about 20 seconds.

4 Drop the cookie dough by the teaspoons onto the baking sheet, spacing the cookies about 3 inches apart as they will spread as they bake.

5 Bake the cookies until they are lightly browned around the edges, 8 to 10 minutes. Be careful not to overbake the cookies as they brown quickly. Remove the baking sheet from the oven and let the cookies cool on the baking sheet for about 45 seconds, then transfer them to a wire rack to cool to room temperature, about 20 minutes. Repeat with the remaining cookie dough.

6 Place the confectioners' sugar in a small bowl and whisk in the remaining 1 tablespoon of orange

juice until smooth. Dip a teaspoon or knife into the glaze and drizzle it lightly over the cookies in a zigzag motion. Let the cookies rest for 15 to 20 minutes for the glaze to set.

EXTRA! EXTRA!

When making a glaze, the rule of thumb for the ratio of confectioners' sugar to liquid is 1 cup of sugar per 2 tablespoons of a liquid such as orange or lemon juice. This recipe uses only half that much glaze, but if you want more, add another ½ cup of confectioners' sugar and another tablespoon of juice.

Coconut Lime Cornmeal Cookies:

For this variation, omit the orange zest and juice. Zest and juice 1 large lime; you will get about 1 teaspoon of zest and 2 to 3 tablespoons of juice. Use 1 teaspoon of lime zest and 1 tablespoon of lime juice in the cookie dough and the remaining juice in the glaze. Fold ⅔ cup of flaked sweetened coconut into the dough after beating in the baking mix and cornmeal.

Dairy-Free:

Substitute margarine for butter and the cookies will be dairy-free.

Sweetened Whipped Cream

MAKES: 2 CUPS
PREP: 5 MINUTES

WHAT WOULD I DO WITHOUT REAL WHIPPED CREAM? It has been a fixture in my kitchen for as long as I can remember. Serve it over warm brownies, fruit pies, and cobblers, and at holiday time alongside pumpkin or pecan pie, or gingerbread. Or just dollop a spoonful on top of sliced summertime peaches. It is the perfect complement to the perfect dessert.

1 cup heavy (whipping) cream
¼ cup confectioners' sugar
½ teaspoon pure vanilla extract

1 Place a clean, large mixing bowl and electric mixer beaters in the freezer for a few minutes while you assemble the ingredients.

2 Pour the cream into the chilled bowl and beat with the electric mixer on high speed until the cream thickens, 1½ minutes. Stop the machine and add the sugar and vanilla.

Beat the cream on high speed until stiff peaks form, 1 to 2 minutes more. Cover and refrigerate for up to 2 hours.

EXTRA! EXTRA!

Cream whips best when the beaters and bowl are chilled. Place them in the freezer for 5 minutes or the fridge for 15 minutes before whipping the cream.

Dairy-Free:
Buy a whipped dairy-free topping, such as Cool Whip.

Conversion Tables

Liquid Conversions

U.S.	IMPERIAL	METRIC
2 tbs	1 fl oz	30 ml
3 tbs	1½ fl oz	45 ml
¼ cup	2 fl oz	60 ml
⅓ cup	2½ fl oz	75 ml
⅓ cup + 1 tbs	3 fl oz	90 ml
⅓ cup + 2 tbs	3½ fl oz	100 ml
½ cup	4 fl oz	125 ml
⅔ cup	5 fl oz	150 ml
¾ cup	6 fl oz	175 ml
¾ cup + 2 tbs	7 fl oz	200 ml
1 cup	8 fl oz	250 ml
1 cup + 2 tbs	9 fl oz	275 ml
1¼ cups	10 fl oz	300 ml
1⅓ cups	11 fl oz	325 ml
1½ cups	12 fl oz	350 ml
1⅔ cups	13 fl oz	375 ml
1¾ cups	14 fl oz	400 ml
1¾ cups + 2 tbs	15 fl oz	450 ml
2 cups (1 pint)	16 fl oz	500 ml
2½ cups	20 fl oz (1 pint)	600 ml
3¾ cups	1½ pints	900 ml
4 cups	1¾ pints	1 liter

Weight Conversions

US/UK	METRIC	US/UK	METRIC
½ oz	15 g	7 oz	200 g
1 oz	30 g	8 oz	250 g
1½ oz	45 g	9 oz	275 g
2 oz	60 g	10 oz	300 g
2½ oz	75 g	11 oz	325 g
3 oz	90 g	12 oz	350 g
3½ oz	100 g	13 oz	375 g
4 oz	125 g	14 oz	400 g
5 oz	150 g	15 oz	450 g
6 oz	175 g	1 lb	500 g

Oven Temperatures

FAHRENHEIT	GAS MARK	CELSIUS
250	½	120
275	1	140
300	2	150
325	3	160
350	4	180
375	5	190
400	6	200
425	7	220
450	8	230
475	9	240
500	10	260

Note: Reduce the temperature by 20°C (68°F) for fan-assisted ovens.

Approximate Equivalents

1 stick butter = 8 tbs = 4 oz = ½ cup

1 cup all-purpose presifted flour or dried bread crumbs = 5 oz

1 cup granulated sugar = 8 oz

1 cup (packed) brown sugar = 6 oz

1 cup confectioners' sugar = 4½ oz

1 cup honey or syrup = 12 oz

1 cup grated cheese = 4 oz

1 cup dried beans = 6 oz

1 large egg = about 2 oz or about 3 tbs

1 egg yolk = about 1 tbs

1 egg white = about 2 tbs

Please note that all conversions are approximate but close enough to be useful when converting from one system to another.

Index